# Milestones

# Automotive

Englisch für Fahrzeugberufe

mit Medien

Herausgeber
Christian Rode

Ernst Klett Verlag
Stuttgart • Leipzig • Dortmund

# So arbeiten Sie mit Milestones

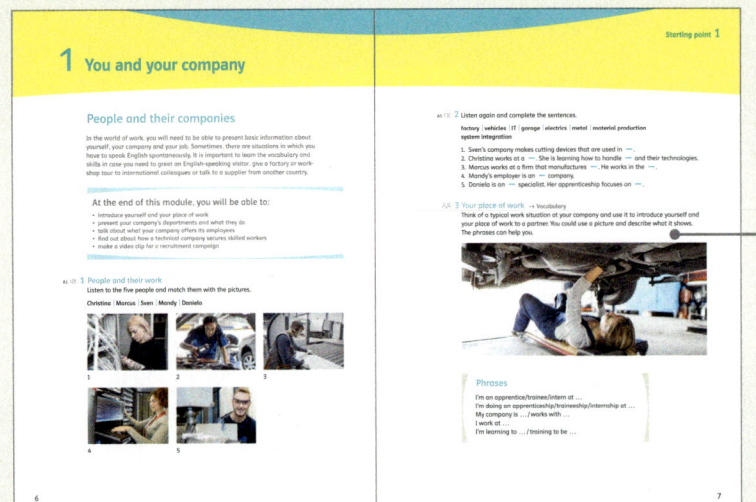

**Starting point**
Einstieg ins Thema und Überblick über die Ziele des Kapitels

Anwendungsaufgabe – wie ist das in meiner Firma?

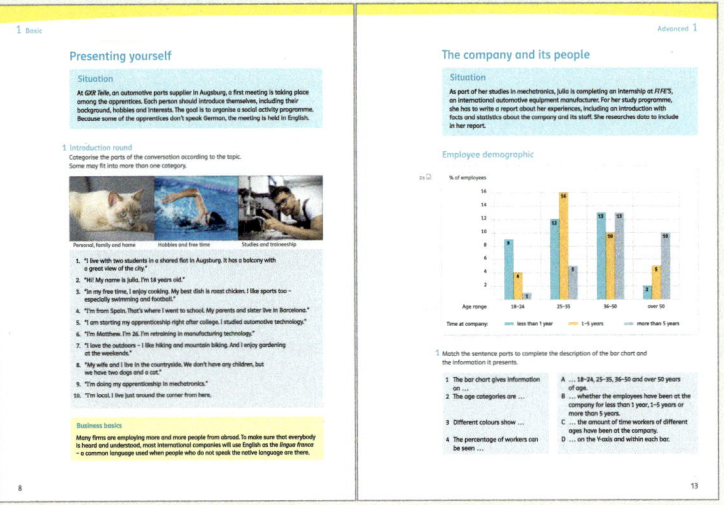

**Basic | Advanced**
Anwendungsorientierte Aufgaben sowie Aufgaben zu den Kompetenzen Leseverstehen, Hörverstehen, Mediation, Sprechen und Schreiben sind eingebettet in authentische Handlungssituationen aus dem Berufsleben

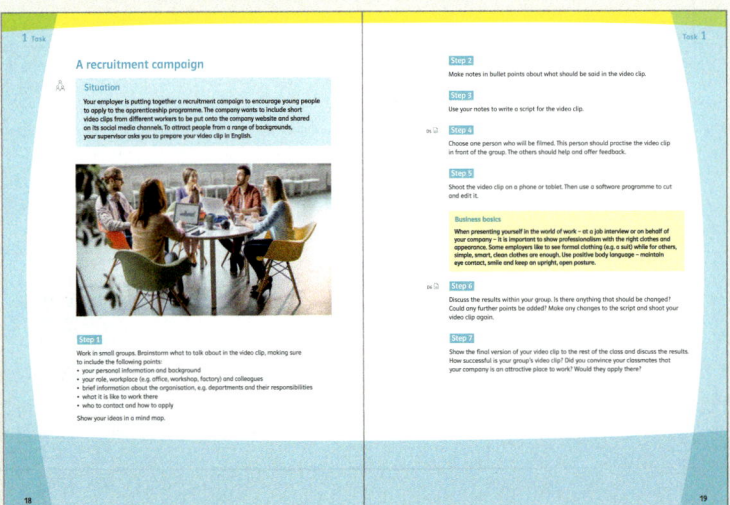

**Task**
Am Ende des *Modules* werden alle zentralen Kompetenzen fachübergreifend angewendet

## Essentials (Modules 1–5)

Die wichtigsten Grundlagen für die Arbeit im Technologiesektor, einschließlich Organisations-, Präsentations- und Kommunikationsthemen

## Specifics (Modules 6–10)

Fachspezifische Kenntnisse, die einen tieferen Einblick in die Arbeit im Bereich der Fahrzeugtechnik geben

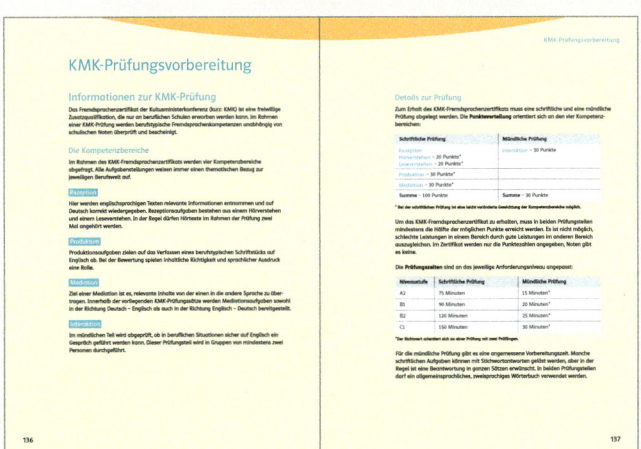

### KMK-Prüfungsvorbereitung
zwei komplette Musterprüfungen – Niveau A2 und B1

## Anhang

### Helping hand
Hilfestellungen zu Aufgaben in den *Modules*

### More
Weiterführende Aufgaben zu den Aufgaben in den *Modules*

### Grammar files
Kompaktgrammatik zum Nachschlagen und Lernen

### Vocabulary
Themenübergreifende *Word banks* sowie chronologische Vokabellisten zu den *Modules*

## Symbole und Medien

| | | | | |
|---|---|---|---|---|
| 👥 | Partnerarbeit | A1 🔊 | Audio | |
| 👥👥 | Gruppenarbeit | V1 ▶ | Video | |
| → ○ 3, p. 40 | Verweis auf *Helping hand* im Anhang | I1 ✋ | interaktiv | |
| → ● 3, p. 40 | Verweis auf *More* im Anhang | D1 📄 | Dokument | |
| → Grammar | Verweis auf die *Grammar files* | | | |
| → Vocabulary | Verweis auf *Vocabulary* | | | |

**Die Medien (Audios, Videos, interaktive Übungen und Dokumente) zum Schulbuch sind online und offline verfügbar.**

1. QR-Code scannen oder Link in einen Browser eingeben
2. Mit den persönlichen Klett-Zugangsdaten anmelden
3. Digitale Medien online nutzen oder in die 📱 **Klett Lernen App** herunterladen

Link

# Contents

## Essentials
## Working in the technology sector

### Module 1
### You and your company

**Starting point**
People and their companies ... 6

**Basic**
Presenting yourself ... 8
The company and its departments ... 10

**Advanced**
The company and its people ... 13
Securing skilled staff ... 16

**Task**
A recruitment campaign ... 18

### Module 2
### Your place of work

**Starting point**
Different workplaces ... 20

**Basic**
Safety at the workplace ... 22
Data security ... 25

**Advanced**
Data protection ... 28
Mobile work ... 30

**Task**
Workplace of the year ... 32

### Module 3
### Tasks and responsibilities

**Starting point**
First tasks ... 34

**Basic**
Tasks, responsibilities and expectations ... 36
Being organised, happy and healthy at work ... 38

**Advanced**
Conflicts and issues at work ... 40

**Task**
A welcome guide for apprentices ... 42

### Module 4
### Working in a global world

**Starting point**
Different locations ... 44

**Basic**
Intercultural awareness ... 46
Meeting international business partners ... 49

**Advanced**
Preparing for an international assignment ... 52
A project abroad ... 56

**Task**
Living and working in Germany ... 58

### Module 5
### Communication

**Starting point**
Media and methods ... 60

**Basic**
Company communication ... 63
Instructions ... 65

**Advanced**
Telephone communication ... 68

**Task**
Product development and communication ... 70

## Specifics
## Working in the automotive industry

### Module 6
### In the workshop

**Starting point**
A workshop tour ... 72

**Basic**
Tools in a car workshop ... 74
Safety measures ... 75
Changing tyres ... 78
Transporting a vehicle ... 80

**Advanced**
Working with electricity ... 84

**Task**
Safety in your workshop ... 86

### Module 7
### Maintenance and repair work

**Starting point**
Servicing a vehicle ... 88

**Basic**
The main inspection ... 91
Brakes ... 93

# Contents

**Advanced**
Engines .................................................... 96
Diagnostic tools in the workshop ....... 98
**Task**
Buying a vintage car ............................. 100

## Module 8
## Servicing a vintage car
**Starting point**
Talking to international customers ..... 102
**Basic**
Researching fuel system problems ..... 104
Planning repairs ..................................... 106
**Advanced**
Ordering a spare part ............................ 108
**Task**
Your favourite vintage car ................... 110

## Module 9
## Customer service
**Starting point**
Roadside assistance .............................. 112
**Basic**
Repair costs ............................................. 114
Upgrading a car ...................................... 116
**Advanced**
Digital vehicle inspection .................... 118
**Task**
Dealing with a complaint ..................... 120

## Module 10
## Electric vehicles
**Starting point**
Modern driving systems ....................... 122
**Basic**
How to handle EVs ................................. 124
**Advanced**
Advanced driver-assistance system
(ADAS) ...................................................... 130
Sensors in EVs ........................................ 132
**Task**
Electric vehicle or petrol car? ............. 134

## KMK-Prüfungsvorbereitung

Informationen zur KMK-Prüfung .......... 136

### A2
**Rezeption – Hörverstehen**
Different braking systems ................... 138
**Rezeption – Leseverstehen**
Electric vehicle technology ................. 138
**Produktion**
An informative leaflet on engine oils .... 139
**Mediation: Englisch – Deutsch**
The most common reasons the A/C is
not working ............................................. 140
**Mediation: Deutsch – Englisch**
The pros and cons of electric vehicles ... 140
**Interaktion**
Technical inspections internationally ... 141

### B1
**Rezeption – Hörverstehen**
A critical look at e-mobility ................. 144
**Rezeption – Leseverstehen**
V2X systems ............................................ 145
**Produktion**
A complaint to a manufacturer ........... 146
**Mediation: Englisch – Deutsch**
What is the difference between LIDAR
and RADAR? ............................................ 147
**Mediation: Deutsch – Englisch**
Autonomous driving levels .................. 147
**Interaktion**
Tyre quality ............................................. 148

## Appendix

Helping hand .......................................... 150
More ......................................................... 163
Grammar files ......................................... 165
Irregular verbs ........................................ 185
List of operators .................................... 186
Vocabulary .............................................. 187
Conversion tables .................................. 220
Classroom phrases ................................ 221
Sources .................................................... 222

# 1 You and your company

## People and their companies

In the world of work, you will need to be able to present basic information about yourself, your company and your job. Sometimes, there are situations in which you have to speak English spontaneously. It is important to learn the vocabulary and skills in case you need to greet an English-speaking visitor, give a factory or workshop tour to international colleagues or talk to a supplier from another country.

### At the end of this module, you will be able to:
- introduce yourself and your place of work
- present your company's departments and what they do
- talk about what your company offers its employees
- find out about how a technical company secures skilled workers
- make a video clip for a recruitment campaign

### A1 1 People and their work
Listen to the five people and match them with the pictures.

Christina | Marcus | Sven | Mandy | Daniela

1

2

3

4

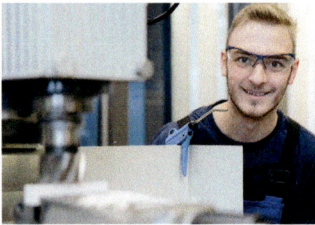
5

## Starting point 1

A1 🔊 **2** Listen again and complete the sentences.

factory | vehicles | IT | garage | electrics | metal | material production system integration

1. Sven's company makes cutting devices that are used in —.
2. Christina works at a —. She is learning how to handle — and their technologies.
3. Marcus works at a firm that manufactures —. He works in the —.
4. Mandy's employer is an — company.
5. Daniela is an — specialist. Her apprenticeship focuses on —.

**3 Your place of work** → Vocabulary

Think of a typical work situation at your company and use it to introduce yourself and your place of work to a partner. You could use a picture and describe what it shows. The phrases can help you.

### Phrases

I'm an apprentice/trainee/intern at …
I'm doing an apprenticeship/traineeship/internship at …
My company is … / works with …
I work at …
I'm learning to … / training to be …

7

# 1 Basic

## Presenting yourself

### Situation

At *GXR Teile*, an automotive parts supplier in Augsburg, a first meeting is taking place among the apprentices. Each person should introduce themselves, including their background, hobbies and interests. The goal is to organise a social activity programme. Because some of the apprentices don't speak German, the meeting is held in English.

### 1 Introduction round

Categorise the parts of the conversation according to the topic.
Some may fit into more than one category.

Personal, family and home | Hobbies and free time | Studies and traineeship

1. "I live with two students in a shared flat in Augsburg. It has a balcony with a great view of the city."
2. "Hi! My name is Julia. I'm 18 years old."
3. "In my free time, I enjoy cooking. My best dish is roast chicken. I like sports too – especially swimming and football."
4. "I'm from Spain. That's where I went to school. My parents and sister live in Barcelona."
5. "I am starting my apprenticeship right after college. I studied automotive technology."
6. "I'm Matthew. I'm 26. I'm retraining in manufacturing technology."
7. "I love the outdoors – I like hiking and mountain biking. And I enjoy gardening at the weekends."
8. "My wife and I live in the countryside. We don't have any children, but we have two dogs and a cat."
9. "I'm doing my apprenticeship in mechatronics."
10. "I'm local. I live just around the corner from here."

### Business basics

Many firms are employing more and more people from abroad. To make sure that everybody is heard and understood, most international companies will use English as the *lingua franca* – a common language used when people who do not speak the native language are there.

# Basic 1

V1 ▶ | I1 ✋  
V2 ▶ | I2 ✋

**2** For each statement, write down a fitting question. Then come up with two more questions that could be asked at a first introduction meeting. → ○ 2, p. 154 → Grammar 1.1, 1.2

1. "I live in a shared apartment in the city centre."
2. "Hello! I'm Karin."
3. "I love wildlife photography. I spend a lot of time outdoors."
4. "I am from Portugal. My family lives in Lisbon."
5. "I'm doing an apprenticeship in IT in systems integration."

 **3** `Over to you` Speed-dating bingo

In class, do speed-dating-style first introductions. You will have 45 minutes and you must talk to each member of your class for two to three minutes. Remember: You can only speak in English!

1. Before you start, make notes on your basic personal information so that you can introduce yourself. You can include your education, skills, hobbies, interests, home or living situation.
2. Introduce yourself to each partner. Then choose and complete one statement from the list to share with your partner and ask them one question.

| Statements | Questions |
|---|---|
| If I had 24 hours to live, I would … | Where in the world would you most like to visit? |
| I'd like to spend a long holiday with … | What is your greatest ambition? |
| Parents should always … | When did you last go to the hairdresser? |
| I like people who … | Which would you rather be – a cat, a dog or a fish? |
| Studying English is … | Who in the world would you most like to meet? |
| The world would be a better place if … | What is your idea of a perfect day? |
| My favourite English word is … | Where did you last go on holiday? |
| I would never eat … | What will you be doing at 9 a.m. tomorrow? |
| I am most afraid of … | How often do you speak English outside of class? |
| The best author/singer/actor is … | In how many languages can you count to ten? |
| If I could choose my name, I'd be called … | How would you describe your English in one word? |

3. Once everybody has spoken to each member of the class, come back together. What did you find out about your classmates? Which information was most interesting?

# 1 Basic

## The company and its departments

### Situation

Tom is an employee at *iBot-SR*, a company which provides software for robotics equipment used in production and manufacturing. He is preparing an introduction in English for a new colleague, Piotr, who has moved from Poland for a job as a software tester. It is Tom's task to explain the company and its departments to Piotr.

### A company website

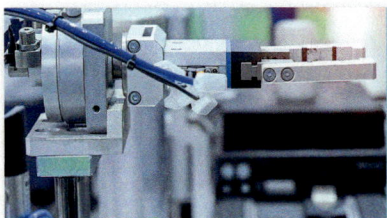

**iBot-SR**

*Compact digital solutions for manufacturing and production robotics*

Based in Berlin, *iBot-SR* has been a leading provider of software and cloud storage services for the manufacturing industry since 2006. Our products and services are made to optimise your company's operations processes – increasing efficiency and security while reducing inactivity and waste.

With our cloud systems, you can immediately access important production data – anywhere, at any time. Across different locations, you can check output, stock records, production capacity, updates and results via the click of a button and share data with business partners, clients or management.

*iBot-SR*'s practical, reliable and secure products and services create the optimum user experience for everybody, robot or human!

**1** Match the English words with the German translations.

| | | | |
|---|---|---|---|
| 1 | solutions | A | Kunden/Kundinnen |
| 2 | based in | B | Betrieb |
| 3 | provider | C | mit Sitz in |
| 4 | products and services | D | Nutzer/-in |
| 5 | processes | E | Anbieter |
| 6 | operations | F | Leistung |
| 7 | security | G | Ergebnisse |
| 8 | locations | H | Abläufe, Prozesse |
| 9 | output | I | Lösungen |
| 10 | stock | J | Sicherheit |
| 11 | production capacity | K | Fertigungskapazität |
| 12 | results | L | Produkte und Dienstleistungen |
| 13 | clients | M | Lagerbestand |
| 14 | user | N | Standorte |

Basic 1

**2** Complete the following assignments with information from the website.

1. State when *iBot-SR* was founded and where the company headquarters are.
2. Write down the products and services provided by *iBot-SR*.
3. State whom the products and services are for.

**3** Write two to three sentences to summarise the company *iBot-SR* and what it does.

A2 🔊 **4** Listen to the audio and complete the tasks.

1. Describe the challenges many production companies are facing.
2. Outline what *iBot-SR* provides that is necessary for robotic equipment to do its job.
3. Name four departments within the company *iBot-SR*.
4. State how many people *iBot-SR* employs and where.
5. List the people who are invited to contact the company.

> ### Words
> **demand** – *die Nachfrage, die Anforderung* | **consumer** – *der/die Verbraucher/-in*
> **timeframe** – *der Zeitraum* | **relief** – *die Entlastung*
> **overstretched** – *überfordert* | **maintenance** – *die Wartung*
> **to record** – *erfassen, aufnehmen* | **to store** – *speichern*
> **everyday operations** – *der Alltagsbetrieb* | **goods** – *die Waren, die Güter*

**5 Company departments**

Match the English department names with the German translations.

1 engineering         A Vertrieb
2 customer service    B Buchführung
3 quality control     C Forschung und Entwicklung
4 purchasing          D Qualitätssicherung
5 research and development (R&D)   E Technik
6 sales and marketing F Personalverwaltung
7 human resources (HR) G Einkauf
8 accounts            H Kundenberatung

**6** What does each department do? Match the words and phrases to make sentences.

Example: Sales and marketing advertises and sells the products and services.

| Purchasing | develops | the company's finances |
| Human resources (HR) | creates | functioning products and services |
| Engineering | buys | new employees |
| Quality control | offers | raw materials |
| Customer service | checks | the products and services |
| Accounts | advertises and sells | the standard of the products |
| Sales and marketing | handles | new products |
| Research and development (R&D) | recruits and trains | advice and support to clients |

**7 Company structures**

In many small companies, the boss makes the main decisions. In large companies with many different departments, there is often a hierarchical structure. In your opinion, which makes more sense? Share your thoughts and experiences and try to convince your classmates.

D1
D2

**8 Over to you** Presenting your company → Vocabulary

Prepare and give a presentation about your company.

1. Collect information that you want to include about your company, e.g. its location, products and services, departments. Make notes to answer the following questions:
   - What does your company do?
   - How are the tasks organised? Who is responsible for what?
   - What do you do? What are your responsibilities?

2. Work in pairs and take turns presenting your company. Try to speak as clearly and freely as possible and use simple, short phrases and sentences.

### Phrases

… people work at my company / in my department/group/team.
My company has …
I am responsible for …
The … department organises the company's …
The colleagues in … manage/develop/create/check/handle …
The … department's mission/goal is to …
I'm not sure who takes care of …

Advanced 1

# The company and its people

### Situation

As part of her studies in mechatronics, Julia is completing an internship at *FIFE'S*, an international automotive equipment manufacturer. For her study programme, she has to write a report about her experiences, including an introduction with facts and statistics about the company and its staff. She researches data to include in her report.

## Employee demographic

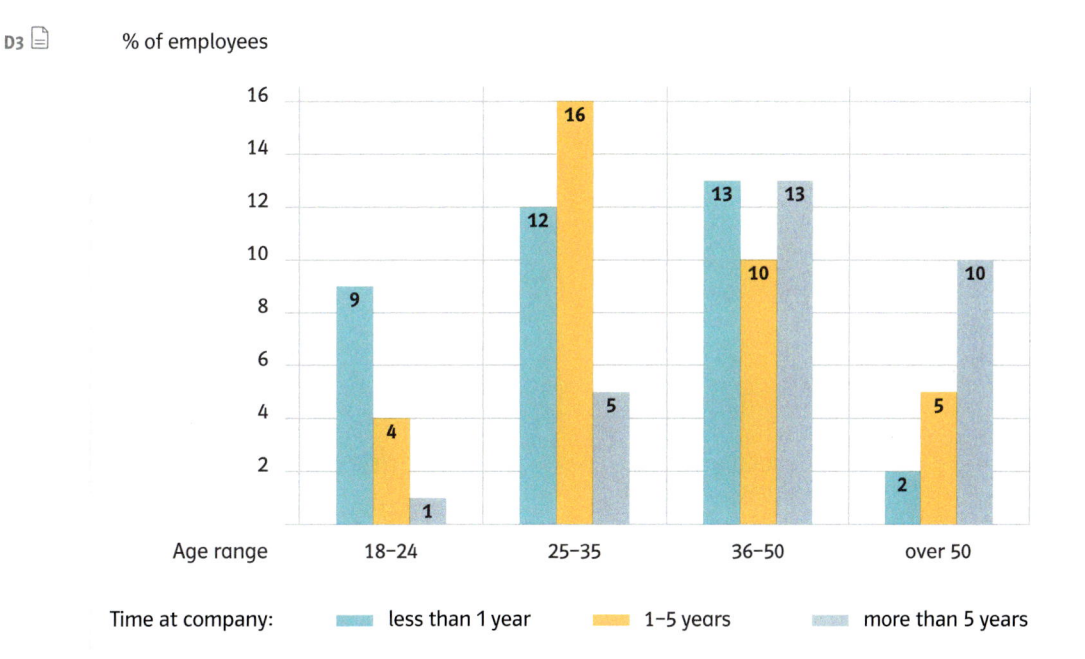

1 Match the sentence parts to complete the description of the bar chart and the information it presents.

1 The bar chart gives information on …
2 The age categories are …
3 Different colours show …
4 The percentage of workers can be seen …

A … 18–24, 25–35, 36–50 and over 50 years of age.
B … whether the employees have been at the company for less than 1 year, 1–5 years or more than 5 years.
C … the amount of time workers of different ages have been at the company.
D … on the Y-axis and within each bar.

13

# 1 Advanced

2 Choose the statements which are correct according to the trends shown in the bar chart.

A Only 4% of workers in the 18–24 age category have been at the company for more than 5 years.
B The age category 36–50 has the highest amount of workers who have been at the company for less than 1 year.
C 14% of the workforce is under 25 years old.
D The most common demographic is workers who are between 25 and 35 years old and have been at the company for between 1 and 5 years.
E The least common demographic is workers who are over 50 and have been at the company for less than 1 year.
F The age range with the highest amount of employees overall is 25–35.

## Company benefits

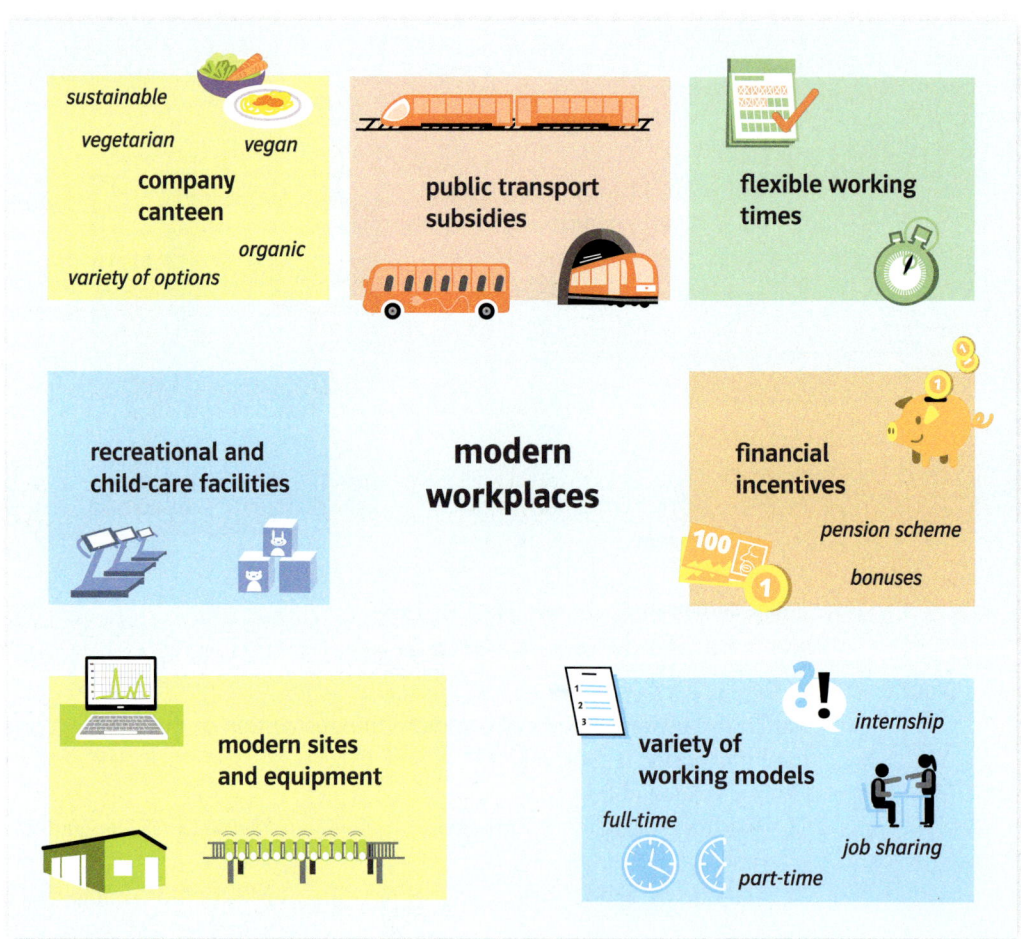

> **Information**
>
> An infographic gives pieces of information in a visual format that makes it quick and easy to read and understand. It uses colours and illustrations to present the topic and make it look attractive.

# Advanced 1

3 Choose the sentence which best summarises the infographic.

   A It shows the ways in which a company recruits different workers.
   B It presents the most important information about a company's business.
   C It presents the benefits offered by a company to show that it is an attractive place to work.

4 Categorise the benefits shown in the infographic.

| Financial benefits | Flexibility | Nice to have |
| --- | --- | --- |
| … | … | … |

5 Use your notes from the previous exercises to describe the infographic in detail.
→ ○ 5, p. 154

6 **Over to you** Discussing your company, its people and benefits

Collect information about your company or department and complete the tasks.

1. Make notes about the following points:
   - the people, their age ranges and backgrounds, e.g. education, experience
   - benefits the company offers, e.g. discounts, canteen, flexible working hours

2. Share and compare your results in class. What is the same and what is different from your classmates' companies? Which points are the most important when choosing an employer?

> **Business basics**
>
> In the European Union, all employers must follow workers' rights. These laws secure fair conditions by regulating standards, e.g. pay, working hours, holiday, sick leave and accident prevention.

15

# 1 Advanced

## Securing skilled staff

### Situation

*EinSchaltTech*, an electrical installations company, has recently updated its offer and recruitment process in the hope of attracting more young people. Manon, a HR representative, has written a text about the successes. It will be shared on the company's intranet. Now she wants to include input from the trainees themselves. So that international employees can contribute too, you mediate the text into English.

### Loslegen bei *EinschaltTech*!

Es ist kein Geheimnis, dass wir bei *Einschalt-Tech* voll und ganz auf junge kluge Köpfe setzen, die innovative Ideen zu unserem stetig wachsenden Unternehmen beitragen können. Deshalb sind wir stets auf der Suche nach neuen Nachwuchstalenten. Diversität wird bei uns großgeschrieben: Nicht nur, weil ein Großteil unserer Auszubildenden aus der ganzen Welt zu uns kommt – beispielsweise aus Indien, Brasilien oder der UK – sondern auch, weil wir wissen, dass es für uns alle ein Gewinn ist. Im Gegenzug bieten wir jedem Auszubildenden die Möglichkeit, wertvolle Fähigkeiten zu erlernen, Erfahrungen zu sammeln, sich angesehene Qualifikationen zu sichern und von einer Vielzahl von betrieblichen Vorteilen zu profitieren.

### Einschalten: Tage der offenen Tür

Von Anfang an: Wir möchten, dass potenzielle Bewerber/-innen direkt ein Gefühl dafür bekommen, warum es großartig ist, für EinschaltTech zu arbeiten. Aus diesem Grund haben wir die vierteljährlichen *Einschalten: Tage der offenen Tür* ins Leben gerufen. Gestaltet von einem Team kreativer und erfahrener Kollegen und Kolleginnen aus verschiedenen Abteilungen bieten die *Einschalten: Tage der offenen Tür* eine Einführung in die Schlüsselprinzipien und Philosophie, Produkte und Dienstleistungen, sowie Abteilungen und Organisationsstrukturen von *EinschaltTech*. Aber es soll nicht nur um theoretische Inhalte gehen: Besucher/-innen sind außerdem herzlich dazu eingeladen, unsere hochmoderne Ausrüstung zu erleben und Räumlichkeiten zu erkunden, Werkzeuge und Geräte zu bedienen und sich sogar an einer kleinen realitätsnahen Projektaufgabe zu versuchen.

### Angebot, Möglichkeiten und Vorteile

*EinschaltTech* bietet Ausbildungsplätze für zahlreiche Berufsprofile an – von Elektrikern, die in der direkten Installation tätig werden, bis hin zu IT-Spezialisten, die Projekte unterstützen. Die Ausbildungsprogramme bieten eine perfekte Mischung aus Theorie und Praxis und werden begleitend zu spannenden Projekten angeboten. Da es uns wichtig ist, dass unsere neuen Mitarbeitenden nicht nur technisches Fachwissen, sondern auch soziale Kompetenzen gewinnen, runden Teamwork, Seminare, Mentoring-Stunden und Zeit für individuelles Lernen das Paket ab. Und nach dem erfolgreichen Abschluss der Ausbildung geht es direkt weiter: 95% unserer Auszubildenden werden mit Vollzeitverträgen übernommen und können ihre professionelle Karriere bei *EinschaltTech* fortsetzen. Alle Angestellten von EinschaltTech, ganz egal ob Auszubildende oder Vollzeitmitarbeitende, profitieren von einem branchentypischen Gehalt, flexiblen Arbeitszeiten und Zuschüssen für den öffentlichen Nahverkehr.

### Anwerbung

Auch unser Bewerbungsprozess geht mit der Zeit: Bewerbungsunterlagen werden in papierloser Form per E-Mail zugeschickt. In manchen Fällen ist eine Abgabe sogar über Social-Media-Plattformen oder im Videoformat möglich. Bewerbungsgespräche finden üblicherweise online statt und beinhalten sowohl eine offene Diskussion als auch kurze Präsentationen beider Seiten.

(392 Wörter)

Advanced 1

> **Business basics**
>
> Many larger companies have an intranet platform. This is a network site which is only visible and accessible to company employees. It is used to provide and share information and resources.

### 1 Attracting new employees

For each of the four phrases from the text, choose the most suitable English version.

1. Loslegen
   - A Product range
   - B Getting started
   - C Open for business

2. Tage der offenen Tür
   - A Open days
   - B First days
   - C Training days

3. Angebot, Möglichkeiten und Vorteile
   - A Many study paths and a great career
   - B Vacancies, recruitment and salary
   - C Offer, opportunities and benefits

4. Anwerbung
   - A Recruitment
   - B Integration
   - C Support

### 2 Match the key terms and phrases from the text with their English equivalents.

| 1 | junge, kluge Köpfe | A | young, bright minds |
| 2 | wertvolle Fähigkeiten | B | specialist technical knowledge |
| 3 | betriebliche Vorteile | C | project task |
| 4 | vierteljährlich | D | full-time contract |
| 5 | hochmoderne Ausrüstung | E | state-of-the-art equipment |
| 6 | Werkzeuge und Geräte | F | tools and devices |
| 7 | Projektaufgabe | G | company benefits |
| 8 | technisches Fachwissen | H | quarterly |
| 9 | Vollzeitvertrag | I | competitive salary |
| 10 | branchentypisches Gehalt | J | valuable skills |

### 3 In English, complete the following tasks with information from the text.

1. Give two reasons why diversity is important to the company.
2. Outline what visitors get at the open days.
3. Describe the training new employees get.
4. State the benefits available to all staff members.

### D4 4 Summarise each section of the text in two to three sentences in English.

### 5 Over to you Sharing experiences

In English, write a short paragraph in which you talk about your own personal experiences training with your company.

# 1 Task

## A recruitment campaign

### Situation

Your employer is putting together a recruitment campaign to encourage young people to apply to the apprenticeship programme. The company wants to include short video clips from different workers to be put onto the company website and shared on its social media channels. To attract people from a range of backgrounds, your supervisor asks you to prepare your video clip in English.

### Step 1

Work in small groups. Brainstorm what to talk about in the video clip, making sure to include the following points:
- your personal information and background
- your role, workplace (e.g. office, workshop, factory) and colleagues
- brief information about the organisation, e.g. departments and their responsibilities
- what it is like to work there
- who to contact and how to apply

Show your ideas in a mind map.

### Step 2

Make notes in bullet points about what should be said in the video clip.

### Step 3

Use your notes to write a script for the video clip.

D5

### Step 4

Choose one person who will be filmed. This person should practise the video clip in front of the group. The others should help and offer feedback.

### Step 5

Shoot the video clip on a phone or tablet. Then use a software programme to cut and edit it.

> **Business basics**
>
> When presenting yourself in the world of work – at a job interview or on behalf of your company – it is important to show professionalism with the right clothes and appearance. Some employers like to see formal clothing (e.g. a suit) while for others, simple, smart, clean clothes are enough. Use positive body language – maintain eye contact, smile and keep an upright, open posture.

D6

### Step 6

Discuss the results within your group. Is there anything that should be changed? Could any further points be added? Make any changes to the script and shoot your video clip again.

### Step 7

Show the final version of your video clip to the rest of the class and discuss the results. How successful is your group's video clip? Did you convince your classmates that your company is an attractive place to work? Would they apply there?

# 2 Your place of work

## Different workplaces

You will spend a lot of time at your workplace. It is important that you feel comfortable talking about it in English to foreign colleagues and clients, including what safety regulations you have to follow and how your company makes sure that its employees stick to different laws and regulations. You should also be able to discuss what makes your company attractive to potential employees.

### At the end of this module, you will be able to:
- describe your own workplace, equipment and tasks
- understand safety measures and regulations across different workplaces
- talk about data security incidents and protection policies
- discuss mobile working, its advantages and challenges
- name and explain things that make a company a good place to work at

**1** Match the pictures with the descriptions of the workplaces.

1

2

3

4

**Starting point 2**

A In a factory, there are lots of tools and machines to work on products. Some machines have fast-moving or sharp parts and might get very hot when in use. Workers must be trained to use the equipment, stick to health-and-safety rules and wear protective clothing.

B In many professions, a van is just as important as the tools and equipment it transports. It gets workers to customers to carry out jobs or to suppliers to pick up materials. Items transported in the vehicle must be secured well. A van can usually be driven with a normal driving licence, but extra qualifications might be needed for large-goods vehicles, trailers, etc.

C A workshop has many different items used to work on cars and other vehicles, like spare parts, oils and sprays. There are also special tools and equipment that help workers. Everything should be organised and the workshop floor should be clean and dry.

D Working in IT often means working in an office, server room or even from home. It is important to understand different electronic components, how they communicate with each other and work together in a wider system. All electronic parts must be checked and meet standard certification requirements.

**2** Match the jobs with the workplaces described.  → Vocabulary

system integrator | mechatronics technician | industrial mechanic | electrotechnican
metalworker | vehicle mechanic | precision mechanic | IT system electronics technician
IT specialist | toolmaker | electrician

**3** What are the potential risks and dangers of each workplace? How might they be reduced? Share your ideas with a partner, then discuss them in class. → ○ 3, p. 155

**4 Your place of work**

Write a short description of your own workplace. What does it look like? What equipment and machines does it have? What tasks are done there?
→ Grammar 1.1, 1.2  → Vocabulary

> ### Phrases
>
> In my workplace there is/are …
> I work with / use …
> My tasks include …
> Often/Sometimes, I have / need to …
> We have access to …

## 2 Basic

## Safety at the workplace

### Situation

At the engineering company *AlloyX GmbH*, a safety training session is taking place to tell employees about potential hazards and ways to prevent accidents at work. It covers a variety of workplaces that can be found across the company's different sites. As some employees do not speak German, the training is being held in English.

### 1 Safety signs

Study the safety signs and match them with the terms.

A Do not alter the switch
B Biological hazard
C Wear respiratory protection
D Emergency exit
E Wear protective gloves
F Corrosive hazard
G Assembly point
H Emergency telephone
I Wear high-visibility vest
J Electrical hazard
K No active mobile phones
L No smoking
M Wear head protection
N Wear eye protection
O Laser beam
P First aid
Q Danger of slipping
R Toxic
S No access for unauthorised persons
T Wear ear protection
U Automated external defibrillator
V Wear protective footwear
W Environmental hazard

**2** Complete the sentences to categorise the signs.

warning | forbidden | help | safety | done | prohibition | worn | triangles | diagonal line

1. Round red signs with a — through them are — signs.
   They inform people of things which are —.
2. Yellow — are — signs. They alert people to dangers.
3. Blue signs are mandatory signs. They inform people of things which must be — or —.
4. Green signs are — signs. They show people where — can be found.

## Safety at different workplaces

### Construction site safety

→ Make sure you have completed and are up to date with all the necessary training and certifications before entering and working on a construction site.

→ You are responsible for your own safety – always pay attention to signs, rules and regulations. If you notice anything dangerous or hazardous, inform your supervisor or another person of authority. Report all accidents immediately.

→ You must wear the correct PPE (personal protective equipment) such as a hard hat, high-visibility vest, non-slip safety boots and gloves.

If you are working at height, you may need extra equipment such as a safety harness.

→ Before using a forklift truck, make sure the forks are straight and not damaged, and that the load is balanced and secure. Always drive with the load as low as is safely possible, paying attention to speed limits and warning signs. Use the horn at intersections and in areas where there may be people.

**3** Summarise the most important points of the text *Construction site safety* in German.

**4** Match the sentence parts to form tips on electrical safety.

| | |
|---|---|
| 1 **Overloaded electrical circuits can cause fire, so …** | A … to avoid electric shocks. |
| 2 Make sure plugs and cables are in good condition, … | B **… do not connect outlets with too many plugs or devices.** |
| 3 Make sure that all electrical parts have enough ventilation … | C … have them installed by a qualified electrician. |
| 4 Make sure that any electrical cords or extension wires are secured … | D … to stop them from overheating. |
| 5 If extra electrical outlets are needed, … | E … without any broken or loose wires. |
| 6 Cover unused sockets with plastic covers … | F … under a desk or along a wall. |

23

## 2 Basic

**5** Complete the rules and guidelines.

drink | tools | fire extinguishers | loud equipment | steel toe cap
safety glasses | emergency exits | gloves | liquids

1. Clean up any spilled oil or other — immediately to avoid the risks of slipping and injury.
2. Wear boots with a strong — to protect feet from falling parts or —.
3. Machine parts can get very hot. Wear protective — before handling machinery.
4. Do not eat or — in the workshop.
5. Wear — to protect your eyes when performing maintenance, services, or repair work.
6. Wear ear protection when using power tools and other —.
7. Keep your work area clean and organised so that the — are not blocked.
8. Make sure the workshop has — for each type of fire – electrical, gas, and oil.

**6 Over to you** Rules and guidelines for your workplace → Grammar 8 → Vocabulary

Write a set of rules and guidelines in English describing the potential dangers and risks at your place of work. The phrases can help you.

1. Brainstorm ideas and note them down. You can use the input from the previous tasks to help you. Think about the following points:
   - tools, machinery, equipment etc.
   - protective clothing
   - hazardous materials, items, temperatures etc.
2. Write one sentence for each point in which you describe the potential risk.
3. Add one sentence to each point saying what you, your colleagues or the company can do to prevent problems or accidents.
4. Put all the points together to create your set of rules and guidelines.

### Phrases

… may present a danger/risk/hazard.
Some … are flammable/dangerous/poisonous/harmful/sharp/hot.
When working with …,
Always/Never …
To prevent …, make sure you …
The company provides … to ensure …
To stay safe, I …

Basic 2

# Data security

## Situation

Grace is a construction mechanics apprentice at *CopperCrest GmbH*, an international metal company with headquarters in Dortmund. Her friend Ashley, who she met on a work and travel trip in Ireland, is asking her about her first week back at work.

## Access denied

> Hi Grace! How was your first week back at work after your holiday?

> Don't ask! 🤦

> Why? What's up? Everything ok?

> Yes and no. I'm fine, I'm not in trouble or anything like that. I've just had a nightmare with access and IT. 😠

> Ok, you had me worried for a minute! What happened?

> First, the security barrier at the main entrance wouldn't accept my card – it had expired, so someone had to let me in. And then when I had finally made it to my desk, I couldn't log onto the intranet!

> Why not?

> My supervisor told me there were some serious security problems and they basically had to reconfigure the whole system. 😤

25

## 2 Basic

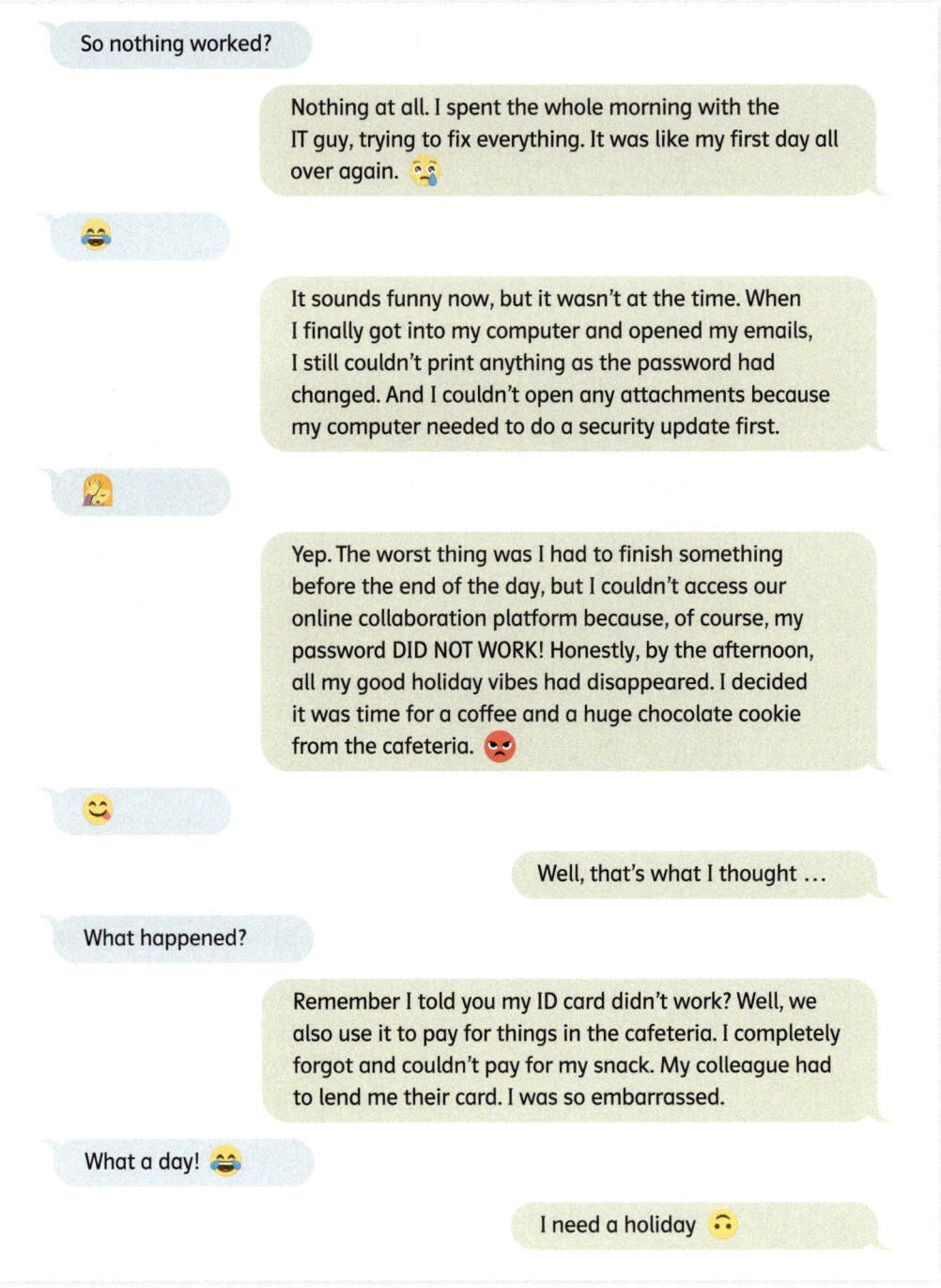

1 Outline and explain the problems Grace faced in the following situations.

1. at the main entrance
2. logging onto the intranet
3. printing and opening attachments
4. using the online collaboration platform
5. paying for her snack

**2** Match the following data security terms with their explanations. → ● 2, p. 166

| | | | |
|---|---|---|---|
| 1 | encryption | A | when an unauthorised person gets access to sensitive information stored online, such as credit card numbers or personal details |
| 2 | firewall | B | software which allows someone to secretly collect information about your online activities without your knowledge or permission |
| 3 | malware | C | when someone tries to trick you into giving them your personal information online by pretending to be someone trustworthy |
| 4 | phishing | D | adding extra security to your online accounts by providing more than one type of identification, e.g. a password and a unique code sent to your phone |
| 5 | two-factor authentication | E | the use of a secret code or software to keep others from understanding your online information |
| 6 | data breach | F | a protective barrier that blocks unwanted or harmful internet traffic from entering your computer or network |
| 7 | spyware | G | software that can harm your computer or steal your personal information when you're connected to the internet |

> **Business basics**
>
> As each country has different laws for data security, it is important to consider the location of a server. The storage of data on a server in a specific country must follow that country's laws. The server's location also determines which rules apply in regards of who can access the data. Moving data between countries comes with rules too: Some countries restrict data transfer to places with less protection. Finally, server location affects how fast data can be accessed – the closer the server, the faster the transfer.

**3** `Over to you` Discussing data security incidents → Vocabulary

Think about the following questions. For each one, make notes about what happened, how it happened, which data were accessed, and the effects.

- Have you or has someone you know ever experienced a data security breach relating to personal data?
- Have you ever known or heard about a data security breach or cyberattack within a company or organisation?

**4** Share your notes with a partner. Then team up with another pair and discuss your results. Which incidents were the most interesting? Why?

## 2 Advanced

# Data protection

### Situation

Louis is a trainee at *TechTronics GmbH*, a tools and equipment manufacturer in Mannheim. Since he is involved in a project with a client who orders power tools from *TechTronics GmbH*, the IT team informs Louis of an accidental breach of data protection rules. Later, Louis' manager asks him to share the details of the situation with his colleagues in the next team meeting.

### Business basics

The *Datenschutz-Grundverordnung (DSGVO)* is a German law that protects personal data and their privacy. It makes sure that organisations are fair and transparent in how they handle data. It also gives people more control over their data – for example, they can access, change or delete them if they want to. Organisations must keep data safe and report any breaches. If they do not follow the law, they can get large fines.

## A data protection breach

| File | Edit | View | Go | Message | Tools | Help |

From: TechTronics GmbH IT Team
To: All TechTronics GmbH Teams involved in customer projects
Subject: Protocol – Notification of a data breach

Dear colleagues,
We are emailing to inform you of a data protection breach in accordance with GDPR. Please be assured that the breach was found and resolved within a short space of time, so no damage was done and no further action is required.
All TechTronics GmbH clients are given access to the RightOrder system. This way, they can view, change and check the status of their orders with TechTronics GmbH, as well as their invoices and other important documentation. They are required to use two-factor authentication to access their accounts.
On Tuesday 4th March from approximately 5 a.m. to 7 a.m., it was possible for one client to access the data of another client. This could have been done by changing the personal client ID found in the download link. The download link is usually encrypted and locked so that it cannot be changed, but on the day in question, the security system was disabled due to a software bug. By changing the download link, all data that clients can see could potentially be viewed, including current and previous orders and invoices.
Through tracing access records and histories, we can confirm that no client's personal data were accessed by anyone else and that no unlawful activity was undertaken. However, we are aware of the potential risk and damage that this incident could have caused had it not been dealt with quickly. TechTronics GmbH is aware of its responsibility to protect and responsibly handle our clients' data and we are sorry to inform you of this temporary error.
Since you are involved in customer projects, you are receiving this communication for reasons of transparency and to encourage awareness and sensitivity regarding data protection rules. You do not need to take action and no further risk is expected.
Please click here to access our data protection information, rules and regulations. If you have any concerns or further questions, please contact your department's data protection officer.
Kind regards,
IT Team

Advanced 2

**1** Match the words from the email with the correct definition or explanation.

| | | | |
|---|---|---|---|
| 1 | breach | A | an event or occurrence |
| 2 | to disable | B | the ability to understand and take into account |
| 3 | unlawful activity | C | an illegal action or series of actions |
| 4 | damage | D | a person responsible for keeping informed about data protection and passing on important information |
| 5 | incident | E | to prevent from working properly |
| 6 | sensitivity | F | unwanted effect caused by a mistake or action |
| 7 | data protection officer | G | the breaking of a rule or regulation |

**2** Complete the assignments in English.

1. State the purpose of the *RightOrder* system.
2. Outline what went wrong on Tuesday 4th March.
3. Explain how the IT team knew that no illegal activity took place as a result of the error.
4. Explain why Louis is informed of the incident.

**3** Listen to the voice message from Paolo. Summarise what he asks Louis to do and why.

> **Words**
>
> **to amend** – *ändern* | **to detect** – *entdecken* | **promptly** – *sofort*
> **reminder** – *die Mahnung, die Erinnerung* | **to contribute** – *beitragen*

**4** Imagine you are Louis. You are going to present the information about the incident in the next team meeting. Pay attention to the instructions Paolo gave and prepare a 5-minute presentation covering the most important points. → ○ 4, p. 155

**5** **Over to you** Discussing data protection in your company → Vocabulary

Make notes about the following questions.

- What personal data does your company collect from customers and clients? For what purposes?
- How and where are personal or sensitive data stored? Who has access to them?
- Which information are you allowed to share with your colleagues? Which, if any, can you share outside of the company?
- Does your company have rules about its own sensitive information? What are they?
- Are employees at your company trained in data protection and privacy best practices?

**6** Share your results with the rest of the class. Which points do you have in common with your classmates? Which are the most important?

# 2 Advanced

# Mobile work

## Situation

Enis wants to work in a technical job and is researching working conditions.
He knows that he will likely have to work irregular hours, sometimes at different locations. He comes across a platform where technical workers talk about their experiences with mobile working.

## Experiences of mobile working

Mobile working presents opportunities and challenges for everyone.
Four professionals talk to us about their working lives.

**Managing customer site visits**
*by Arthur, field service electronics technician*

My job involves visiting different locations to install, maintain, service or repair various electrotechnical systems for smart homes and buildings. Mobile working gives me an exciting working environment and allows me to work closely with customers. One advantage is the freedom to manage my own schedule. But this flexibility comes with responsibilities. I need to make sure that I complete all my tasks on time. I have to handle the reimbursement process for my travel expenses and materials too. So I need to keep careful records and stick to company guidelines.

**Weekend and night work**
*by Deliah, IT professional*

In IT, mobile working means more than just working remotely. As I am responsible for system updates and maintenance, I may have to complete critical software updates at weekends or during the night so I don't disturb daily operations. This requires effective communication to make sure everyone is aware of the scheduled maintenance work. It is important to maintain a good work-life balance and find time for personal activities.

**Shift work and personal well-being**
*by Matthias, machine operator*

Being a machine operator in a factory often means working shifts to keep production going. For me, mobile working is the ability to move between different sections of the production floor and operate various machines. My work is physically demanding, but the flexibility to change workstations within the facility helps. HR emphasises the importance of a healthy work-life balance. Employees are encouraged to take regular breaks and do physical activities to reduce the stresses of shift work.

**On the road to support and assist**
*by Tuana, roadside mechanic*

My company offers roadside assistance and towing services for vehicles that have broken down or been in an accident. I'm also responsible for cleaning up accident sites, like removing harmful chemicals from the road. The roads don't have closing hours, so I have to be available at the weekend and at night too. It's exciting being the first port of call for people in need of assistance. Also, every case is a little bit different, so you never know exactly what to expect. Sometimes it can be frustrating when I can't relax or go to social events because it's my turn to be available. But my team plans the shifts according to a rota, so it's always fair. And in return, I've learned many useful skills and I have great job satisfaction – as well as a company phone!

Advanced 2

**1** Read the texts. Match each person with the right picture.

Tuana | Matthias | Deliah | Arthur

1

2

3

4

**2** Read the texts and complete the assignments. Use your own words as much as possible.

1. State one advantage of mobile working for Arthur.
2. Describe Arthur's responsibilities in terms of cost reimbursement.
3. Describe a situation in which Deliah has to work outside of regular working hours.
4. Explain how Deliah makes sure that everyone knows about scheduled maintenance work.
5. List the things Tuana finds exciting about her job.
6. Explain how Tuana's team makes sure the on-call system is fair for everyone.
7. Give one advantage of mobile working for Matthias.
8. Explain how HR supports Matthias in maintaining a healthy work-life balance.

**3** Use the information from the text to find at least three advantages and three disadvantages of mobile working.

**4** Think about your own job in relation to flexibility and mobility.
Do you have any advantages or disadvantages to add?

**5** Over to you Managing mobile working → Grammar 8

Write a list of three simple, practical time management tips for someone who is new to mobile working. Think about strategies that could help you stay organised and focused.

## 2 Task

 **Workplace of the year**

> **Situation**
> 
> Your boss has asked you to research ways to promote your company. You find a podcast on what makes a good workplace. It mentions a *Workplace of the year* competition, which you think would be a great way to promote your company.

### Step 1

Listen to the podcast and select the factors that it mentions.

A community involvement
B research and development
C employee training
D a guaranteed job
E diversity and inclusion
F working atmosphere
G location
H modern technology and equipment
I company canteen
J sustainability
K pay and benefits
L interesting projects
M flat hierarchies
N work-life balance

### Step 2

Listen again. Take notes on each of the factors mentioned and write down any examples. Compare your results with a classmate and add any missing information.

### Step 3

In small groups, discuss the application *RevolutionRecycle*. Think about:

- positive aspects – what do you like about it?
- weaknesses or limitations – what could be improved?
- examples and evidence – does the application back up its claims?

## Task 2

### RevolutionRecycle

 **RevolutionRecycle** is a top contender for the *Workplace of the year* title. Our focus on our **people** and **projects** in combination with the **environment** and **community** sets us apart from the rest.

 Our **PEOPLE** are at the heart of our success. That's why we prioritise their well-being and a healthy work-life balance. Our offer includes healthcare benefits, wellness initiatives and retirement plans as well as Christmas and holiday bonus programmes.

 Every one of our **TEAMS** fosters a collaborative culture, ensuring a positive working atmosphere where everyone's voice is heard. Employees and leadership teams organise regular staff parties and events to help create a unique bond.

 Innovative **PROJECTS** are led by experienced and skilled research teams. Access to top-quality, cutting-edge technology and equipment drives them onwards and upwards. Our track record of patents in recycling and environmental technologies speaks for itself.

 **SUSTAINABILITY** and the **ENVIRONMENT** are at the core of what we do. We minimise waste, promote a circular economy and achieve high recycling rates. Our commitment shows in our practices.

 **COMMUNITY** involvement extends our impact beyond the workplace. We aim to raise awareness, educate and empower others to make a greener world.

### Step 4

You have decided to enter the competition. Decide for which company you would like to write your application – one of your training companies, a well-known firm or an imaginary company.

### Step 5

In your group, choose five to eight factors to mention and illustrate in your application. Research and collect information about each one.

### Step 6 → Grammar 5, 6

Write your application and prepare to present it in class, pointing out the strongest and most important points.

### Step 7

Present your applications in class. Then decide together which application should enter the competition.

# 3 Tasks and responsibilities

## First tasks

Starting an apprenticeship means learning new skills and balancing your responsibilities. Being organised and flexible will help you to succeed. Cooperation and support are also important for a positive work environment. Time management, task prioritisation and regular breaks will help you to be productive, confident and happy at work.

### At the end of this module, you will be able to:
- talk about your first experiences as an apprentice
- understand different tasks, responsibilities, rights and obligations
- understand the challenges apprentices might come across and ways to deal with them
- analyse and evaluate workplace conflicts and resolution strategies
- identify and present essential information for new apprentices

### Tech Talk: Apprentice Special – How was your first year as an apprentice?

In my first year as an IT apprentice, I've been lucky enough to have a fantastic mentor. She's been patient and supportive, so I can learn at my own pace. The workload has been manageable, and I've had the opportunity to work on some interesting systems integration projects. My colleagues are always happy to help, which makes me feel like a valued part of the team. The only downside is the occasional boring task, like helping employees when their Wi-Fi password isn't working, but the overall experience has been rewarding.

My first year as an apprentice car mechanic has been tough. My boss is very demanding and can be quite impatient with me. The workload is often overwhelming, and I sometimes have to work on several cars at once. I'm given a lot of responsibility, which can be stressful. I feel like I have been thrown in at the deep end. Luckily my colleagues are friendly and helpful, and I've learned a lot despite the challenges. I hope that next year will be more balanced and that my boss will give me some space to learn at my own pace.

My first year as an apprentice in metalwork has been a mix of highs and lows. My boss is strict but fair, and she is good at pushing me to develop my skills. The workload is heavy, but it keeps me busy and engaged. Some tasks are repetitive and boring, like cutting sheet metal, but I've also had opportunities to work on complex projects where I've been able to improve my skills with the hand tools. My colleagues are generally happy to help, but they don't always have time to explain things to me in detail. It's been a rollercoaster, but I've definitely learned a lot!

I had a tough start to my apprenticeship in electrical systems. Of course, I expected to be doing basic tasks at the beginning, but I spent so much time making coffee for the rest of my team that it felt more like I was training to be a barista! Luckily things improved and I was slowly given more stimulating tasks. I even accompanied some more experienced colleagues to construction sites and helped them with installation jobs. Working on-site was really interesting, but I enjoyed the troubleshooting tasks the most. My colleagues are friendly, but I think there's room for improvement with regards to teamwork.

# Starting point 3

**1** Read the expressions from the texts and match them with their explanations.

| | |
|---|---|
| 1 at your own pace | A made to do new things without support |
| 2 thrown in at the deep end | B to give somebody time to themselves |
| 3 to give somebody space | C when positive changes could still be made |
| 4 highs and lows | D at a speed that allows you to process things |
| 5 room for improvement | E positive and negative experiences |

**2** Complete the sentences.

rewarding | demanding | experienced | chance | overwhelming | appreciate | mentor

1. My — has been a great source of guidance and encouragement.
2. Although some tasks are boring, I've had the — to work on interesting projects.
3. Working with a — supervisor can be difficult at times.
4. I — the support of my colleagues when I don't understand a task.
5. The apprenticeship journey can be both challenging and —.
6. The workload can feel —, especially in the first year.
7. It is important to be stimulated and to have the chance to work on projects with more — colleagues.

**3** List the positive and negative experiences the apprentices had in their first year.

**4 First experiences** → Grammar 1.3, 9 → Vocabulary

Write a short text describing the first few weeks of your apprenticeship.

- What tasks and responsibilities did you have?
- What were your colleagues and supervisor like?

Get into small groups and share your experiences.

## Phrases

My apprenticeship was …
On my first day / In my first week/month, I …
I was often asked to / I had to …
Some of my typical tasks included …
My supervisor was …
My colleagues were generally …
One thing I enjoyed / didn't enjoy was …

## 3 Basic

# Tasks, responsibilities and expectations

> **Situation**
>
> Liam has just started his apprenticeship as an electronics technician for automation technology at *AutoNexa GmbH*. He wants to hear from employers and other apprentices about what to expect. His classmate recommends a podcast with some insights into his responsibilities and how to succeed in his apprenticeship.

### 1 Company and classroom
Work with a partner and discuss the following questions.

- Which skills do you learn in the classroom and which do you learn during an apprenticeship? Is there any overlap?
- What do you expect from your internship and from your school? What do they expect from you?

### 2 Listen to the first part of the podcast. Explain the following phrases in your own words.
→ ○ 2, p. 156

1. hands-on experience
2. work ethic
3. cheap labour

### 3 Listen again and choose the correct answer to each of the following questions.

1. What does Benjamin say is the main motivation for doing an apprenticeship?
   A  to have job security
   B  to be financially independent
   C  to get on-the-job experience and knowledge of a profession

2. According to Jens, what else should apprentices learn about during their training?
   A  how they can build a career and progress within the company
   B  networking with colleagues and superiors
   C  contracts, health and safety and environmental issues

3. What do companies need to do to keep their apprentices satisfied?
   A  offer competitive salaries
   B  provide regular feedback
   C  evolve and adapt to industry changes

4. How does Jens suggest companies should view apprentices?
   A as an investment in the company's future
   B as a source of new perspectives and ideas
   C as a way to increase productivity and innovation

5. According to Anna-Lena, what kind of apprentices do companies look for?
   A people who want to learn
   B people who are detail-oriented
   C people with good communication skills

6. What does Jens say about how apprentices should think and behave?
   A Apprentices should focus on learning new information.
   B Apprentices should prioritise teamwork and communication.
   C Apprentices should be independent and think for themselves.

**A6  4** Listen to the second part of the podcast and complete the sentences.

responsibility | energy efficient | customised | diagnose | troubleshooting

1. Jolien's apprenticeship involves many different tasks, including —.
2. Leroy enjoys being creative and working on — projects for clients.
3. Anastasia's team has been focusing on making electrical systems more —.
4. Anastasia had to — a problem and find a solution without any help.
5. Jolien's supervisor encourages her to take — and work independently with customers on smaller software updates.

**A6  5** Listen again. Write down the name, job and daily tasks of each apprentice interviewed.
→ ● 5, p. 166

**V11 | I11  6 Over to you** Your apprenticeship experience → Grammar 4 → Vocabulary

Think about the following questions and make notes.

- What kinds of tasks do you find most motivating and rewarding?
- In which situations can you take responsibility and work independently?
- What makes a good mentor or supervisor?
- What else can you do to make the most of your apprenticeship?

## Phrases

I really like/enjoy …
I find … interesting/useful/stimulating/rewarding because …
When …, I was responsible for …
I have the opportunity to work independently when …
In my opinion, a good mentor/supervisor should be …
I think I will get the most out of my apprenticeship by …

# 3 Basic

## Being organised, happy and healthy at work

> **Situation**
>
> Kannika is two months into her apprenticeship as a construction mechanic at *ProMetal GmbH*. She is finding the change from being a student to being an apprentice difficult at times. She has found an online forum where apprentices share their experiences and advice.

### Life as an apprentice

**Paula_J** My first few months as an apprentice have been really cool. The train ride to work is very long, but I love listening to podcasts, so it's not too bad. I love the company and I'm desperate to impress everyone, so I don't mind staying late or skipping lunch sometimes to finish a task.

**Sr2005** Sounds perfect. Any tips?

**Paula_J** Try to stick to a routine, be organised and save some money each month if you can.

**Jaz** Hi Paula. It sounds like you are taking on a bit too much. You don't need to be perfect right away! Make sure you take the breaks and look after yourself.

**Emre** The last few months have been tough. Work starts at 7:30 a.m., but I have to leave the house just after 6 because the site is so far away. I have to take an early train because if I took the next one I wouldn't get to work until 7:40. I'm always exhausted and in the evenings I'm too tired to do anything except lie on the sofa and watch TV. I miss my friends. We all have different working hours so it's hard for us to meet up. We sometimes play games together online, but it's not the same.

**KT** Hi Emre. Maybe you could talk to your supervisor and ask if you could start 10 minutes later? Sounds like it would help you a lot. Just an idea.

**Emre** Thanks, maybe I'll do that. 30 minutes of extra sleep would definitely make a difference!

**Joey** If you're having trouble getting up in the morning, go easy on the late-night gaming ;)

**Nicci98** My apprenticeship has been a mix of ups and downs. The daily commute is a drag, but one of my colleagues lives in the next village, so we take turns driving. There's a lot to learn. My supervisor is nice, but I don't always understand things right away and I feel stupid when I keep asking questions. I don't want him to think I'm useless, and I definitely don't want to bother my colleagues – they always seem very busy and stressed. I'm also the only woman here and I sometimes feel a bit isolated. What should I do?

**Sami** Talk to your supervisor. After all, it's his job to train you – nobody can expect you to know everything already. Cut yourself some slack!

**Zoe** Try to show confidence through your voice, body language and behaviour. This really helped me to start believing in myself more. Maybe you could also join in with some team activities and social events. They're good opportunities to build relationships with your colleagues.

**Chrissi** I'm generally happy with my apprenticeship. I'm based at a small, family-run company, so I'm given quite a lot of responsibility, which is great, but I struggle to prioritise my tasks! Any advice?

**Kah_EE** I had a similar experience. I make a daily to-do list and work through it one by one. Every new task I get is added to the list. I just use a piece of paper, but one of my colleagues has an app.

Basic 3

**1** Find words from the texts that match the definitions.

1. extremely keen, eager
2. to convince somebody you are good at something
3. a regular way of doing something
4. very tired
5. the journey to and from a place of work
6. not serving a purpose
7. alone
8. to find something difficult

**2** Complete the tasks, using your own words as much as possible.

1. Summarise Paula's attitude towards her apprenticeship.
2. Outline the main problem Emre is experiencing.
3. Explain why Nicci doesn't want to ask her supervisor or colleagues too many questions.
4. Summarise the advice Nicci gets.
5. Describe what Chrissi is finding difficult and what might help her.

**3** Write a reply to two of the people. Comment on what they have written, offer some advice or ask them a question.

**4** **Over to you** Starting working life → Grammar 1.3, 9 → Vocabulary

Which post on the forum can you most relate to? Why?
Share your thoughts with a partner.

**5** Write your own post based on the first few months of your apprenticeship.
You can use the following ideas:

- your experiences, feelings and the biggest challenges
- strategies you use to manage your workload
- how important work-life balance is to you and how you maintain it
- support, tips or advice you would like to share or receive

## Phrases

At the beginning I felt …
The biggest challenge I faced was …
I had to get used to the …
I found it useful to …
… is a good way of prioritising tasks / managing your workload.
Having a healthy work-life balance is …
Some good ways of maintaining a healthy balance are …
Do you have any tips/advice for …?

**6** Give your text to your partner to read. They should write a comment replying to your post before passing it on to another classmate to do the same. Afterwards, see what your classmates have written and report back to the class.

# 3 Advanced

# Conflicts and issues at work

> **Situation**
>
> Benji is doing an apprenticeship to become an automotive mechatronics technician at *DriveTech GmbH*. He is taking part in a training session on workplace dynamics, communication and teamwork. There, they are looking at some examples of different types of conflicts.

**1** Brainstorm conflicts, problems or difficult situations that might come up in the following contexts. You can use examples from your own experience. Share your ideas with a partner.

- at school
- at your place of work
- at a club (e.g. a sports team)
- when spending time with friends, family or a partner
- when dealing with official processes

**2** Study the diagram and look up the meanings of any expressions you don't know. In which categories would you place the conflicts, problems or difficult situations you came up with?

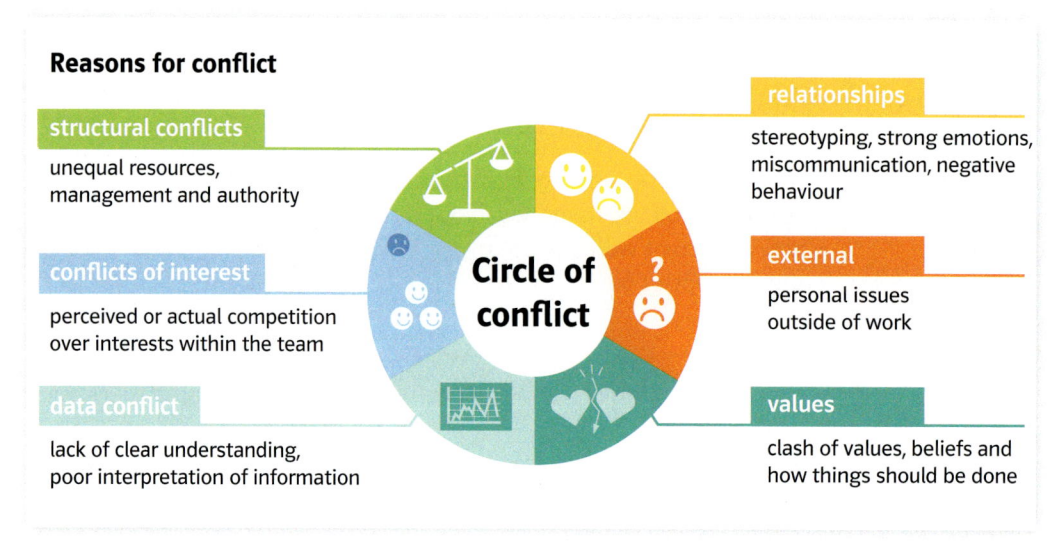

**Reasons for conflict**

**Circle of conflict**

- **structural conflicts**: unequal resources, management and authority
- **conflicts of interest**: perceived or actual competition over interests within the team
- **data conflict**: lack of clear understanding, poor interpretation of information
- **relationships**: stereotyping, strong emotions, miscommunication, negative behaviour
- **external**: personal issues outside of work
- **values**: clash of values, beliefs and how things should be done

Source: Gary Ferlong and The 10 Minute Leader

**3** Listen to three people talking about work-related problems. Explain the marked expressions in English. → ○ 3, p. 156

1. "I **think twice** about asking for help."
2. "She is **supposedly** there to help me."
3. "I've started to feel **left out**."
4. "They **don't take me** as **seriously** as they do one another."
5. "They **jump in** to do things for me."
6. "I don't feel like I can **join in**."
7. "Work has **put a strain on** my relationships."
8. "I need to **put myself first**."
9. "I don't want to **let anyone down**."

Advanced 3

A7 🔊 **4** Listen again and complete the table with bullet points.

| Name | Job / Place of work | Conflict / Issue |
|---|---|---|
| Julian | … | … |
| Erika | … | … |
| Luis | … | … |

> **Words**
>
> pharmaceutical – *arzneilich*
> impatient – *ungeduldig* | discriminated – *diskriminiert*
> to hesitate – *zögern* | to assume – *glauben*
> to split up – *sich trennen* | to carry on – *weitermachen*

**5** Decide which category from the diagram best fits each problem described in the audio. Share and discuss your ideas with a partner. → ◯ 5, p. 156

**6** With the same partner, think about how you would try to solve each problem and make notes on the first steps you would take. Then team up with another pair and compare your ideas. Which suggestions do you think would work best? Why?

A8 🔊 **7** Listen to the next audio. Make notes on how the problems were dealt with and who was involved. Compare your notes with the solutions you came up with.

**8** With your partner, discuss how effective you think the solutions in the audio are. How long will they last and why? Discuss them in class and decide on the best solution to each problem.

V10 ▶| I10  **9** **Over to you** Conflicts in your workplace → Grammar 2, 8
V12 ▶| I12

What does your company do to avoid problems at work? What solutions or strategies are used if problems do come up?

> **Phrases**
>
> At our company, we try to …
> Conflicts are avoided by …
> Our supervisor makes sure that …
> We have a rule that …
> If there is an issue at work, we / our supervisor …
> If I have a problem at work, I ususally …

41

## 3 Task

# A welcome guide for apprentices

### Situation

Leandro moved to Munich from Italy to complete an apprenticeship at *ProMetal GmbH* and he is now a metal-cutting mechanic at the company. He has been asked to make a welcome guide in English for new international apprentices. It should help them to understand their rights and obligations and give them some useful points of contact and resources so that they can access information about contracts, orientation plans, the curriculum, company policies and *ProMetal's* wiki.

Task 3

### Step 1

Think about what new apprentices should learn from your guide. In groups, brainstorm what information they need to know and where it can be found. The following categories can help you:

- company policies and regulations, e.g. working hours
- company sites, locations etc.
- tasks, responsibilities, obligations and rights
- important points of contact

### Step 2

Choose which company from your group you want to make the welcome guide for. Gather the information and put it into categories.

### Step 3

Decide how to present the information. You could create a list, table, chart, mind map, or something else. Think about what style would make the information easiest to understand.

### Step 4

Arrange the information clearly so that readers can follow it. Use short sentences or bullet points. Add colours, pictures or icons to make your guide interesting and enjoyable to read. Make sure the text and pictures work well together to help people understand the information.

D7
D8

### Step 5

Check your guide to make sure that everything is correct and makes sense. Ask another group to look at it and tell you if they think something is missing, or if they find anything confusing. Make any necessary changes and then share your welcome guide with the rest of the class.

# 4 Working in a global world

## Different locations

As you enter the global world of work, you will need to understand how intercultural differences can affect you and your colleagues. It is not only important to get your message across clearly, but also to avoid misunderstandings and causing offence. International partnerships are necessary for any company and as the world becomes more connected, you will need to be ready to deal with a wide range of people and cultures.

### At the end of this module, you will be able to:

- talk about opportunities to work with international colleagues
- make appropriate small talk in work situations
- understand company hierarchies and how to deal with them
- plan and prepare for an international project
- offer advice about living and working in Germany

### A9 🔊 1 International workers in Germany
D9 📄
Listen to four international workers talk about their experiences working on a construction site in Germany. Match the people with the correct information.

| | |
|---|---|
| 1  Adrian … | A  … talks about the importance of good communication. |
| 2  Jakub … | B  … works as a surveyor on construction projects. |
| 3  Lena … | C  … works in Germany because of its working conditions and wages. |
| 4  Raddhi … | D  … likes the sense of teamwork and friendship in Germany. |

#### Words

**to suppose** – *vermuten* | **to vary** – *sich ändern*
**male-dominated** – *von Männern dominiert*
**instruction** – *die Anweisung*

### A9 🔊 2 Listen again and complete the tasks, using your own words as much as possible.

1. Write down one positive thing and one negative thing Adrian says about working in Germany.
2. Describe when communication problems might happen even when English is used as a common language.
3. Write down three roles mentioned by Raddhi.
4. Describe Raddhi's feelings about his team and his working life.

Starting point 4

### 3 Working with people from around the world

How international is your company? In class, discuss the opportunities you have to work with people from different countries and share your experiences. The questions and phrases can help you.

- How many international workers does your company have? Where are they from?
- What are your experiences of working with people from different countries?
- What trends, similarities or differences have you noticed while working with people from abroad?
- How do you think having workers from different countries benefits a company?
- What challenges might workers and companies experience when working with their international colleagues?
- What does your company do to accommodate its international workers?

### Phrases

My company has some / a few / lots of workers from …
In my experience, working with people from … has been …
I find it … to work with people from …
I have noticed that …
One benefit/challenge of having workers from different countries could be …
To make sure that workers from abroad are …, my company/colleagues …

# 4 Basic

## Intercultural awareness

### Situation
Tom works as a toolmaker at *Eberhardt's*, a company which produces power tools for domestic and industrial use. His supervisor has invited him to a Meet and Greet with employees from the company's branches across Europe. At the end, there will be a dinner for all attendants. Before he goes, Tom wants to find out more about intercultural differences in work and social settings.

### Information
You should be aware of intercultural differences when working with people from other countries, but you should never generalise their behaviours and attitudes. There are always individual similarities and differences.

### European work and travel

**Teppei**
One of our suppliers is based in Bursa. Heiko is my first point of contact and we often visit each other. I think most people know about the warmth and hospitality of Turkish people,
5  especially if they have visited Turkey or have Turkish friends, and that doesn't just apply to social situations. From Heiko, I've learned that establishing a trusting, sincere relationship is crucial to us working together – taking the time to get to know one another and build a connection. Turkish people usually like it when you ask questions and show an interest in their culture, traditions and personal lives. I guess it could be because these things can also
10  have a direct influence on their work, which is just as important to them. When I discuss something with Heiko, he often takes his time, and there's often some back and forth before we reach an agreement. It's important to be positive and proactive, but more than anything else you need to be respectful and patient.

**Fabian**
15  I spent a year in Alicante, where I worked for a small company that installs solar panels. The Spanish siesta took a while to get used to. But I soon understood – we had a long break while the sun was at its highest point, and then continued working into the early evening. The Spanish are generally very outgoing, friendly and relaxed – but they're also incredibly hard working and will often keep going until the job is done. They also try to involve everyone
20  as much as they can. When we went for dinner together after work, it felt like everybody was there – colleagues, locals, families and children!

**Anastasia**
I worked in Brighton for a while. At the beginning, when I went for lunch with my colleagues, I was surprised when they just started eating without saying anything. I said, "Have a nice
25  meal," and they all looked at me a bit strangely. Eventually I asked someone about it and found out that in the UK, it's not customary to say things like that before a meal. They aren't being rude – if you ask them about it, they probably won't even know what you're talking about! It's polite to wait until everyone at the table has their food before you start eating, but if you wait for someone to say something, your food will go cold!

## Basic 4

**V8 | I8 | 1** Look up the meaning of any words you don't know and write down all of the positive adjectives you can find in the texts. → Grammar 5

**2** Find the German equivalents for the following words and phrases from the texts. Share your results with a partner. Did you come up with the same answers?

1. hospitality
2. to establish a relationship
3. crucial
4. to build a connection
5. just as
6. back and forth
7. to reach an agreement
8. to get used to
9. to involve people
10. surprised
11. strangely
12. eventually
13. customary
14. rude

**D4 | 3** Complete the following tasks in German.

1. Nennen Sie zwei Beispiele, wie eine positive Beziehung zu türkischen Kolleginnen/Kollegen aufgebaut werden kann.
2. Beschreiben Sie was oft passiert, wenn Teppei und Heiko etwas diskutieren.
3. Erklären Sie, wie sich Fabians Haltung zur *Siesta* verändert hat.
4. Fassen Sie Fabians Eindrücke von Spanierinnen und Spaniern zusammen.
5. Fassen Sie Anastasias Erfahrung in der UK und was sie daraus gelernt hat zusammen.

**4** Discuss the following points with a partner and report back to the class.

- Compare which of the customs mentioned in the blog you already knew about and which are new to you.
- Explain why you agree or disagree with the opinions given in the blog.
- Share any interesting intercultural experiences you have had, e.g. at work, at school or on holiday.
- Name similarities and the biggest differences you have noticed between your own culture and the culture of other countries.
- Come up with at least two challenges someone from another country may face when working in Germany.

47

## 4 Basic

### 5 Small talk
Work with a partner and complete the following tasks.

1. Brainstorm situations in which you might make small talk with someone in English.
2. What experiences have you had with small talk? What do you find easy and what do you find difficult about it?

### 6
Listen to the podcast and write down the small talk topics that are mentioned. Sort them into suitable and unsuitable topics.

> **Words**
>
> **interaction** – *der Umgang miteinander* | **glue** – *der Klebstoff*
> **to feel at ease** – *sich wohlfühlen*
> **to build rapport** – *ein gutes Verhältnis aufbauen*
> **daunting** – *beängstigend* | **shy** – *schüchtern*
> **insincere** – *heuchlerisch* | **to bond** – *eine Beziehung aufbauen*

### 7 Listen again and choose the correct answer to each question.

1. Why is small talk so essential to our daily interactions?
   A to establish relationships with colleagues and clients
   B to decide if somebody is trustworthy or not

2. Why do some people find small talk challenging?
   A They worry about running out of topics.
   B They don't like discussing cultural differences.

3. Which of the following is the least suitable small talk topic?
   A personal appearance
   B travel experiences

4. When is it appropriate to compliment somebody?
   A If you compliment something somebody is wearing.
   B If a woman compliments another woman.

5. What does Tom say about making jokes?
   A It is best not to make jokes with people you don't know very well.
   B Only make jokes if you are sure they are funny.

### 8 Over to you  Small talk → ○ 8, p. 157

Work with a partner to create two small talk dialogues. Come up with a situation and a setting. Then have a short conversation. One dialogue should be an example of good small talk and the other should be an example of bad small talk. Be creative!

### 9
Team up with another pair and perform your dialogues in front of the class. Ask the other pair to explain the mistakes that were made in your example of bad small talk.

Basic 4

# Meeting international business partners

## Situation

Dilara is doing an apprenticeship in mechatronics at *TechnologieTräger*, a company which develops medical robots for microsurgery. Her boss, Louise, has asked her to accompany her to a technology fair in Hannover, where they will display a new prototype. It will be a good opportunity for Dilara to practise explaining the prototype to representatives from other companies. Since Dilara will be meeting people from different levels, she wants to prepare by finding out about the hierarchical structures of an organisation.

## Hierarchical structures

### Business basics

Many companies have a hierarchical structure to assign responsibilities and ensure smooth workflows. The titles and roles can vary between companies. Some have flat structures with fewer hierarchical levels, while larger corporations may have more defined levels.

D3

↑ POWER / RESPONSIBILITY

**CEO***
The executive makes major decisions about the company.

**Chief Technology Officer (CTO)**
This person defines the company's direction in their area of expertise and collaborates with other executives to align its technical goals.

— Executive

**Director**
Directors oversee a department or multiple teams, set strategic targets, manage budgets, and ensure that everything aligns with the company's objectives.

**Manager**
Managers are in charge of teams, administrative duties and complex projects. In the technical sector, they are experts in their field, making significant technical decisions and leading teams in projects or initiatives.

— Senior

**Electrician / Construction Mechanic / IT System Integrator / …**
Qualified workers with some experience, capable of handling tasks independently and managing their own workload.

— Mid-level

**Junior Mechanic / Trainee Sheet Metal Worker / …**
These are people in entry-level positions who are not fully trained or qualified. Under supervision, they develop essential skills and learn how to handle basic tasks.

— Junior

*CEO = Chief Executive Officer

49

## 4 Basic

**1** Match the terms from the diagram with their definitions.

| | | | |
|---|---|---|---|
| 1 | to align | A | to watch over |
| 2 | to oversee | B | to deal with, to manage |
| 3 | administrative duties | C | important, fundamental |
| 4 | to handle | D | tasks relating to the organisation of a business |
| 5 | independently | E | supported by somebody more experienced |
| 6 | workload | F | without support |
| 7 | under supervision | G | to set in order to support a specific purpose or direction |
| 8 | essential | H | how much work needs to be done |

**2** Complete the following tasks and questions.

1. Briefly describe the four levels of hierarchy shown in the diagram.
2. What might be the characteristics of a manager or director?
3. How are the characteristics of a mid-level staff member different from those of a senior staff member?
4. How might somebody progress from a mid-level position to a senior position?
5. Which hierarchical levels might not exist in a medium-sized company?
6. What do you think the levels of hierarchy would look like in a small, family-run company?

**3** In English, staff are said to **report to** their supervisor or manager, who is usually one level above them. → ● 3, p. 166

1. Use the diagram to write two sentences using the verb **to report**.
   *Example: The Chief Technology Officer reports to the Chief Executive Officer.*
2. Who do you report to? Who does your supervisor report to? Talk to a partner.

### 4 Greeting people

Louise is introducing Dilara to Will McCarthy. Louise and Will already know each other. Put the conversation in the correct order.

A Louise: Let me introduce you to my colleague, Dilara Güler. Dilara, this is Will McCarthy.

B Louise: Not bad thank you, how are you?

C Dilara: It's a pleasure to meet you too. Please call me Dilara.

D Will: Good morning Louise, how are you?

E Will: Pleased to meet you, Dilara. Please call me Will.

F Will: I'm fine, thanks.

G Louise: Good morning, Will. It's nice to see you again.

## Basic 4

**5** Match the places with the descriptions of how people usually greet each other. Do some research if you are unsure.

USA | Spain | Japan | United Arab Emirates

A The traditional greeting is a bow. A handshake may be acceptable in a business context. Business cards are key and should be received with both hands and a slight bow.
B The most common greeting is a handshake which is lighter than the firm handshake you might expect in Western countries.
C Greetings are usually warm and friendly. If people already know each other, they might kiss each other on the cheek.
D A firm handshake with direct eye contact and a smile is the standard greeting in a business setting.

### 6 International business cards

Study the four business cards Dilara receives from company representatives at the fair and complete the following assignments.

**FutureTech LLC**
AHMED AL MANSOORI *Mechatronics Engineer*
Al Rigga Road, Deira
Dubai, United Arab Emirates
+971 4 8881 881
a.almansoori@futuretechinnovations...ae

*Hiroshi Tanaka*
Senior Medical Engineer,
**HealthMech Solutions K.K.**
Minato-ku 1-1-1, Tokyo 105-0011, Japan
+81 3 8815 2634
h.tanaka@dynamechsolutions...co.jp

**FUTUREBUILDERS INC**
*Samantha McCarthy*
Construction Manager
123 Pearl St, San Francisco CA 94102, USA
+1 415 9561347
s.mccarthy@futurebuildersinc...com

Luisa Martinez
*Junior Developer*
Calle San Jorge 50
28003 Madrid, Spain
+34 91 5594 223
lmartinez@quantumcodeglobal...es

Quantum Code
Global S.A.

1. Talk about each business card with a partner. What does the person do? What are their responsibilities? What sort of background might they have?
2. Assign a level of hierarchy to each person. Give reasons for your decision.
3. What should Dilara be aware of when talking to these people?

**7 Over to you** Hierarchy levels at your company → Grammar 4

Work with a partner. Describe your company's hierarchical structure. Are there strict rules about how to communicate with people above you? At what level might employees need to be able to introduce themselves and talk about their job or the company in English?

**8** With your partner, act out a conversation at the technology fair. One person takes on the role of their supervisor and the other takes the role of an international business partner. Introduce yourselves and talk about your companies and the tasks and responsibilities involved in your jobs.

# 4 Advanced

## Preparing for an international assignment

### Situation

Helena works at *Precision Mechatronics GmbH*, a firm that specialises in packaging machines. Her department has received an assignment to assemble a machine for a sunflower oil manufacturer in Budapest. Helena's boss is sending some technicians there for three weeks to set up the machine, adjust it to the manufacturer's needs and train the staff how to use it. He asks Helena to help them prepare.

---

<u>F</u>ile   <u>E</u>dit   <u>G</u>o   <u>V</u>iew   <u>M</u>essage   <u>T</u>ools   <u>H</u>elp

From: Alexander Fredriksson afredriksson@precisionmech...com
To: Helena Müller hmueller45@precisionmech...com
Subject: Arany Q-Fill 25 assignment

Dear Helena,

Thanks for helping the team prepare for the trip to Hungary. As you know, we want to install and calibrate the Q-Fill 25 machine for the manufacturing company Arany Virág kft. in Budapest. I'm sending Georg and Benjamin to complete the job. It's the first time they'll be going over, so they might need some tips for travelling and working in Hungary (e.g. anything they need to prepare for or watch out for).

The guys will also need to instruct the staff at Arany on how to operate and maintain the machine so that they can use it independently. The company's working languages are Hungarian and English. As before, Georg and Benjamin will use VR and AR software and hardware to carry out the training – the mixed reality applications provide digital manuals and instructional videos. These cover the majority of the training but the guys will need to know the key technical terms and phrases in English in case the staff at Arany have any specific questions. Can you provide Georg and Benjamin with some support for learning the relevant words and phrases? Maybe you could put together a kind of technical phrasebook?

Any questions or problems, let me know. Thanks again!
Alex

Advanced 4

1 For each of the following verbs, choose the most accurate translation.

1. to assemble
   A  zusammenbauen
   B  zusammenfassen

2. to adjust
   A  einstellen
   B  ausstehen

3. to watch out for
   A  beachten
   B  veranschlagen

4. to instruct
   A  anweisen
   B  vorgeben

5. to operate
   A  bedienen
   B  einschalten

6. to maintain
   A  warten
   B  bereitstellen

7. to carry out
   A  ausführen
   B  wegtragen

2 Complete the following tasks in English.

1. Write down three things Georg and Benjamin need to do during their trip to Budapest.
2. Explain what the mixed reality training software does.
3. Explain what Georg and Benjamin might need to do alongside the training software.

3 Georg and Benjamin send Helena a list of the most important terms for the packaging machine. Search for the correct English equivalents and check your results with a partner.

1. Höchstleistung
2. Stromversorgung
3. Energieverbrauch
4. elektrische Schalttafel
5. Systemsteuerung
6. Trennschalter
7. Näherungssensor
8. pneumatisches Stellventil
9. Heizelement
10. Sicherheitshinweise
11. Siegelbacken
12. bewegliche Teile
13. Ventil
14. Dichtung
15. Transportband

### Information

Translation tools and platforms often come up with different proposals for one term. If you are not sure which is the most accurate, narrow down the options by checking them in a dictionary with precise descriptions. You can also enter them into a search engine and see which images or illustrations come up. When you think you have a fitting translation, check it again by entering it back into a different tool or platform and making sure that the original term comes up.

## 4 Advanced

**4** Complete the following sentences and phrases with the English equivalents.

1. Regular maintenance ensures the machine's Höchstleistung.
2. Connect the machine to a Stromversorgung.
3. Energieverbrauch can be regulated and optimised by …
4. The elektrische Schalttafel is located …
5. The Systemsteuerung is responsible for …
6. The voltage is cut when the Trennschalter is activated.
7. The Näherungssensor can be set and readjusted if necessary.
8. The Heizelement has a protective panel.
9. The Siegelbacken are heated by the heating element.
10. The Ventil is operated by an actuator.
11. Pay attention to the Sicherheitshinweise.
12. Watch out for bewegliche Teile.

**5** Use your results from the previous exercises to create a document with useful terms and phrases in English for the packaging machine.

## Advanced 4

### 🇭🇺 Travelling and working in Hungary

**VISAS**
Check the visa requirements for travelling to Hungary from your home country. Apply for a work visa or residence permit if required and ensure your passport is valid for the duration of your stay.

**TRANSPORT AND TOLL ROADS**
Research the toll system for Hungarian motorways and buy the necessary vignette online or at a border crossing. Ensure that it is correctly displayed on your vehicle. You can also register your vehicle online. (Note: If you are driving through Austria, make sure you are properly informed about Austrian toll roads as well!) Familiarise yourself with national traffic laws. Pay attention to speed limits, especially on motorways.

**LANGUAGE**
Learn some basic Hungarian phrases and download a translation app to facilitate communication. Make sure you are confident communicating in English, and learn any important specialist terms you may need.

**WORKING HOURS**
Confirm your working hours with your employer and/or client in advance.

**CURRENCY**
Familiarise yourself with the Hungarian forint (HUF) and consider exchanging some currency before departure.

**ACCOMMODATION**
Make sure you book your accommodation well in advance of your trip. Choose a location as close to the client as possible to avoid long journeys.

**GIFTS**
Bring small gifts for your hosts as a sign of appreciation where appropriate, for example when you are finishing a meeting or a project. Generally, a speciality from your home country is appreciated.

---

**6** Find German terms for the following words and expressions from the flyer. Compare your results with a partner.

1. residence permit
2. currency
3. toll road
4. border crossing
5. traffic laws
6. sign of appreciation
7. specialist terms
8. well in advance of

**7** Which of the tips are important to consider before travelling and which are relevant during a trip?

**8** In German, write an email from Helena to Georg and Benjamin. Summarise the most important points from the flyer and recommend what they should consider before travelling. Offer help and attach your document with useful terms and phrases for the packaging machine.

# 4 Advanced

## A project abroad

### Situation

Ezra is in his last year as an industrial mechanics apprentice at *Green Circuit GmbH*, an e-waste recycling facility in Freiburg. Ezra has already been offered a permanent position at the company. He sees the following advert on the company website and decides to apply.

### PROJECT OPPORTUNITY
### Green Horizons – e-waste solutions for India

We are pleased to announce an upcoming opportunity which represents an important step in our commitment to global sustainability. Based in New Delhi, our new project Green Horizons aims to set up innovative e-waste recycling facilities in India, one of the world's fastest-growing economies, to deal with the growing problem of electronic waste. With this initiative, we aim to establish a scalable and affordable model for responsible e-waste management, including the recovery of valuable metals and the safe disposal or recycling of hazardous components.

**This pilot project will challenge our team to:**
- design and implement an advanced e-waste recycling process which is made for the specific challenges of the Indian market
- innovate in the field of material recovery, maximising the extraction of valuable metals from e-waste
- develop effective methods for the safe disposal or recycling of hazardous components
- supervise and train local technicians so that they can implement and maintain the solutions
- collaborate with local communities and authorities to ensure the sustainability and social acceptability of the project

**WE NEED YOUR EXPERTISE!**
This is an exciting opportunity, particularly for mechanics and electricians who want to make a real impact on tackling the global e-waste problem while developing their technical and intercultural skills. We're looking for problem-solvers with a passion for sustainable development and a detailed understanding of recycling technologies. If you are looking for a challenge that combines technical innovation, environmental leadership and international cooperation, this project could be for you!

**HOW TO APPLY**
Applicants are invited to hand in their applications via the company website. Please provide your current CV and a short covering letter explaining your interest in the project and any relevant experience or skills you can bring to the team. Please note: The application window closes in four weeks. Don't miss your chance to be part of this ground-breaking initiative!

**Let's reshape the future of e-waste recycling together.**
**Your contribution to global sustainability starts here.**

Advanced 4

> **Culture**
>
> Due to the rapid growth of India's cities, it faces significant waste management challenges. More and more people are consuming products like mobile phones, which create huge amounts of e-waste. Waste is often not disposed of correctly and there is no recycling infrastructure. This causes environmental damage and poses health risks for the population.

**1** Explain the terms from the advert in your own words. Use a dictionary to help you.

1. sustainability
2. e-waste
3. scalable model
4. material recovery
5. hazardous components
6. safe disposal
7. social acceptability
8. extraction

**2** Complete the sentences summarising the most important points from the text.
→ ○ 2, p. 157
1. The *Green Horizons* project aims to set up — in India, designing and implementing an advanced recycling process made specifically for the market.
2. The goals of the project are to maximise the extraction of — from e-waste and develop effective methods for the safe disposal or recycling of —.
3. The project team will train — and collaborate with — in India.
4. The project is especially suitable for — who want to develop their skills, are good at solving problems and have a good understanding of —.
5. Applicants are invited to hand in — via the company website within —.

**3** Discuss the following questions with a partner before sharing your ideas with the rest of the class.

- Why might the *Green Horizons* project be attractive to employees?
- What might be challenging for the project team that goes to India?
- Which qualities and characteristics might the company look for when selecting people?

**4** Write a covering letter for the *Green Horizons* project. Explain why you would like to be part of the team going to India and why you would be a suitable candidate.
→ ○ 4, p. 157

**5** **Over to you** Taking part in a project abroad

Discuss the following questions in class.

- Which companies do you know of that work on international projects? What are their projects?
- Would you be interested in going abroad to work on an international project? Why or why not?
- What opportunities and challenges might be involved in working on a project abroad?
- What advice would you give to someone who is about to take part in their first international project? → Grammar 8

57

4 Task

## Living and working in Germany

### Situation

Your employer has recently hired a lot of employees from abroad. To help them adjust to life in Germany, she has asked you to put together an informative flyer for them. It should include the most important information about working in Germany, as well as general advice about rules and customs in everyday life.

Task 4

### Step 1

Work in groups. Brainstorm which areas of working and private life the flyer should include. You can use the ideas below as well as your own.

- working hours and breaks
- recycling rules and practices
- local authorities

### Step 2

Decide how long each of the points you want to include should be.
Divide them between the members of your group.

### Step 3

Do some research to find out more about each of the points you have chosen.

### Step 4

Write your paragraphs. You may wish to use a collaborative online tool.

### Step 5

Bring all of your paragraphs together and design your flyer. Use images and colours to make it more engaging. Pay attention to the structure of your text, e.g. by adding headings and subheadings.

### Step 6

Share your flyer with another group and ask them for feedback.
Is there anything you should change? Could you add any further points?

### Step 7

Share the final version of your flyer with the rest of the class and then discuss it.

- Does it sound friendly?
- How helpful is it for new employees from abroad?
- Would your classmates pass it on to people who have recently started working in Germany?

# 5 Communication

## Media and methods

Navigating a company's methods of communication can be challenging. Internally, you will need to understand instructions and communicate with different team members about tasks and problems. You might also take part in meetings and offer fresh perspectives. The way a company presents itself to the outside world is also shaped by communication, so it's important to maintain a professional image and use clear messages that align with the company's values, products and services. Internal and external communication are linked when insights gained from customer feedback are shared and used for improvement.

### At the end of this module, you will be able to:
- talk about different media and methods of communication
- understand the collaborative tools used in professional situations
- recognise the role of communication in giving and receiving instructions
- communicate key information about a product to a customer
- suggest a new technology and a communication strategy for a smart city project

**1** Listen to the audio. Write down the communication media that the apprentices talk about and organise them into categories.

| verbal | written | programs and systems |
|---|---|---|
| … | … | … |

**2** Listen again and complete the sentences about the different communication methods.

ticketing systems | trust | email | ask questions | working from home | document
face-to-face | messaging apps

1. Speaking to a supervisor — means you can get answers and feedback quickly.
2. Sending complicated questions via — means you can look up the answers again later.
3. Speaking face-to-face to customers helps build —.
4. — help employees in different areas or locations to communicate.
5. Meeting software helps people to connect with their colleagues even when they are —.
6. — track the status of different IT issues.
7. Project management apps can help organise and — projects where lots of people are working together.
8. Online meetings keep everyone up to date and give people the chance to —.

**3** Listen again and complete the tasks.

1. Write down two ways James' company can order parts from suppliers.
2. Write down two situations in which Samira uses the company messaging app.
3. Explain how the meeting software that Samira uses is helpful.
4. Outline the best communication tool that is used at Ruben's company.

**4** Explain the following expressions in your own words in English.

1. "… I prefer a **hands-on approach**."
2. " … if I am **out and about**."
3. "… for **keeping an eye on** all the projects …"

# 5 Starting point

**D3 📄 5 Workplace communication survey** → ⭕ 5, p.158

The graph shows the results of a survey on communication in the workplace. Describe it and outline the most significant results.

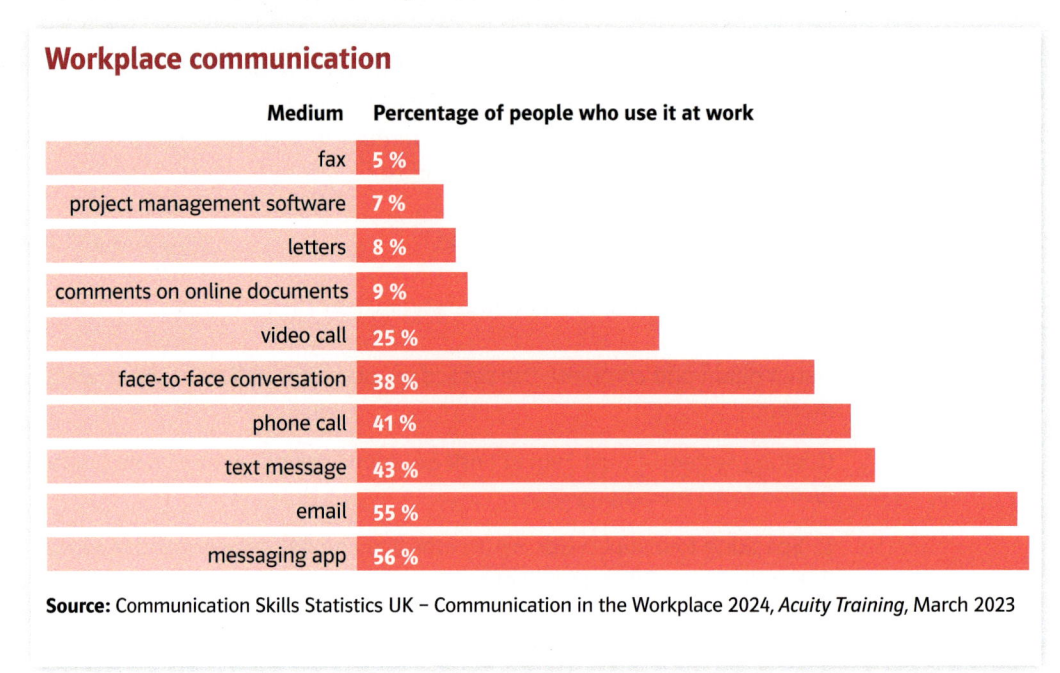

**Workplace communication**

| Medium | Percentage of people who use it at work |
|---|---|
| fax | 5 % |
| project management software | 7 % |
| letters | 8 % |
| comments on online documents | 9 % |
| video call | 25 % |
| face-to-face conversation | 38 % |
| phone call | 41 % |
| text message | 43 % |
| email | 55 % |
| messaging app | 56 % |

**Source:** Communication Skills Statistics UK – Communication in the Workplace 2024, *Acuity Training*, March 2023

**👥 6** With a partner, discuss which results you are most surprised about and why. How do the results of the survey compare to the situation at your company?

**V1 ▶ | I1 ✋ 7 Your communication situations** → Grammar 1.1

1. Make a mind map showing the different people you communicate with at work and for what purposes. Try to include formal and informal situations, for example with colleagues, supervisors, customers or suppliers.

👥 2. Present your mind map to a partner. Talk to them about how the modes and methods of communication are different for each of the people and situations.

### Phrases

I have to talk to … about …
When I communicate with …, I use …
I would (not) use … to …
It's better to communicate with … via … because …

Basic 5

# Company communication

## Situation

Sarah has started an apprenticeship as a mechatronics technician at *AutoBright GmbH*, a mid-sized manufacturer of modern car lighting systems. The language spoken at the company is English. During her apprenticeship, she will need to develop her technical skills and learn to use the communication tools.

### 1 Collaborative tools
Match the communication options shown with their functions.

1. Voice over Internet Protocol (VoIP)
2. instant messenger 
3. online collaboration 
4. AI chatbot 
5. video conferencing 
6. email 

A longer, text-based electronic messages and files sent to individuals and groups anywhere in the world
B real-time text-based method of communication between users which enables quick and direct conversations and includes features like emojis
C supports teamwork and communication, enabling individuals and teams to work together on projects, share documents, schedule tasks and coordinate work in a virtual environment
D allows individuals and teams to have face-to-face meetings over the internet, with features such as video and audio calls, screen sharing and collaboration tools
E enables users to make cost-effective digital calls instead of using traditional phone lines
F automated text-based or voice conversations with users to answer questions, provide information and help with tasks

### 2 Discuss the communication tools with a partner. In which situations might Sarah use them?

## 5 Basic

> **Business basics**
>
> In smaller companies, personal and direct forms of communication (e.g. face-to-face discussions, phone calls) are more common since employees often work at the same location. Larger companies often need to invest in communication and collaboration tools because they have employees in different countries and locations working together on the same projects. Confidential documents and legal contracts that require handwritten signatures may still be sent by post, but digital alternatives have become far more common.

**3** Choose the most suitable communication option for each situation.
Compare your results with a partner and explain your reasons to each other.

1. A team of engineers with colleagues in Germany, India and the US needs to have a real-time discussion about a project update.
2. A group of employees in Spain needs to work on a project task with some colleagues in Brazil. The work will take several days.
3. The HR department needs to interview people for a new role at the company.
4. The IT helpdesk is handling a large amount of user enquiries.
5. Two software developers are working from home and need to have a quick exchange about a coding issue.
6. The IT department needs to send out some information about a software update to all employees.
7. A supervisor needs to schedule some meetings with the new apprentices.
8. The sales team wants to do some training sessions about a new product.
9. A technician needs to use the manufacturer's hotline to describe a problem with a product supplied to the company.

**4** **Over to you** Your company's communication tools → ○ 4, p. 158 → Grammar 8

V10 | I10

Think about the communication options at your company.
Make notes to answer the following questions:

- Which communication tools, programs and apps are available?
  Which ones do you use the most? When and why?
- How do you access the tools? Do you have one central device, workspace or platform?
  Can you access them when you are working offsite?
- Are any of the tools linked?
- Have you had any problems with any of the tools or programs?
  Which of them do you avoid and why?

Share your notes with a partner. Together, discuss how the communication options might be improved, e.g. in terms of organisation, user-friendliness or efficiency.

> **Phrases**
>
> At my company, workers have access to …
> You can log in to the platform via …
> We almost always use … for …
> I use … sometimes / occasionally / rarely.
> I find … useful / practical / difficult because …

Basic 5

# Instructions

> **Situation**
>
> Alex has completed the first part of her training as a field service technician at *Sparks GmbH* and is ready to start going to client sites with senior technicians. The company van plays an important role in these visits, as it is stocked with tools, equipment and sensitive technology. Alex's supervisor, Mr McKenzie, introduces her to the electric van she will be driving.

A12 🔊 **1** Listen to the dialogue and write down the key topics included in the training.
D9 📄

A12 🔊 **2** Listen again and take notes to answer the following questions:

- What kinds of questions does Mr McKenzie ask Alex? Why?
- How does Mr McKenzie make sure that Alex has understood what he has told her?
- What questions does Alex ask? Why?

Compare your notes with a partner.

A12 🔊 **3** Find the opposites of the following words from the dialogue.

1. available
2. nearest
3. secured
4. evenly
5. regular
6. sure
7. comfortable

A12 🔊 **4** Listen one more time and decide whether the following statements are true or false.

A This is Alex's first time driving an electric van.
B Another colleague is responsible for securing the equipment transported in the van.
C Electric vehicles are not as loud as fuel-system vehicles.
D Alex feels like she needs more information before she can drive the van.

65

## 5 Basic

D13

# ELECTRIC DRILL

## Main components

**Drill bit:** The cutting tool that attaches to the front of the drill to make holes in various materials.
**Chuck:** Holds the drill bit in place; often adjustable to fit different bit sizes.
**Speed trigger:** A trigger on the handle that controls how fast the drill bit spins; more pressure means higher speed.
**Handle grip:** Where you hold the drill; designed for comfort and control.
**Torque adjustment:** Allows you to change the drill's turning force for different materials and tasks.

**Motor:** Powers the drill, converting electrical energy into the rotational force that turns the drill bit.
**Reverse switch:** Changes the direction of rotation of the drill bit; useful for removing screws or extracting the bit from a hole.
**Battery:** Provides power to the drill without needing to plug it into the mains; removable and rechargeable.
**Power:** Switch or button that turns the drill on and off; sometimes integrated with the speed trigger.

## Use

Secure the drill bit, adjust torque as needed, press the speed trigger to activate the motor and begin drilling. Use the reverse switch to remove screws or the drill bit from the material.

## Safety

- Always wear safety goggles to protect your eyes from debris and gloves to protect your hands from sharp edges and increase grip.
- Make sure that the material you're working on is clamped down or securely held in place to stop the material from moving unexpectedly, which could cause the drill to slip.
- Select a drill bit that is appropriate for the material you're drilling. Using the wrong type of drill bit can lead to accidents or damage the material.
- Set the torque and speed according to the material and task. Using too much force or speed can cause the drill bit to slip or the material to splinter.
- Make sure your work area is free of clutter and well lit. A clean, bright environment helps you see what you're doing and avoid potential hazards.

Basic 5

4 Read the text and look up any words you don't know. With a partner, brainstorm some questions that someone learning about this device might have.

5 Work in pairs. Use the cards to perform a role play about how to use the drill. → ○ 5, p. 159

| Supervisor | Apprentice |
|---|---|
| Explain the electric drill to the apprentice. Use the key information and the picture to describe the tool's features and functions. Answer their questions and make sure that they have understood. Offer them some tips and explain how to use the drill safely. | Show interest in learning about the tool and listen carefully to the supervisor's explanations. Ask relevant questions to deepen your understanding and clarify information. |

D10  6 Report back to the class about your role play. Did the supervisor communicate the information clearly? Were they able to answer the apprentice's questions? Did the apprentice react appropriately? What could be improved?

7 **Over to you** Experiences receiving and giving instructions

Receiving and giving instructions can be a challenge.

1. Have you ever been in a situation where you were introduced to a new technical concept or a new piece of equipment? How was the information presented to you? How did you make sure you understood everything? What did you do about any points that were unclear? Make notes.
2. Have you ever had to give another employee instructions about how to do something? How did you make sure you were clear and respectful, and that they understood what you were saying?

### Phrases

I showed my colleague how to …
When they didn't understand what I meant, I …
They found it difficult to …, so I …
I tried to …
I made sure … by …

## 5 Advanced

# Telephone communication

### Situation
The automobile manufacturer *Britannia Motors Ltd.* is interested in *AutoBright*'s latest energy-efficient lighting systems. A caller from *Britannia Motors* wants to find out more about the systems' compatibility with its new car models, their energy consumption and durability. Sarah needs to answer the caller's questions and provide further information and technical advice.

### LUX-Beam LED car lighting system: Providing superior road illumination with energy-efficient technology

**Model:** LUX-Beam 500
**Item code:** LB-500-XE
**Features:** adaptive brightness | integrated heat management | flicker-free technology
**Benefits:** enhanced visibility and safety | reduced energy consumption | long-lasting performance | easy installation

**Light output:** 3000 lumens per bulb
**Power consumption:** 35 watts per hour
**Voltage:** 12–24V DC
**Lifespan:** 50,000 hours
**Light colour:** Cool white (6500 kelvin)
**Material:** Aerospace-grade aluminium
**Certifications:** E-Mark, RoHS, CE
**Compatibility:** Compatible with most modern car models

**1** Match the nouns with their definitions.

| | | | |
|---|---|---|---|
| 1 | compatibility | A | the amount of time for which something lasts |
| 2 | consumption | B | use of something, usually energy or fuel |
| 3 | durability | C | ability to function for a long period of time |
| 4 | enhanced | D | how well something fulfils its function |
| 5 | performance | E | ability to work together |
| 6 | lifespan | F | improved in comparison to an older version |

**2** Use the product profile to write five sentences summarising the key information about the lighting system.

**3 Problems on the phone** → ○ 3, p. 159
Look at the possible challenges Sarah might come across during her phone call with the customer. With a partner, discuss how she might deal with each situation.

- lack of knowledge or information
- caller is rude or unfriendly
- poor signal or internet connection
- difficulty understanding the caller due to language

Advanced 5

4 Use the cards to act out the telephone conversation with a partner.
→ Grammar 1.2, 1.10, 11.2

**AutoBright GmbH**
customer service desk

1. Greet the caller professionally, introduce yourself and politely ask the reason for their call.
3. Outline the product and ask what specific details they need.
5. Explain the compatibility of the lighting system with new, complex car models. Use precise figures to talk about energy efficiency.
7. Spell out the product name, technical terms and a quotation number using the phonetic alphabet.
9. Thank the caller for their enquiry and confirm the next steps.
11. End the call.

**Britannia Motors Ltd.**
representative

2. Start the call with a professional greeting and say you want to enquire about the *LUX-Beam 500* lighting system.
4. Ask for technical details about energy consumption, durability and system compatibility.
6. Express interest in placing an order and ask for a quote.
8. Spell out your company name and contact details using the phonetic alphabet.
10. Thank the service agent and ask for information about the next steps.

## Phrases

Hello, this is … from … speaking. How can I help you?
All our lighting systems are compatible with …
The *LUX-Beam 500* is a state-of-the-art system that will …
It consumes … watts per hour and has a durability estimate of …
Let me spell that out for you: …
Thank you very much for your call. I will now …

I am calling to ask for some more information about …
Could you explain/provide …?
Can I assume that it is …?
I would be interested in ordering …

5 **Over to you** Communicating with external partners

Think of a situation where a customer, supplier or other external partner might contact your company by phone, e.g. to find out about a product or the status of an order. Note down the key points of their enquiry and some typical questions they might ask. Give your notes to a partner and ask them to play the role of the external party while you practise your answers accordingly. Invent extra details about the situation and the company if you need to.

# 5 Task

## Product development and communication

### Situation

You are an apprentice at *EuroTech Solutions GmbH*. The company is working on a project with city officials, local businesses, community organisations and other partners to develop a smart city infrastructure in Sarajevo. Your team has been asked to research and present an innovative product for the smart city infrastructure and to suggest a communication strategy for its integration into the project. All documentation and communication will be in English.

### Business basics

Project management means planning and organising a project to make sure it is completed successfully and on time. It involves setting goals, managing resources, leading teams and solving problems. Various methods and approaches can be used.

### NEXTGen Cityscape Project Sarajevo

**NEXTGen Cityscape Project Sarajevo** will transform Sarajevo into a smart city, integrating advanced technologies to modernise its infrastructure. Sarajevo is rich in history and cultural significance but has faced challenges when it comes to technological development. **NEXTGen Cityscape Project Sarajevo** will focus on improving connectivity, sustainable development and quality of life for its residents, while respecting and protecting the city's unique character. The initiative presents an opportunity to pave the way for a more connected and efficient future. IoT (Internet of Things) solutions will be used to increase energy efficiency, introduce intelligent transportation systems, reduce traffic and develop digital platforms to improve public services. The project will focus on the central district of the city, covering an area of eight square kilometres and directly impacting around 100,000 residents.

| Phase | Goals | Timeframe | Budget |
|---|---|---|---|
| 1 | Planning and infrastructure assessment | 6 months | 50 m EUR |
| 2 | Implementation of core technologies | 12 months | 120 m EUR |
| 3 | Growth and optimisation | 18 months | 50 m EUR |

Task 5

### Step 1

Work in small groups. Study the project description and divide up the following points among the members of your group:

- basic concept of a smart city
- needs and challenges of Sarajevo
- goals of the smart city project
- timeline, phases and budget
- people and groups involved

Do some research on the points you have been given and make notes.

### Step 2

Brainstorm innovative technological ideas, products or applications within your field of work that could be implemented in a smart city. Discuss your ideas as a group and then choose one.

### Step 3

Develop a basic project plan for how your chosen technology could be implemented in Sarajevo. Consider the following points:

- its location within the city
- which groups of people would use it
- requirements for its implementation
- an approximate timeline and budget

### Step 4

Plan a communication strategy for how you would explain your idea to stakeholders. This might include presentations, project management software or social media. Consider any written documents that would need to be created and think about the internal and external communication needed for each phase of the project.

D1
### Step 5

Create visuals to explain your idea and its benefits for Sarajevo, as well as your communication strategy. Put the most important information into a presentation and practise it. Use the visuals to make your presentation more engaging.

D2
### Step 5

Share your presentation with the rest of the class. Ask for feedback and improve your idea and presentation accordingly.

# 6 In the workshop

## A workshop tour

Mechanics in a car workshop use a wide variety of tools and machines. To be able to work efficiently they need to know how and when to use these tools and machines, and where they are kept in the workshop. Safety plays an important role as well. Knowing how to use tools and machines safely is essential.

### At the end of this module, you will be able to:
- describe the floor plan of a car workshop
- name tools that are used in a car workshop
- explain how to change tyres
- talk about safety instructions in general and for work that involves electricity
- talk to a customer about safely transporting a vehicle

A13
D9

**1 A workshop floor plan** → Vocabulary

Paul Erichsen, the chief mechanic at *Erichsen KFZ-Service*, is taking two trainees from Sweden on a tour of the workshop. Listen to the first part of the tour and match the words with the correct parts of the floor plan (1–12).

break room | toilets | changing room | inspection pit | reception area | shelves | workbenches car lift | storage room | spare parts and tyres store | waste and recycling bins | working area

**Starting point 6**

A14 🔊 **2 Workshop equipment** → Vocabulary
Listen to the second part of the workshop tour. Write down the tools, machines, and equipment that you can find on the shelves and the tool trolleys.

> **Words**
>
> **socket spanner set** – *das Steckschlüsselsortiment*
> **torque wrench** – *der Drehmomentschlüssel*
> **pneumatic impact wrench** – *der Druckluftschlagschrauber*
> **car lift** – *die Hebebühne*
> **tyre pressure gauge** – *der Reifendruckmesser*

**3** Work with a partner. Ask each other questions about the places, tools and machines in the *Erichsen KFZ-Service* workshop. Where can you find them?

Examples: Where can I find the reception area?
– It's right here next to the entrance.
Where is the impact wrench kept?
– It is kept on shelf B.

**4 Your workshop**
Go online and find a video in which a car workshop is presented. Look up any words you don't know and note down the main points that are mentioned. Share them with your group. What did you like and what did you not like about the way the car workshop was presented?

**5** Now draw a rough floor plan of your own car workshop. Describe the workshop to your
V8 ▶ | I8 👆 partner, including information about the different machines and tools that are used in
V9 ▶ | I9 👆 your workshop. → Grammar 5, 6

> **Phrases**
>
> I'm going to tell you about the different facilities and explain to you …
> In front of / Beside / To the left / right of … you will find …
> The door / gate leads to …
> After you have passed … you will come to …
> Now we are entering …
> The area is organised into …
> This is where we keep …

# 6 Basic

## Tools in a car workshop

### Situation
Cem, an apprentice at *Erichsen KFZ-Service*, is preparing for the arrival of two trainees from Sweden. He is researching the English names of the different tools used in the workshop.

**1 Hand tools and power tools** → Vocabulary

The tools in the pictures are used in every car workshop. Match the words with the pictures.

(outside) micrometer | torque wrench | oscilloscope | pneumatic impact wrench
dial gauge | cranked ring spanner | diagnostic tester | multimeter

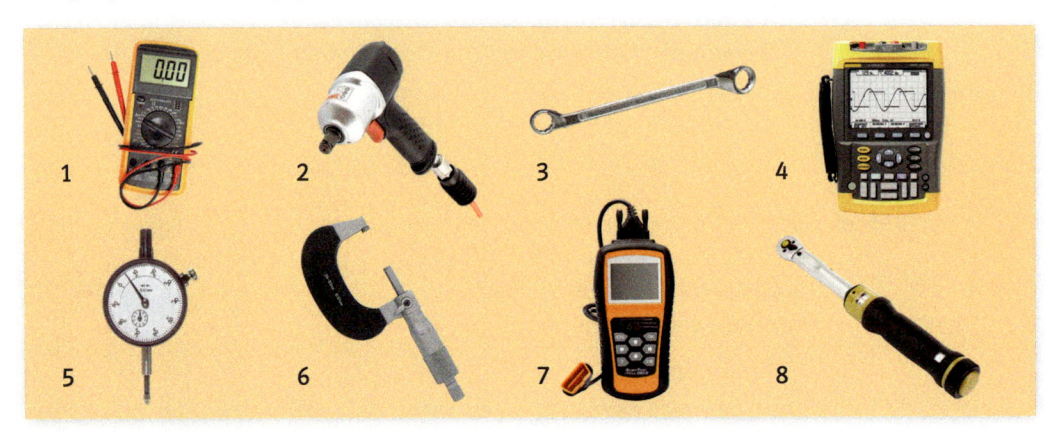

**2** Which tools would you use for the different tasks? Match the sentence parts.

1. For checking and filling up tyres …
2. If you need to change the wheels on a car, …
3. If you need to measure electrical voltage, …
4. To replace batteries …
5. For disassembling car parts …
6. To fix dents …
7. To find a problem with a car …

A … you use a rubber hammer.
B … you use an engine diagnostic tool.
C … you need screwdrivers, ratchets, wrenches, a hammer, pliers, a spanner, and an outside micrometer.
D … you will use a multimeter and an oscilloscope.
E … you use a compressor and a tyre gauge.
F … you will use a wrench, a wheel balancer, a tyre changer, and a spanner.
G … you use pliers, a socket wrench and a hammer.

**3 Over to you** Using tools in your workshop → Grammar 1.3

Describe which tools you have recently used in your workshop and explain what you used them for. Write full sentences in the past tense.

Basic **6**

# Safety measures

### Situation
*Erichsen KFZ-Service* is taking part in the EU's *Erasmus+* programme and is hosting two trainees from Sweden. They will be at the company for two weeks. Before they can start working in the workshop, they need to learn the basic safety rules, including what kind of safety clothing and safety equipment they should use. Paul Erichsen has asked his apprentice Cem to explain the safety measures to the new trainees, so Cem does some research to find the English vocabulary he needs.

### Information
The *Erasmus+* programme is a European Union (EU) exchange programme which enables trainees in EU countries to gain valuable work experience in another EU country.

## 1 Protective workwear → Vocabulary
Match the words with the pictures.

safety shoes | safety goggles / safety glasses | overall | kneepads | protective mask
protective gloves | flame-resistant clothing | ear protection | face shield | safety helmet

## 2 Complete the sentences with words from the previous exercise.

1. Did you know that the colour blue, which is used often for mechanics' —, is supposed to increase the customer's trust?
2. A mechanic often comes into contact with hot and sharp objects. Therefore, they have to wear —. These often have rubber grips on the palms for holding tools.
3. In a workshop, there are a lot of big, heavy objects that could fall or roll onto your feet. That is why mechanics have to wear —, which are also waterproof and electrical hazard-resistant.
4. When grinding or sanding parts of a vehicle — are often not sufficient. Consider wearing a — instead.
5. If you have to raise your voice to be heard, — should be worn to avoid damaging your hearing.

## 6 Basic

### Safety rules for automotive repair shops

[...] The following is a list of general safety tips every repair shop should use to keep everyone safe.
- Never smoke in or near repair bays or garages. Vehicles contain flammable and combustible fluids that can easily be set on fire if hot ash from a cigar or cigarette were to come into contact with such materials.
- Keep work areas clean and organized. Pick up tools and use tool cabinets to keep walkways clear and free from clutter. Whether it's a workbench, the workshop floor, toolboxes, or the office, keeping your workspace free from clutter and organizing tools and equipment correctly can prevent a number of dangerous workplace risks and help maintain overall shop safety. [...]
- Never wear loose clothing or clothing that is ripped or torn. To prevent employees from wearing unacceptable attire, it is recommended to obtain customized uniforms and work apparel from a qualified uniform service company.
- Wear protective gear at all times, as appropriate for the repair. Goggles, gloves, and ear protection should be worn when making certain types of repairs.
- Make sure fire extinguishers are easily acceptable and appropriate for all potential fire types. In the event of a fire, extinguishers need to be accessed quickly and be charged with the right materials to put out the type of fire: i.e., gas, oil, electrical, and so on. [...]
- Never work underneath a vehicle unless it has been properly supported. Raising the vehicle off the ground to access the underside requires verifying it is stable, and that there is no risk of the vehicle falling on top of the mechanic. [...]
- Be aware of the vehicle's temperature before beginning any work. The engine, manifold, exhaust system, and radiator could be hot and cause skin burns. Plus, the radiator coolant is still pressurized.
- In addition to wearing chemical and fire resistant clothing, workers should be educated on the right procedures to follow in case of common auto shop safety risks. These include fires, electrical issues, and chemical spills. Regularly retrain new and existing employees in the right steps to take in case of such safety risks to minimize the damage they cause when they happen. [...]

(360 words)
*Prudential Overall Supply, USA,* 2023

### 3 Safety rules

Match the words from the text (1–8) with their synonyms (A–H).
Then translate them into German.

1 torn
2 to prevent
3 to verify
4 manifold
5 combustible
6 attire / apparel
7 fluid
8 loose

A clothing
B to check
C ripped
D flammable, burnable
E to stop, to avoid
F not fixed, baggy
G elbow
H liquid

**4** Complete each sentence with the correct word from the text.

appropriate | customized | acceptable | properly | correct

1. If the fuel gauge does not show the — fuel consumption value, there could be a problem with the fuel supply sensor.
2. A car mechanic has to carry out all repairs to an — standard.
3. — workwear gives a car workshop a professional look.
4. Tools must be stored — to avoid corrosion or damage.
5. You should always wear protective gear which is — for the work you are doing.

**5** Complete the workshop safety rules by putting in *Do* ✅ or *Don't*. ❌

1. — smoke in the workshop as it contains many flammable fluids.
2. — keep walkways clear and free from things lying around.
3. — put tools away properly so that other people will not fall over scattered parts or tools.
4. — wear loose clothing.
5. — forget to check if a vehicle is properly supported before it is raised off the ground.
6. — make sure you know where the nearest fire extinguisher is.
7. — inform yourself about all safety procedures to avoid putting yourself or others at risk.

**6** Find words in the text that fit into the following categories. → ○ 6, p. 156

| Car parts | Areas and equipment in a workshop | Safety attire and equipment | Safety risks and possible accidents |
|---|---|---|---|
| … | … | … | … |

**7** Complete the sentences with words you collected in the previous exercise.

1. A car mechanic can easily get burnt if they come into contact with a hot —.
2. You can find the tools you need in the —.
3. Sometimes, engine oil, coolants or brake fluids can leak from cars and cause a —.
4. When welding, a mechanic should wear —.
5. You should always wear the right attire in the workshop and never wear —.
6. I had forgotten to switch off the car and received an — shock.

**8 Over to you** Safety in your workshop → Grammar 8

Copy and fill in the following form. Are you satisfied with how safety is handled at your workplace or do some things need to be improved? Discuss with a partner.

| | Always | Sometimes | Never |
|---|---|---|---|
| 1. First aid kits are provided and well kept. | … | … | … |
| 2. Employees are regularly trained in first aid. | … | … | … |
| 3. Emergency exits are well signposted. | … | … | … |
| 4. Fire extinguishers are available and in good condition. | … | … | … |
| 5. Workspaces are tidy. | … | … | … |

## 6 Basic

## Changing tyres

### Situation
One of the first tasks the Swedish trainees are asked to do is to change tyres. As they do not have much experience, Cem gives them some information about how to change a tyre and what tools to use.

### Information
Unless you have all-season tyres, tyres have to be changed twice a year. This ensures safety, improved grip and optimal fuel consumption, as well as reducing wear and tear. Keep tyres inflated according to tyre pressure specifications to avoid accidents. EU tyre labelling helps to choose more fuel-efficient tyres.

D3 **1 Car tyres** → Vocabulary
Look at the two drawings and complete the sentences with the correct car tyre parts.

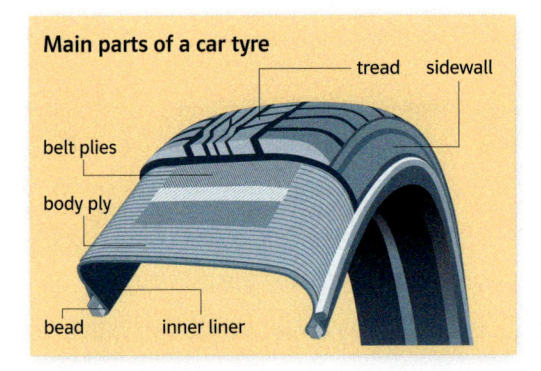

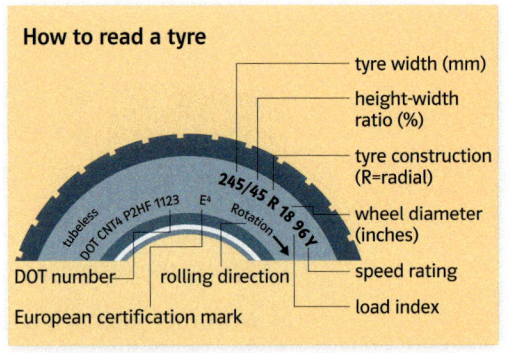

**Main parts of a car tyre**: tread, sidewall, belt plies, body ply, bead, inner liner

**How to read a tyre**: tyre width (mm), height-width ratio (%), tyre construction (R=radial), wheel diameter (inches), speed rating, load index, DOT number, rolling direction, European certification mark

1. The — is made of rubber. It's the part of the tyre that comes into contact with the road.
2. Between the tread and the body ply you will find the —. These are rubber-coated layers of steel, fibreglass and other materials which hold the plies in place.
3. On the —, which protects the body ply, you will find the tyre markings and other important information such as the tyre size and type.
4. The — is made up of several layers of fabric, also called plies, and is coated with rubber to seal in air and strengthen the structure of the tyre.
5. The — is the inner layer of a tubeless tyre. It is made of rubber and the air pressure inside it is very high.
6. The — is a rubber-coated loop of high-strength steel cable that allows the tyre to stay "seated" on the rim.

**2** Work with a partner. Take turns explaining to each other what the different numbers and symbols on a car tyre mean. Use the *Words* and *Phrases* to help you.

### Words
**date of production** – *das Herstelldatum* | **age of the tyre** – *das Alter des Reifens*
**calendar week** – *die Kalenderwoche* | **rolling direction** – *die Laufrichtung*

Basic **6**

### Phrases

One of the most important details you can find on a tyre is …
The … is given in millimetres.
The … tells you how old a tyre is; it consists of four numbers.
It is important to pay attention to the … when fitting tyres.

### 3 How to change a tyre

Look at the pictures showing how a car driver should change a tyre.
Match the steps (A–F) with the pictures (1–6).

1
2
3
4
5
6

A Attach the spare tyre and screw the wheel nuts back on by hand.
B Remove the wheel cover and loosen the nuts with the wheel wrench.
C Turn the wheel nuts anti-clockwise, remove them and put them in a safe place. Now you can remove the wheel.
D Check that you have all the necessary parts and tools. You will need: a spare tyre, a wheel wrench, a car jack, and a hazard triangle if you are changing the tyre at the roadside. You should always check your car manual to be sure about the steps before you start. Park your car: For a manual transmission, use first or reverse gear, for automatic transmission use the parking brake.
E Lower the vehicle carefully and remove the jack. Tighten the wheel nuts in a star or cross pattern using the wheel wrench.
F Place the jack under the car. The car manual might tell you the best place to put it. Then raise the jack to lift the car off the ground.

### Words

**to loosen** – *lockern, aufdrehen* | **wheel wrench** – *das Radkreuz*
**clockwise / anti-clockwise** – *im / gegen den Uhrzeigersinn*
**car jack** – *der Wagenheber* | **transmission** – *das Getriebe*
**reverse gear** – *der Rückwärtsgang* | **to tighten** – *anziehen*

## 6 Basic

### 4 Over to you Changing tyres professionally

In a professional environment, mechanical and hydraulic tools make changing tyres easier and faster. Which tools do you use to change tyres in your workshop? How do you use them? Write full sentences. The *Words* can help you.

> **Words**
>
> **chock** – *der Unterlegkeil* | **pneumatic car jack** – *der pneumatische Wagenheber*
> **to raise** – *anheben* | **wheel bolt** – *die Radschraube*
> **torque wrench** – *der Drehmomentschlüssel* | **torque value** – *der Drehmomentwert*
> **tyre valve** – *das Reifenventil*

5 Explain the steps of changing a tyre in your workshop to a partner. Take turns.

## Transporting a vehicle

> **Situation**
>
> A customer from Denmark left his SUV at *Erichsen KFZ-Service* after having an accident. He now wants to transport his car back to Denmark himself and have it repaired there. As he has no experience of towing a car, Cem is going to explain to him what he needs to do.

### 1 Different types of cars  → ○ 1, p. 156

Car workshops often repair a wide range of vehicles. Match the vehicle types to the pictures.

**lorry | pickup truck | estate car | convertible / cabriolet | sedan / saloon | SUV**

1　　　2　　　3

4　　　5　　　6

> **Information**
>
> Car workshops often work with transport services to move vehicles quickly and at good prices to different locations. The costs depend on many factors including the type of vehicle, the mode of transport and the distance between locations.

## How auto transport companies load cars onto their trailers

Loading expensive exotic cars onto a trailer takes patience, care, and skill. The goal [...] is to get your car from point A to point B without a scratch on it. [...]

There are two ways to get a car onto a trailer. A company will use either ramps or hydraulic lifts. Those two methods have major differences that can affect the condition of your car. Some carriers prefer using car hauling ramps because they're cheaper than hydraulic lift gates. That might decrease the cost of shipping your car in the short term, but there are dangers associated with ramps. Ramps pose a risk to vehicles that sit low to the ground. The possibility of scraping the underside of the car increases during loading due to the ramps steep incline. Some loaders use blocks of wood in addition to the ramps to cut the incline. The blocks can shoot up, after the car rolls off them, and hit the car. Hydraulic lift gates [...] are the safest way to load a vehicle. They're literally an elevator for the car during loading and unloading. They lower completely to the ground, so low clearance vehicles can drive on to the ramp without the risk of scraping the undercarriage. They also give the driver much more control over the car. Instead of the driver having to drive up two thin ramps, he can slowly drive on and off the liftgate. There are no inclines that require aggressive acceleration or excessive brake control. Burning up a clutch happens when loading cars on ramps, so lift gates are the best option.

When securing your car [...] only use nylon wheel tie downs, never chains. Nylon tie downs are the only way to secure a classic car for transport because they won't damage the car. The straps go over the tire and never meet the frame or chassis. Chains get attached to holes underneath the vehicle, on the frame, and then onto the trailer. Putting chains on too tight could bend the frame, which could result in thousands of dollars of damage. By attaching chains to the wrong place underneath the car, they could slip out and allow the car to roll in transit or possibly scratch the paint. Attaching to the wrong spot can also bend the frame and chassis.

(390 words)
*Intercity Lines, Inc.*, 2023

## 2 Loading cars onto trailers

Read the text and match the verbs with the correct nouns.

| | |
|---|---|
| 1 take | A the cost |
| 2 affect | B patience |
| 3 decrease | C the car |
| 4 scrape | D chains |
| 5 burn up | E a risk |
| 6 secure | F the condition |
| 7 attach | G the paint |
| 8 bend | H the underside/undercarriage |
| 9 scratch | I a clutch |
| 10 pose | J the frame and the chassis |

## 6 Basic

**3** Read the text again and answer the questions about loading cars onto trailers in German.

1. Welche Gefahren können durch den Gebrauch von Rampen auftreten?
2. Welche Vorteile hat ein hydraulischer Lift?
3. Welche Vorteile hat die Radbefestigung mit Nylongurten?
4. Welche Probleme kann es geben, wenn Ketten am Fahrzeug befestigt werden?

**4** The Danish customer calls the workshop to explain that he wants to transport his SUV back to Denmark himself. Cem gives him some helpful advice.
Act out the dialogue with a partner and give additional information if possible.

| Cem | Danish customer |
|---|---|
| 1. Answer the phone call. | 2. Give your name and explain that you have found a way to transport your car back to Denmark – trailer. |
| 3. Explain that loading and driving with a trailer is not easy. | 4. Say that you have watched some videos and that you will practise driving and braking with the trailer before you start your journey. |
| 5. Warn the customer that the total weight must not be higher than 3,5 t. Ask about the specifications of the trailer. | 6. Answer: weight 600 kg, payload 2 t, size approx. 5x2 m |
| 7. Give a hint: low angle and ramps useful when loading. | 8. Answer: ramps 1,500 mm, angle 6 degrees |
| 9. Mention accessories necessary for loading / unloading, e.g. wheel chocks. | 10. Say that relevant accessories are included, e.g. ropes. |
| 11. Ask if the loading area is tiltable. | 12. Reply that your trailer has a tiltable loading area. |
| 13. Tell the customer that there is no crane at the workshop, so a cable winch will be necessary. Offer to help with loading. | 14. Say that the ramp is equipped with its own electrical winch. |
| 15. Say that you have lots of experience of loading / unloading trailers. Explain that you normally use a car manoeuvring aid. | 16. Say you are grateful for Cem's help. |
| 17. Remind the customer that the indicators and brake lights on the trailer must be working properly. | 18. Explain that the trailer has its own braking system. Ask about additional regulations for transporting cars in Germany. |
| 19. Explain that there are no special regulations and that you can transport a car on a trailer with a normal driving licence. | 20. Thank Cem and finish the call. |
| 21. Say that you will pass on all the information to the chief mechanic and thank the customer for his call. | |

## Basic 6

### Words

**angle** – *der Winkel* | **ramp** – *die Rampe* | **accessories** – *das Zubehör*
**loading area** – *die Ladefläche* | **tiltable** – *kippbar* | **crane** – *der Kran*
**cable winch** – *die Seilwinde* | **car manoeuvring aid** – *die Rangierhilfe*
**indicator** – *der Blinker* | **driving licence** – *der Führerschein*

### 5 Over to you How to jump-start an old car → ○ 5, p. 157

Discuss the questions with a partner.

1. Why might it be necessary to jump-start a car?
2. Have you ever jump-started a car? If you have, was it easy to do?
3. What equipment do you need to jump-start a car?
4. Is it a good idea to jump-start a modern car?
5. How do you jump-start a car? Take turns explaining the steps.

### Words

**jumper cable** – *das Starthilfekabel* | **grounded** – *geerdet*
**clamps** – *die Klammern* | **to connect** – *verbinden* | **to recharge** – *aufladen*

# 6 Advanced

## Working with electricity

### Situation

Electrical systems in a car include the battery, alternator, lighting and ignition systems, starting motor, wires, fuses, sparks etc. It is very important to be aware of the dangers involved in repairing electrical systems in cars. Cem has been asked to inform the Swedish trainees about the risks and necessary precautions associated with repairing electrical systems.

A17

**Must-have safety tips for working with automotive electrical systems […]**

The ability to work with automotive electrical systems is an important part of every auto technician's job. However, it can also be one of the more complex and risky tasks you will face. […]
1. …
It is a lot easier to abide by safety standards if you understand what they are meant to prevent. Electrical safety is largely in place to prevent an event in which your body or the body of another person completes an electrical circuit, which is what leads to electricity-related injuries. Like water, most metals, and several other materials, the human body can conduct electricity, which puts us as at risk. Exposure to electrical currents can result in four main types of injuries: painful electric shocks, electrical burns, fatal electrocution, and falls caused by any of the above. […]
2. …
[…] One factor that increases the likelihood of you becoming a part of an electric circuit is contact with conducting materials, such as water or metal. Never do electrical work with wet hands, and survey your surroundings for puddles or unusual moisture before beginning your work. When working with metal, be sure to use tools with insulating materials like rubber, as well as protective and insulated gloves and eyewear, to avoid accidentally coming into contact with electrical currents.
3. …
Once you have a safe environment and the right tools, make sure you have de-energized the engine or piece of machinery that you are working with.
De-energizing involves the obvious step of simply unplugging or turning off the power source. However, you should also use a specialized tester in order to make sure there is no additional electricity flowing through the circuit before you begin handling wires.
4. …
[…] Smoking on the job is incredibly dangerous, as gasoline and many other fluids involved in vehicle work and repair are extremely flammable. While the fire hazard of electrical work is not nearly as high as with smoking, you should be similarly cautious when doing electrical work near flammable materials, as sparks can fly – especially when other electrical safety standards are neglected. Moreover, escaping vapors may form decomposition products such as hydrocyanic acid on contact with fire and glowing objects (cigarette!). Make sure you are working in a well-ventilated area, and that you know where the fire extinguisher in your workstation is. […]
5. …
Finally, electrical safety applies not only to the electrical system that you are working on, but also to the devices you are using. Make sure that you assess the cords on your equipment for damage, and either repair or discard equipment with exposed wires. […]

(469 words)

*Automotive Training Centre, Canada,* 2023

Advanced **6**

**1 Electrical systems in cars**
Read the text and match the headings (A–E) with the paragraphs (1–5).

A Know to disconnect power sources
B Do not use devices with frayed cords or wires
C Electrical safety is also fire safety
D Avoid water and other conducting materials when working with electricity
E Know the risks of electrical hazards

**2** Match the words from the text with their definitions.

| | | |
|---|---|---|
| 1 to prevent | A | to allow to flow |
| 2 to conduct | B | coming into contact with sth |
| 3 exposure | C | careful |
| 4 to insulate | D | flow of electricity |
| 5 electrical current | E | to stop sth from happening |
| 6 electrical circuit | F | to disconnect |
| 7 to de-energize | G | to cover sth in order to prevent electricity from travelling |
| 8 flammable | H | to let air flow through |
| 9 cautious | I | catches fire easily |
| 10 to ventilate | J | a closed path for electricity to flow through |

**3** Complete the following rules with words from the text.

1. Never do electrical work with —.
2. Survey your surroundings for —.
3. Use tools with insulating materials and wear —.
4. Make sure you do not accidentally come into contact with any —.
5. De-energize the —.
6. Unplug or turn off —.
7. Make sure you are working in —.
8. Make sure you know where —.
9. Assess the cords on your —.
10. Repair or discard equipment with —.

**4 First aid after an electric shock** → Grammar 11
Put the words into the right order to make sentences about what to do if someone gets an electric shock in a workshop.

1. are still in contact with | the person | Do not touch | the electrical source | if they
   Do not touch the person if they are still in contact with the electrical source.
2. the casualty | the electrical source | without touching | Disconnect
3. if the person | Check | and if they | is still breathing | have injuries
4. someone else | to call them | the emergency services | Call | or ask | immediately
5. the emergency services | you must | until | arrive | perform CPR | If you can't feel a pulse

85

## 6 Task

## Safety in your workshop

### Situation

There have recently been some small accidents in your workshop. The chief mechanic has asked you to create a poster explaining the most important safety rules and tips. He wants it to be in English so that non-German-speaking colleagues and trainees can understand it too.

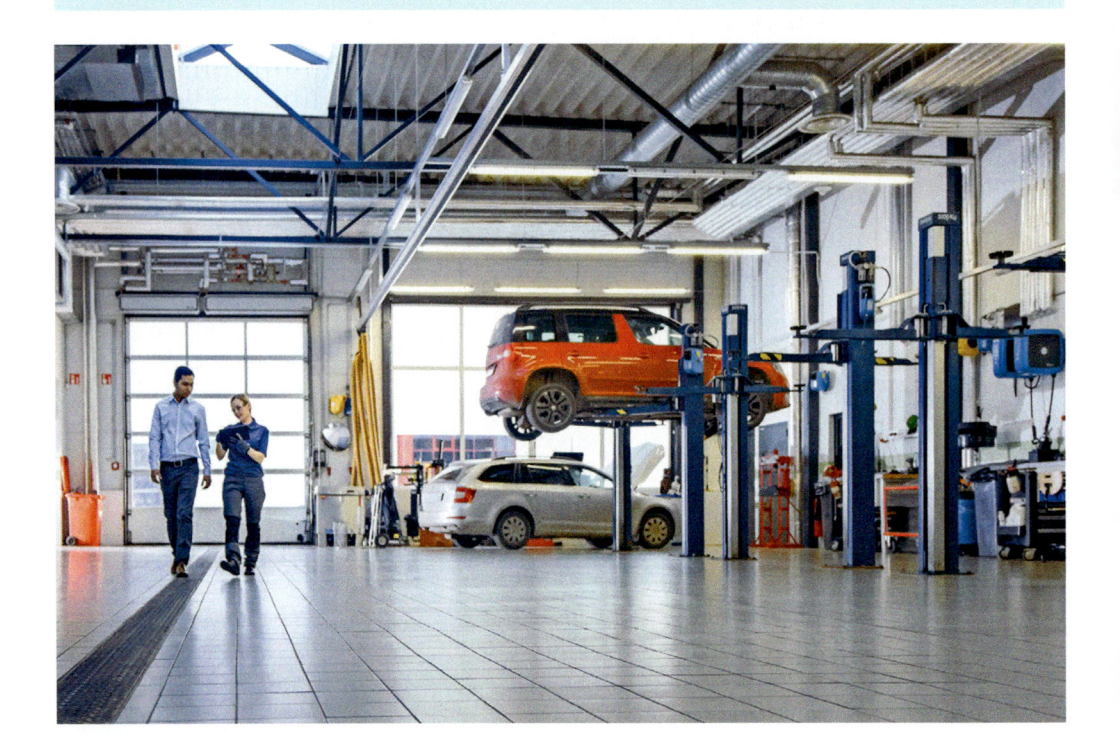

### Step 1

Work in small groups. Talk about the kind of accidents that happen most frequently in your workshops. Then research the most common kinds of accidents.
Make a list of the ten most common accidents.

### Step 2

What could cause the accidents on your list? Discuss in your group and write down the possible causes for each of the accidents.

### Step 3

Based on the causes you identified in Step 2, discuss how to prevent each of the accidents on your list.

### Step 4

Put your ideas from Step 3 into categories.

| What is forbidden | What to be careful about |
|---|---|
| Don't … | Caution! |
| **What is advised** | **Where to find things** |
| Do … | |

### Step 5

Now think about how you could present the rules on a poster. Think about the structure, symbols and colours you might use.

### Step 6

Make a poster about the ten most important workshop safety rules. Make sure your poster is:

- clear
- easy to understand
- informative
- eye-catching

> **Phrases**
>
> You should protect yourself by … | It's a good idea to …
> Make sure that … | Use … properly …
> Be careful … | Avoid … | You are required to …

# 7 Maintenance and repair work

## Servicing a vehicle

Servicing a car regularly ensures that a vehicle is safe to drive and that it fulfils all criteria to protect passengers and the environment. Car manufacturers often recommend service intervals and prepare checklists for servicing. In the European Union, vehicles must be regularly tested and must also undergo exhaust emissions tests.

### At the end of this module, you will be able to:
- explain technical problems to a customer and arrange for repair work to be done
- describe different types of brakes and how to repair them
- describe an internal combustion engine and ways to improve it
- understand and explain diagnostic codes

**1 What is checked during servicing?** → Vocabulary
Match the parts of a vehicle that are typically checked during servicing to the pictures.

braking and steering systems | chassis and body | coolant | engine | exhaust system
lights and signalling devices | wheels and tyres | windscreen wiper

1

2

3

4

Starting point **7**

5

6

7

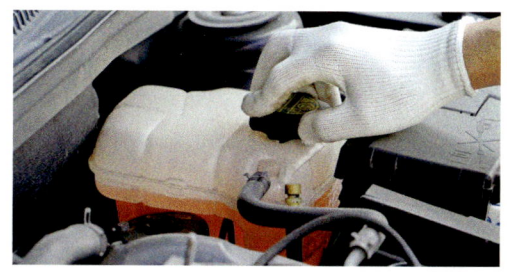

8

v7 | 17 **2** Put the words in the right order to make sentences about testing car parts. → Grammar 11

1. from under the bonnet | the brakes | The mechanic | for wear and from beneath the vehicle | inspects
2. must be | must work | and the wiper system | Windscreen wipers in good condition | properly
3. There | or any other fluids | no leakage of | must be | engine oil, gear oil
4. and reverse lights | be working | e.g. low and high beam, | All lights must properly, | parking lights
5. is 1.6 mm | for tyres | The minimum tread depth
6. that the chassis, doors, | from excessive corrosion | makes sure engine mounts etc. | The mechanic | are free

### 3 Car maintenance schedule

Customers can also follow maintenance schedules as recommended by car manufacturers. Read the text on the next page and answer the questions below. You do not need to use full sentences.

1. What are the risks of not having a maintenance schedule?
2. Where can you often find your car manual?
3. How are service appointments scheduled?
4. How can your car remind you of your maintenance schedule?
5. What is checked or replaced after roughly 60,000 miles and what is checked or replaced after 90,000 miles?
6. Where can you find specific information about a car's maintenance schedule?

89

# 7 Starting point

## Car maintenance schedule: Everything you need to know

[...] Service requirements can vary significantly from one car make and model to another. Depending on your car, your service appointment may be at 5,000 miles – or 15,000. Skipping service appointments can be inconvenient, dangerous, expensive, or all three. So grab that manual out of the glove box, and let's break down the details of keeping your car in great shape.

Typically, service appointments are scheduled either by time (how long it's been since your last appointment) or miles (how many miles you've driven since your last appointment). The manual will tell you the specific time or mileage windows, and most new cars come equipped with dashboard alerts to jog your memory.

[...] During the service appointment, your mechanic will work through the checklist provided by your manual. The newer your car – and the fewer miles it has – the less service it'll require. For your car's first 30,000 to 60,000 miles, simple services are enough: oil changes, tire rotations, and other low-cost inspections and updates. With more miles, more involved servicing becomes necessary. Your 90,000-mile service is usually the first big one, [...] requiring spark plugs, transmission fluid, and axle fluid, as well as replacements for the cabin filters (if your car has them). The specifics for your particular car are outlined in the manual, so take it with you to your appointment. Or, write down a list before you head into the mechanic's shop. (Lost the manual? Just search online for a PDF version using your car's make and model.) [...]

(256 words)

Madeleine Burry, *AAA American Automobile Association*, 2023

### Words

maintenance schedule – *der Wartungsplan / der Serviceplan*
car make – *die Automarke* | to skip – *auslassen*
glove box – *das Handschuhfach* | to break sth down – *etw. aufschlüsseln*
mileage – *der Kilometerstand* | to jog your memory – *deinem Gedächtnis nachhelfen*
spark plug – *die Zündkerze* | transmission fluid – *die Getriebeflüssigkeit*
axle fluid – *die Achsenflüssigkeit* | cabin filter – *der Innenraumfilter*

### 4 Repairs in your workshop

Think about your own workshop and answer the questions. Discuss your answers with a partner.
1. What are the most common reasons for cars to need repairs?
2. Which special tools do you use to carry out maintenance work?
3. Can you give one example of troubleshooting, testing, maintenance or repair work you have done in your workshop recently? What did you do and which tools did you use?

### Phrases

We often have to perform detailing work / replace spare parts / change ...
It is always necessary to check / inspect ...
Sometimes we diagnose ...

Basic 7

# The main inspection

### Situation

Aylin is working as an apprentice in a car workshop in Germany. Today, she is on the reception desk taking phone calls. Mr Singh, an English-speaking customer, had his car checked before its main inspection, and Aylin now needs to explain the problems with his car to him.

**A19 D9  1 Discussing repairs with a customer** → ● 1, p. 164 → Vocabulary

Listen to Aylin's phone conversation with Mr Singh. Say whether each of the following car parts needs to be repaired or not.

1. engine
2. transmission
3. drive axle
4. steering
5. braking
6. catalytic converter
7. tyres
8. headlights
9. indicators
10. oil level

### Words

cost estimate – *der Kostenvoranschlag* | warranty plan – *der Garantieplan*
to recommend – *empfehlen* | contract – *der Vertrag*
to come in handy – *gelegen kommen* | to take sth seriously – *etw. ernst nehmen*
dipstick – *der Ölmessstab*

**D4  2** Aylin's boss wants to know what she discussed with Mr Singh. In German, explain what repair work they have agreed on. → ○ 2, p. 157

**3** Besides the lights on the dashboard, there are other ways to detect problems with a car. Match the car parts to the problems.

| | | |
|---|---|---|
| 1 | electrical components | A unusual noises and vibrations, overheating, loss of power |
| 2 | fuel pump | B burning smell, vibrating, car being pulled to one side |
| 3 | engine | C difficulty shifting gears, grinding noises |
| 4 | suspension | D car struggling to start, flickering lights, smell of burnt plastic |
| 5 | brakes | E engine stalling, rust, poor fuel economy |
| 6 | gas tank | F rising temperature gauge, power surges, sputtering engine |
| 7 | transmission | G bouncing, creaking noise, uncomfortable driving |

## 7 Basic

> **Information**
> In the UK, the main inspection is called the MOT test (Ministry of Transport test). Once a car is three years old (or four years old in Northern Ireland), it must be tested every year. MOT tests are carried out at authorised test centres which display an official blue sign with three white triangles.

V1 | I1  **4 Talking to a customer** → Grammar 1.1, 1.2, 11.2 → ● 4, p. 164
V2 | I2
A car mechanic is telling an English-speaking customer about the main inspection in Germany. Write a dialogue using the prompts below.

| Customer's questions | Car mechanic's answers |
|---|---|
| • when necessary? | • every 2 years, after 3 years if new |
| • costs of main inspection? | • regional differences (around €149) |
| • if repairs are necessary? | • repairs, another test after one month |
| • if no valid main inspection and emissions badge? | • e.g. points in Flensburg |

**5 Over to you** Organising inspections at your workshop

Work with a partner and discuss the following questions.

1. How are main inspections organised at your workshop? Do you carry out the tests in your workshop or do you take the cars to an authorised test centre?
2. What kind of vehicles were brought to your workshop for inspection in the last couple of months?
3. What is your experience of the age and models of the cars that have the most problems passing their inspections?
4. Do your customers follow the maintenance schedules recommended by manufacturers?
5. Would the car in the photo pass its main inspection? Explain your answer.

Basic **7**

# Brakes

### Situation
Customers who come to Aylin's workshop often have problems with their brakes. Aylin wants to be prepared for her next conversation with an English-speaking customer, so she collects English words for the braking systems of different types of vehicles as well as maintenance work on brakes.

### Information
Car brakes are needed for stopping and slowing down. The braking system turns kinetic energy into heat, applying friction to the wheels in order to slow down. As brakes are exposed to wear and tear, they have to be serviced regularly. Two important brake types are disc brakes and drum brakes.

**1 Disc brakes and drum brakes** → Vocabulary

Look at the drawings of a disc brake and a drum brake. Match the words with the correct parts.

brake pad | brake rotor | return spring | backing plate | caliper | brake shoe

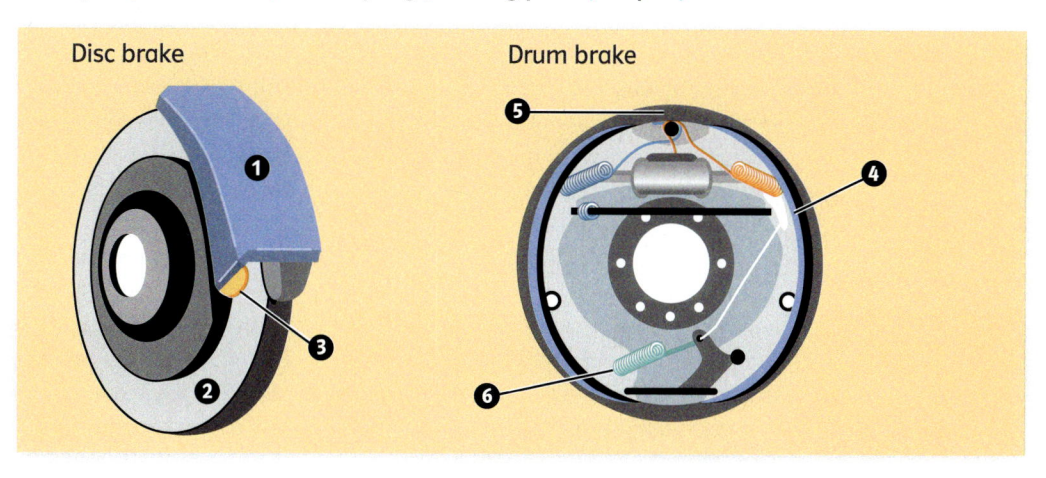

Disc brake                    Drum brake

**2** Use the following words to complete the sentences describing how disc brakes and drum brakes work.

increases | drum | front | hydraulically | slow down | bicycles | rear wheels | squeeze | principle

1. Disc brakes work like the brakes on some —, except that the brake pads — the brake rotor instead of the wheel.
2. The pressure is transmitted —.
3. The friction between the pads and the disc can — the disc and finally stop it moving.
4. Drum brakes work using the same — as disc brakes. The brake shoes press against a spinning surface called the —.
5. The overrunning brake shoes are pulled into the drum which — the braking effect.
6. Cars often have drum brakes on the — and disc brakes on the — wheels.

93

## 7 Basic

### 3 Different braking systems → ● 3, p. 164

Aylin has found a text about brakes in conventional cars and EVs. Find words in the text that describe hydraulic brakes and regenerative braking and how the two systems work. Translate the words into German.

|  | English | German |
|---|---|---|
| hydraulic brakes | hydraulic brakes | Hydraulikbremse |
|  | … | … |
| regenerative braking | … | … |

A20 🔊
D13 📄

**How brakes in electric cars are different**

[…] The brakes in a car, SUV, or pickup are called hydraulic brakes. They use hydraulic pressure to push a braking material <u>surface</u> against a metal rotating part. In a car with disc brakes, a bracket called a caliper squeezes two brake pad surfaces against an iron rotor. The rotor is <u>attached to</u> the <u>hub</u> and spins at the same speed as the wheel. Squeezing the brake pad against the rotor creates heat. Your forward motion becomes braking heat, and you stop. […]
So what's different about the brakes in your EV? In the basic part of the system, almost nothing. Your electric vehicle still has a brake pedal, hydraulic brakes, and disc <u>brake calipers</u> that <u>clamp</u> your brake rotors to help you stop.
But EVs have an extra system, one that is a complete game-changer when it comes to stopping. The system is called <u>regenerative braking</u>. It uses your EV's electric motors to stop your vehicle instead of just making it go. […] This means that the electric motor that gives you power when you're driving can actually generate power to send to the battery when you're slowing down. It works automatically, though the vehicle's computer system can change how much of the power from the motor is turned into electricity (and how quickly it happens) by changing how much power the motor is able to make and send to the battery. So every time you <u>lift off the accelerator</u> or gently apply the brakes in your EV, you're recovering up to 70% of your forward movement as electricity to put in the battery. Instead of wasting it as heat that is sent into the air.
Then why does your EV need regular hydraulic brakes? Because regenerative braking is limited. It can't stop a vehicle as quickly as hydraulic brakes because of limits to how much power it can recover. So in an emergency, you still need hydraulic brakes. Regenerative braking is also limited by the capacity of your EV's battery. If you've ever <u>headed downhill</u> with a full charge, you've probably noticed there is very little regeneration when you <u>let off</u> the accelerator. The same can happen at very low temperatures and after some steep hills. […]

(372 words)
*AutoGuide*, 2022

### 4 Explain in German why EVs still need hydraulic brakes.

## Words

**surface** – *die Oberfläche* | **attached to** – *befestigt an* | **hub** – *die Nabe*
**brake caliper** – *der Bremssattel* | **to clamp** – *festklemmen*
**regenerative braking** – *die Rekuperationsbremse*
**to lift off the accelerator** – *vom Gas gehen* | **accelerator** – *das Fahrpedal*
**to head downhill** – *bergab steuern* | **to let off sth** – *etw. loslassen*

## 5 Braking system malfunctions

Complete the sentences about different problems with the braking system.

1 If the brake fluid runs dry, …
2 If you can push the pedal to the floor without resistance, …
3 When a brake caliper is stuck because of rust or corrosion, …
4 If it is difficult to press the brake pedal down, …
5 A common cause of the car being pulled to one side when braking …
6 Brakes often squeak when …
7 If the parking brake does not prevent the vehicle from moving, …
8 When the ABS warning comes on, …

A … a cable may be broken or loose.
B … is a defective brake caliper or a broken piston.
C … there is a leak or a defective master cylinder, air in your brake system, too much water in the brake fluid, or a brake fade.
D … it might help to lubricate the caliper mechanism.
E … there may be a leak in the brake fluid line.
F … you should have your car checked as soon as possible.
G … the engine vacuum could be too low and the vacuum hose could have a leak.
H … the brake pads are of low quality, too old or dirty.

## Words

**malfunction** – *die Störung / der Defekt*
**resistance** – *der Widerstand* | **leak** – *das Leck*
**to lubricate** – *ölen* | **vacuum hose** – *der Vakuumschlauch*

## 6 Over to you  How to change disc brakes → ○ 6, p. 157

Do you have any experience changing disc brakes? Work with a partner. Make a list of the tools and materials you might need. Then write down the steps for changing brake rotors and brake pads.

# 7 Advanced

## Engines

### Situation
Most of the vehicles that are repaired at Aylin's workshop have internal combustion engines (ICE). A customer has come to the workshop because he has noticed oil patches on the ground beneath his car, and the engine sometimes stalls while idling. The chief mechanic suspects there is a problem with the engine, so Aylin has been asked to check the engine thoroughly.

### Information
The engine converts fuel into mechanical power. There are different types of combustion engines which transfer power to the transmission and then to the wheels. Modern engines have to meet certain emission and fuel economy requirements, as well as demonstrating high performance and reliability. Nevertheless, they may not be on the roads forever.

### D3  1 Parts of an engine  → Vocabulary

Complete the sentences using the words from the drawing. You can use the words more than once.

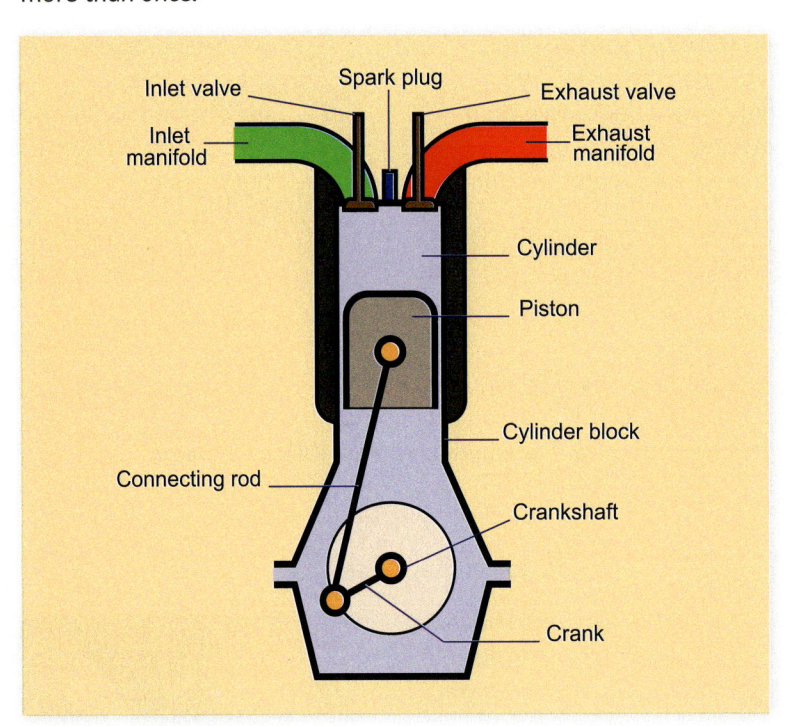

*Diagram labels: Inlet valve, Spark plug, Exhaust valve, Inlet manifold, Exhaust manifold, Cylinder, Piston, Cylinder block, Connecting rod, Crankshaft, Crank*

1. The — transfers the energy produced by the combustion cycle to the —.
2. The — uses an electric spark from the ignition system to ignite the fuel.
3. The parts that regulate the entry of the air-fuel mixture into the — and the exhaust gases from the cylinder are known as —.
4. — are connected to the — and transport the air-fuel mixture and the exhaust gases.
5. The — converts the linear movement of the piston into the circular movement of the —.

**2** Match the parts of an engine to their German translations.

1 spark plug
2 inlet valve
3 exhaust valve
4 inlet manifold
5 exhaust manifold
6 cylinder
7 piston
8 cylinder block
9 connecting rod
10 crank
11 crankshaft

A der Abgaskrümmer
B die Pleuelstange
C die Kurbel
D die Zündkerze
E der Zylinderblock, der Motorblock
F das Auslassventil
G das Einlassventil
H der Kolben
I der Zylinder
J die Kurbelwelle
K das Ansaugrohr

### 3 Optimisation of internal combustion engines

Read the text and match the nouns in bold to the following verbs.

to reduce … | to increase …

#### Combustion engines – trends and innovations

How to make engines more powerful, use less **fuel**, and generate fewer **emissions**.

**USING TURBOCHARGERS**
A turbocharger forces more air into the cylinders, increasing the **pressure** and **temperature**. This allows the engine to generate more **power** with less fuel.

**DOWNSIZING**
Using **smaller engines** with fewer cylinders but a higher specific output reduces **weight** and **friction**, so less energy is lost through **heat** and **pumping**.

**ADJUSTING THE COMPRESSION RATIO**
The compression ratio is the ratio between the volume of the cylinder with the piston in the bottom position and its volume with the piston in the top position.
A low compression ratio does not generate as much power as a high compression ratio, but it is safer and more straightforward.
The compression ratio can be adjusted to driving conditions. A variable compression ratio that changes depending on load, speed and fuel quality is ideal because it enables the engine to work optimally.

**4** Complete the sentences with the comparative forms of the adjectives in brackets. → Grammar 5

1. Engine downsizing means using a *smaller* (small) internal combustion engine with the same power capacity as a — (large) one.
2. Since the turbo is driven by exhaust gases, it is — (efficient).
3. The — (high) the octane number of the fuel, the — (good) the compression ratio should be.
4. Traditional fuel injection systems are — (efficient) than direct injection.

### 5 Over to you Typical engine problems

Talk to a partner about engine problems you have experienced in your workshop.

# 7 Advanced

## Diagnostic tools in the workshop

### Situation
After a visual inspection and some basic tests, Aylin needs to check the diagnostic trouble codes. For this, Aylin uses some advanced automotive diagnostic tools.

### Information
Integrated systems diagnose faults and show warnings on the dashboard of the car. An OBD (on-board diagnostics) tool accesses the error memory of the car and reads out the fault codes so that mechanics know what they need to repair or replace.

### 1 Understanding diagnostic trouble codes → ○ 1, p. 158
Read the text and complete the sentences with the correct forms of the verbs.

categorise | correspond | cover | decode | depend | identify | notify

1. The system uses codes to — the mechanic about an issue.
2. A code — to a fault with the car.
3. The code helps the mechanic to — the issue.
4. The codes are — into four different systems.
5. Each category — certain functions of the car.
6. Some digits — on the system that is being used.
7. Some codes are — automatically and some are not.

A21 🔊
D13 📄

**Diagnostic trouble codes explained**

Diagnostic Trouble Codes or OBD2 Trouble Codes are codes that the car's OBD system uses to notify you about an issue. Each code corresponds to a fault detected in the car. When the vehicle detects an issue, it will activate the corresponding trouble code. A vehicle <u>stores</u> the trouble code in its memory when it detects a component or system that is not operating within acceptable limits. The code will help you identify and fix the issue within the car. Each trouble code consists of one letter and four <u>digits</u>, such as P1234. [...]

**Format of the OBD2 Trouble Codes**
*System or Category*
The OBD2 Trouble Codes are categorised into four different systems.
- Body (**B**-codes) category covers functions that are, generally, inside of the <u>passenger compartment</u>. These functions provide the driver with assistance, comfort, convenience, and safety.
- Chassis (**C**-codes) category covers functions that are, generally, outside of the passenger compartment. These functions typically include mechanical systems such as brakes, steering and suspension.

- Powertrain (**P**-codes) category covers functions that include engine, transmission and associated drivetrain accessories.
- Network & Vehicle Integration (**U**-codes) category covers functions that are shared among computers and systems on the vehicle.

The first letter of the code will mark the system related to the trouble code.

*Generic and manufacturer specific codes*

The first digit in the code will tell you if the code is a generic or manufacturer specific code. Codes starting with **0** as the first digit are generic or global codes. It means that they are adopted by all cars that follow the OBD2 standard. These codes are common enough across most manufacturers so that a common code and fault message could be assigned. Codes starting with **1** as the first digit are manufacturer specific or enhanced codes. It means that these codes are unique to a specific car make or model. These fault codes will not be used generally by a majority of the manufacturers.

The first digit might be also **2** or **3**. In this case the type depends on the system. [...]

*Fault description*

The last two or nowadays three digits define the actual fault description. These numbers will tell the particular problem and each code is defined separately. There's no formula to decode these codes automatically. [...]

(376 words)
*OBD Auto Doctor*, 2020

## Words

**to store** – *speichern* | **digit** – *die Ziffer* | **passenger compartment** – *der Fahrgastraum* | **generic code** – *der Standardcode* | **to assign** – *zuweisen* | **enhanced** – *erweitert*

**2** One of Aylin's colleagues has sent her an email with some questions about diagnostic trouble codes. Answer the questions for Aylin in German.

1. Was ist die Bedeutung der „OBD2 Trouble Codes"?
2. Woraus besteht jeder dieser Fehlercodes?
3. Was überwachen die vier Code-Systeme im Allgemeinen?
4. Was bedeuten generische und herstellerspezifische Codes?

**3** Over to you **Diagnostic tools** → Grammar 4

Think about the different kinds of diagnostic tools you use at work and describe one of them to a partner. Talk about some of the following ideas:

- types of cars they are suitable for
- which system/-s they are used for (engine, transmission, …)
- connection type
- updates
- display

# 7 Task

## Buying a vintage car

### Situation

You are a big fan of American vintage cars and you are thinking about buying one for yourself. Together with a partner you find a car you like on the internet, prepare a checklist, and talk to an American seller, until you finally decide whether you will buy the car.

### Step 1

With a partner, discuss what kind of vintage car you would like to own.
Talk about the brand, type, size, features etc.

### Step 2

Go online and find a car model that interests you. Talk to your partner and explain what you like about the car and why this would be a good choice for you.

### Step 3

Listen to the conversations between a salesperson and a customer in a car dealership. Answer the following questions. For each question, you should give one answer for each dialogue.

1. What kind of car are they talking about?
2. Why does the customer want to buy the car?
3. What technical details do they talk about?
4. What are the possible negative aspects of the car?
5. What do they decide at the end of the conversation?

## Step 4

Using the details from the two conversations from Step 3, create a checklist for the most important things to consider when buying a used car.

## Step 5

You have found an American living near your hometown who wants to sell his car but does not speak German. You arrange a phone call with him. Use the ideas below to act out the telephone conversation with a partner. Add any extra information that you think is important.

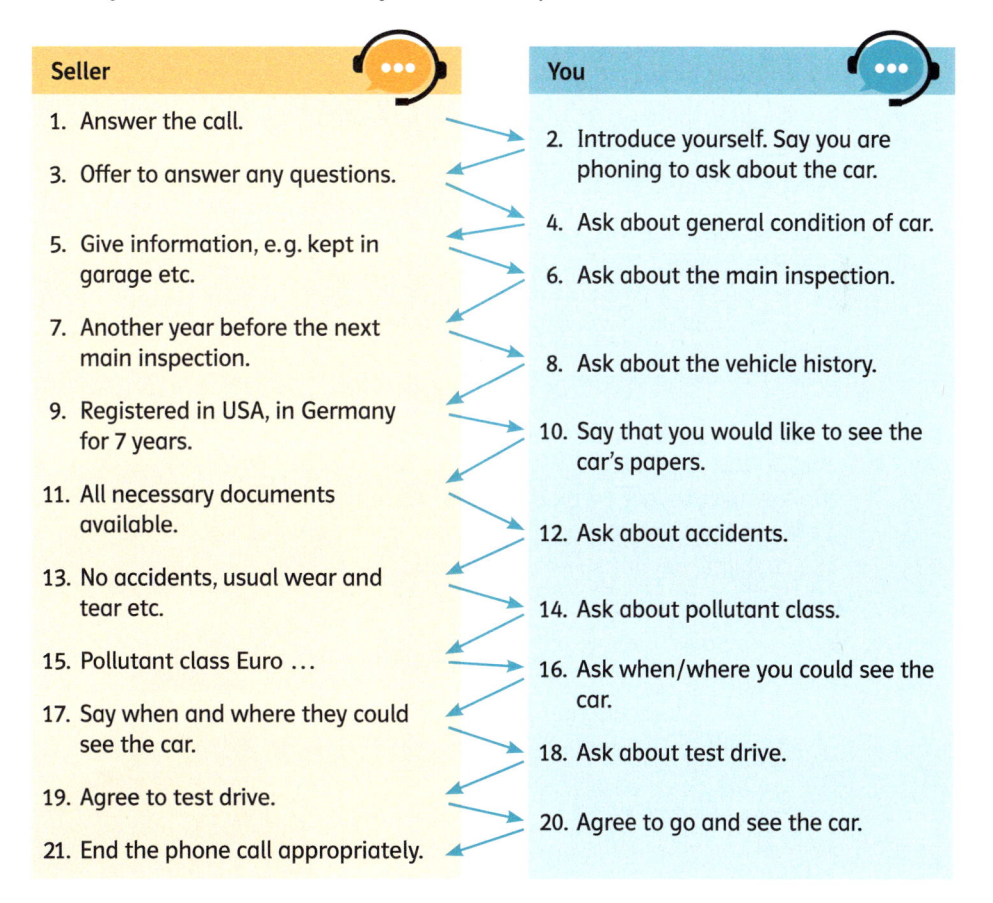

| Seller | You |
|---|---|
| 1. Answer the call. | 2. Introduce yourself. Say you are phoning to ask about the car. |
| 3. Offer to answer any questions. | 4. Ask about general condition of car. |
| 5. Give information, e.g. kept in garage etc. | 6. Ask about the main inspection. |
| 7. Another year before the next main inspection. | 8. Ask about the vehicle history. |
| 9. Registered in USA, in Germany for 7 years. | 10. Say that you would like to see the car's papers. |
| 11. All necessary documents available. | 12. Ask about accidents. |
| 13. No accidents, usual wear and tear etc. | 14. Ask about pollutant class. |
| 15. Pollutant class Euro … | 16. Ask when/where you could see the car. |
| 17. Say when and where they could see the car. | 18. Ask about test drive. |
| 19. Agree to test drive. | 20. Agree to go and see the car. |
| 21. End the phone call appropriately. | |

## Step 6

Do you want to buy the car? Why/why not? Discuss as a group.

# 8 Servicing a vintage car

## Talking to international customers

At your company, you will not always be working with regular types of cars. Sometimes unusual or rare vehicles present special challenges. It is important that you can read and understand service and instruction manuals, and that you know how to contact international customers and suppliers.

### At the end of this module, you will be able to:

- talk about the parts and common faults of fuel systems
- plan repairs
- read an English car manual
- contact an international supplier and order spare parts

**A23** **1 Receiving a phone call**

**D9** Workshop manager Frank Hoffmann receives a call from an English-speaking customer. Listen to the conversation about a vintage car and note down the information to complete the customer service sheet in German.

*KFZ Hoffmann*

**Gesprächsnotiz**

- Datum: …
- Anrufer/-in: …
- Kontaktdaten: …
- Fahrzeugmarke: …
- Fahrzeugtyp: …
- Baujahr: …
- Fehlerbeschreibung: …
- weitere Informationen: …

### Words

**relieved** – *erleichtert* | **fuel tank** – *der Benzintank*
**to splutter** – *stottern* | **incline** – *die Steigung*

## 2 Starting a conversation

What do you normally say when a customer enters the workshop? Work in a group and make a list of German words and phrases to start a conversation. Then translate the words and phrases into English.

## 3

Compare your list in class and add any useful ideas to your list.

> **Information**
>
> Although "old-timer" is an English word, it is not used by people in English-speaking countries to describe very old cars. Instead, they use "vintage" / "antique" (American English) or "classic" / "veteran" (British English). The term "old-timer" is used to refer to an older person or someone who is very experienced.

Vintage cars play a central role in the famous *James Bond* franchise. One of the many cars that appear in the *James Bond* books, written by British author Ian Fleming, is the Bentley 4½ Litre. Around 720 of these British sports cars were made between 1927 and 1931, 55 of which were "Blower Bentleys" with supercharged engines. The Blower Bentley is considered the most iconic Bentley model produced before the Second World War. The spy James Bond (also known as "007") drives a 1930 Blower Bentley in the three novels *Casino Royale* (1953), *Live and Let Die* (1954), and *Moonraker* (1955). Today, a Bentley 4½ Litre sells for around €100,000.

## 4 Famous vintage cars

Can you think of any other cars that play an important role in a book or a film? Discuss in class.

# 8 Basic

## Researching fuel system problems

### Situation

In order to find out what is wrong with the customer's vintage car, Frank Hoffmann from *KFZ Hoffmann* asks his apprentice Ben to do some research into what could have caused the symptoms the customer is describing.

1
2
3

A24
D13

### Common fuel system problems explained

As any auto professional knows, the fuel system is a critical part of the engine. Without fuel, the engine cannot run, and any problem that affects the fuel system is likely going to result in poorer engine performance. [...] Here's a closer look at how and why the most common fuel system problems occur.

**Trouble with fuel injectors**
One of the most common fuel system problems in a car is the fuel injectors. [...] Normally, the fuel injectors inject a fine mist of fuel. If an injector cannot open, the engine may lack power, while an injector that is stuck open can cause a raw gas leak. Luckily, the symptoms of faulty fuel injectors are very noticeable. A driver may experience difficulty in kick starting the engine, fluctuating engine revs, or rough running conditions. Additionally, the vehicle may experience a sudden increase in fuel consumption.
Professionals in automotive careers can diagnose a poorly performing fuel injector by checking to see if it is stuck in an open or closed position. [...] If you suspect the fuel injectors are dirty, they can be cleaned using specialized additives to clear clogged contaminants. Otherwise, a mechanic can replace the faulty part if the injector is beyond repair.

**Faulty fuel pumps**
[...] Fuel provides lubrication and cooling for the pump. Continually driving with low fuel levels can cause the fuel pump to dry out or overheat, and potentially break down. Another cause of the malfunction could be loose or worn connections when the pump doesn't receive the right current flow.
A faulty fuel pump exhibits many of the same symptoms as the fuel injectors. If the engine feels hard to start, the pump may have difficulty getting sufficient fuel for the engine. Likewise, if the vehicle experiences any misfires or sudden fluctuation in power while driving, there may be a malfunction with the fuel pump. Slow acceleration and increased fuel consumption are other obvious indicators that something is up. [...]

**Clogged filters**
Most vehicle manufacturers will recommend that you replace the fuel filter every two years or so. Over time, dirt can

become trapped in the fuel filter, affecting both the pressure and flow of the fuel system. The very purpose of the filter is to provide protection for the entire fuel system, designed to block any contaminants from getting into the fuel. Dirt in the fuel system can affect the smooth performance of the engine and ultimately damage it. Once again, the symptoms may include difficulty starting the engine, or an engine that stalls or struggles to remain idle. [...]

(426 words)
*Automotive Training Centre*, 2023

## 1 The fuel system

Match the following German words with their English translations from the text.

| | |
|---|---|
| 1 abwürgen | A fuel injector |
| 2 der Benzinaustritt | B to remain idle |
| 3 verstopft | C acceleration |
| 4 der Stromfluss | D to stall |
| 5 die Einspritzdüse | E contaminants |
| 6 die Motordrehzahl | F gas leak |
| 7 die Beschleunigung | G engine revs |
| 8 die Schmierung | H lubrication |
| 9 im Leerlauf bleiben | I current flow |
| 10 die Verunreinigung | J clogged |

## 2

The following statements summarise key points from the text, but some of them contain mistakes. Identify which are true, and correct the false statements. → ● 2, p. 164

1. A malfunctioning fuel system can cause weak engine performance.
2. The symptoms of a faulty fuel system can include problems when starting the engine and slow acceleration.
3. The fuel injectors are rarely involved in problems with the fuel system.
4. A sudden increase in fuel consumption may be caused by faulty fuel injectors.
5. If there are problems with a fuel system, mechanics should check if a fuel injector is stuck in position (either open or closed).
6. Driving with low fuel levels does not harm the fuel pump.
7. The fuel filter protects the entire fuel system by keeping any contaminants out of the fuel.
8. It is important to change the fuel filter every year.

## 3 Over to you  Fuel system problems at work

Think about a fuel system problem you have experienced at work. How did you deal with it? Make notes and tell your partner about it. Take turns.

### Phrases

I remember one problem we had …
We once had a car with a dried-out fuel pump / a clogged fuel injector / …
There was a customer who couldn't start her engine anymore because …
We exchanged / cleaned / repaired / …

# 8 Basic

## Planning repairs

### Situation

Ben and his boss have worked out that the vintage car has a faulty fuel pump. Now they need to find out how to remove it and fit a new one. They find the manual in the glove box of the car.

A25

**Description**

On S1 and S2 cars, the fuel pump unit, which consists of two electrically operated pumps, is mounted on the outer side of the right-hand chassis frame member. Each pump has a flexible Neoprene fabric diaphragm, a solenoid, a trip mechanism and suction and delivery valves. Although each of the pumps works independently, they both deliver fuel into a common delivery chamber. [...]

**Fuel Pump – to remove and fit**

– Disconnect the battery leads.
– Remove the cover from the rear filter; this will prevent loss of fuel by siphoning, as the level of the fuel in the tank is above the pump.
– Disconnect the delivery and feed pipes from the fuel pump.
– Disconnect the following electrical leads: the supply lead from the rear pump terminal, the lead to the radio interference suppressor, the connecting lead to the front pump terminal and the suppressor lead from the front pump.
– Remove the two nuts and spring washers securing the pump unit to the mounting bracket on the chassis frame.
– To fit the fuel pump, reverse the procedure given for its removal. It is essential to ensure that when fitting the fuel pump, the delivery and feed pipes of the fuel system are kept clear of the chassis frame between the insulated mounting clips, in order to prevent excessive transmission of noise from the pumps. [...]

(227 words)

*The Technical Publications Department, Rolls-Royce Limited,* 1961

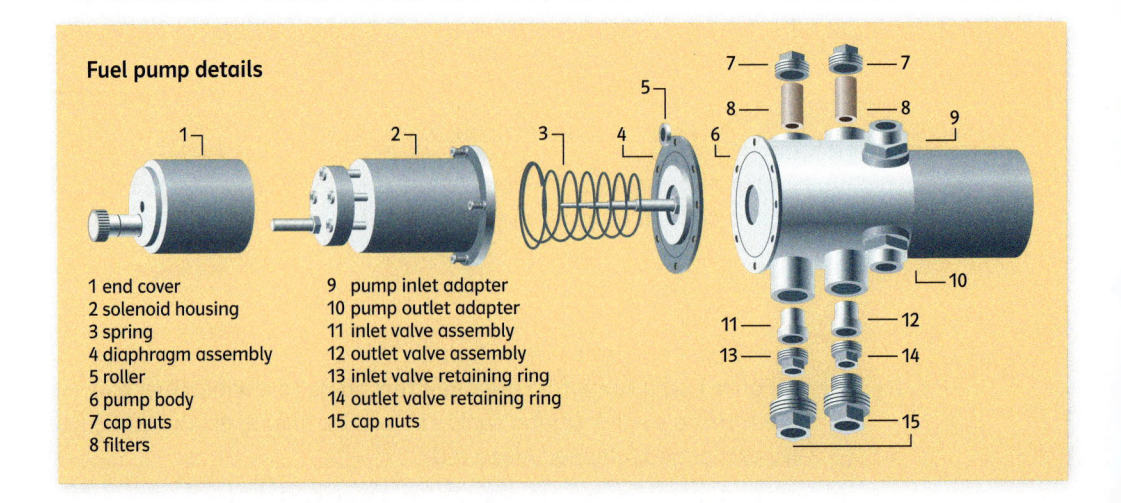

**Fuel pump details**

1 end cover
2 solenoid housing
3 spring
4 diaphragm assembly
5 roller
6 pump body
7 cap nuts
8 filters

9 pump inlet adapter
10 pump outlet adapter
11 inlet valve assembly
12 outlet valve assembly
13 inlet valve retaining ring
14 outlet valve retaining ring
15 cap nuts

# Basic 8

**1 A car manual** → ◯ 1, p. 158

Read the text and note down any words you don't know. Try to guess their meaning before looking them up in a dictionary.

D4 **2** Ben's colleagues ask him to write a step-by-step guide in German on how to remove the fuel pump and fit a new one. Write the guide for him.

> **Information**
>
> Mediation (*Sprachmittlung*) is not the same as translation (*Übersetzung*).
> When you translate a text, you put it word for word into another language.
> With mediation, you only communicate the main ideas of a text.

**3** Over to you **Environmental guidelines** → ● 3, p. 164

When working with a fuel system, you have to make sure you handle the fuel according to environmental guidelines. Look at the poster and summarise what you need to remember when dealing with gasoline.

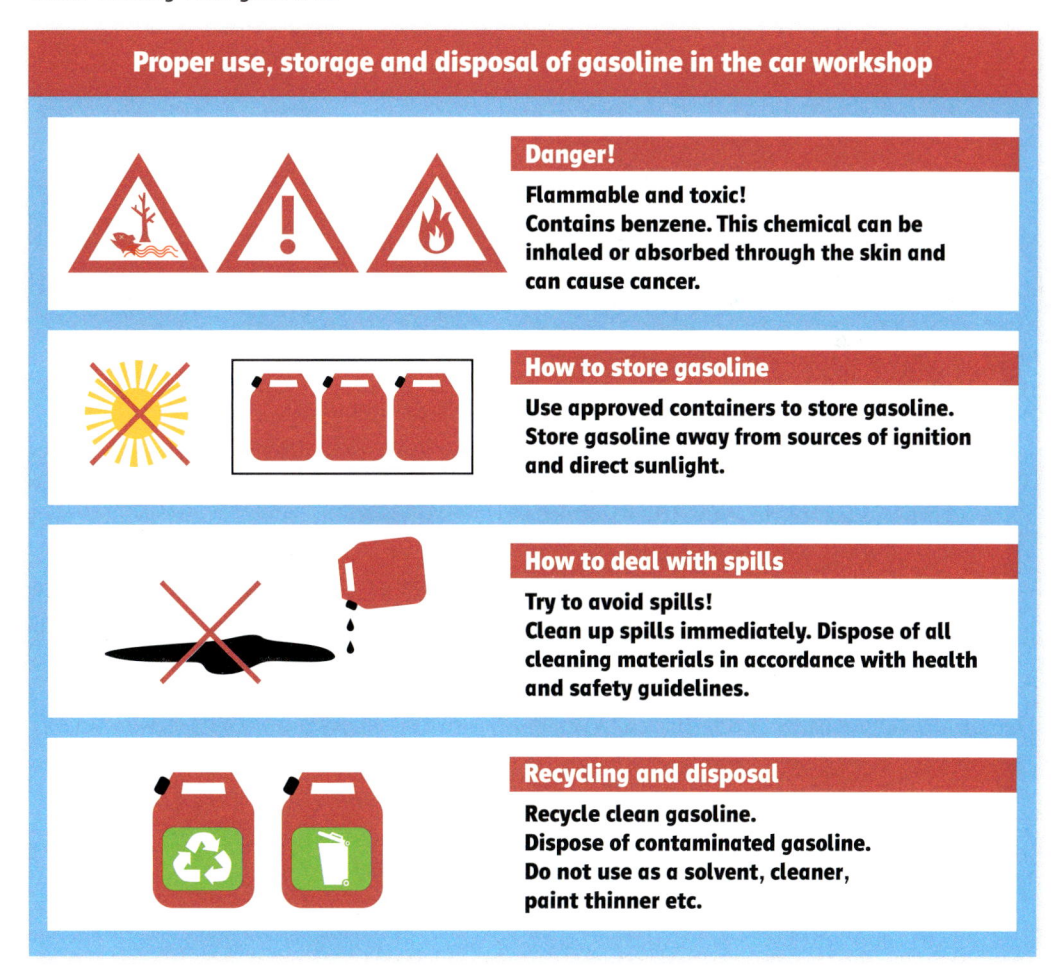

### Proper use, storage and disposal of gasoline in the car workshop

**Danger!**
Flammable and toxic!
Contains benzene. This chemical can be inhaled or absorbed through the skin and can cause cancer.

**How to store gasoline**
Use approved containers to store gasoline.
Store gasoline away from sources of ignition and direct sunlight.

**How to deal with spills**
Try to avoid spills!
Clean up spills immediately. Dispose of all cleaning materials in accordance with health and safety guidelines.

**Recycling and disposal**
Recycle clean gasoline.
Dispose of contaminated gasoline.
Do not use as a solvent, cleaner, paint thinner etc.

**4** What rules do you have in your workshop? Are they different to the ones on the poster? Is there anything missing from the poster? Discuss in class.

# 8 Advanced

## Ordering a spare part

### Situation

Workshop manager Frank Hoffmann from *KFZ Hoffmann* has searched online for suppliers of the new fuel pump he needs. Since he could not find a suitable pump in Germany, he has asked Ben to get in touch with *NLParts* in the Netherlands.

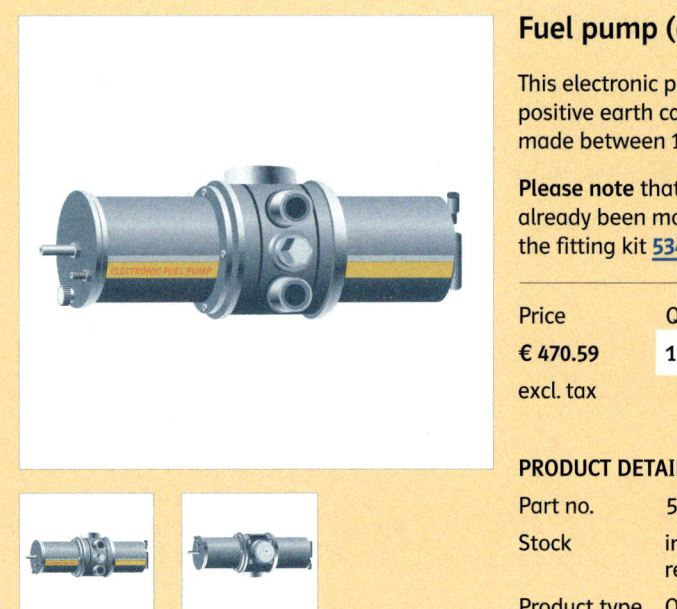

### Fuel pump (electronic)

This electronic pump cannot be used in a positive earth car. It is suitable for all cars made between 1945 and 1980.

**Please note** that if your car has not already been modified you will need the fitting kit **534BT878-PA**

Price: € 470.59 excl. tax
Quantity: 1

Add to cart

**PRODUCT DETAILS**
Part no.        534BT533-PA
Stock           in stock
                ready for dispatch
Product type    OEM part

### 1 Contacting an international supplier → Grammar 1.2

Unfortunately, the website is out of order. So Frank Hoffmann asks Ben to write an email to *NLParts* to ask about the fuel pump. He has given Ben some notes on what he should include. Write the email for Ben.

- nach Verfügbarkeit fragen
- Lieferkosten/-zeit nach Deutschland?
- Expresslieferung möglich?
- welche Zahlungsmöglichkeiten?

#### Words

**availability** – *die Verfügbarkeit* | **delivery costs** – *die Lieferkosten*
**delivery time** – *die Lieferzeit* | **shipment** – *die Lieferung*
**payment options** – *die Zahlungsmöglichkeiten*

#### Phrases

I am writing to you to … | Is it possible …? | We look forward to hearing from you.

Advanced **8**

**A26** **2** You have received a voicemail from *NLParts*. Listen to the voicemail and take notes.
**D9** Who is calling? What information does the caller provide? Compare your notes with a partner. → ○ 2, p. 158

**3** It's time to give Dennis from *NLParts* a call. Ben is a bit nervous about speaking on
**D15** the phone in English, so he practises with another apprentice. Act out the conversation between Ben and Dennis.

### Ben

1. Give your name, the company you work for and ask for Dennis.
3. Refer to voicemail, express wish to discuss shipment of fuel pump.
5. Explain that normal delivery would be too slow as customer is travelling to an event, so express delivery is needed.
7. Thank Dennis and ask how much express delivery will cost.
9. Say that that is not a problem and ask about possible payment methods.
11. Let Dennis know that your company does not have an online payment account or credit card, so you will transfer the money after the call.
13. Ask Dennis to repeat the IBAN.
15. Thank Dennis and tell him that the full payment will be transferred in the next few minutes.
17. Say that that is all for today and thank Dennis.

### Dennis at *NLParts*

2. Say that you are speaking and ask how you can help.
4. Ask which shipment type the company would like: normal or express.
6. Say that express delivery can be arranged immediately and the part will arrive in Germany tomorrow.
8. Say that you charge around €20 for a part of that size and weight.
10. Suggest online payment, credit card, or bank transfer.
12. Give the company's bank details:
IBAN NL91 ABC 0007 6851 07
BIC NL854786755 B01
14. Repeat the IBAN.
16. Thank Ben and say that the part will be prepared for shipment immediately. Ask if you can help with anything else.
18. Thank Ben and say goodbye.

**D4** **4 Customer feedback** → ○ 4, p. 158

The spare part has arrived, and Ben and his boss have successfully fitted the new fuel pump. After the customer has picked up his car, he leaves some feedback on the *KFZ Hoffmann* website. Note down what he says in German.

★★★★★
What amazing service! The super friendly and knowledgeable staff went the extra mile to fix my car. I would recommend KFZ Hoffmann to anyone, especially if you've got a rare vintage car!

# 8 Task

## Your favourite vintage car

### Situation

When the customer arrives at the workshop to pick up his car, you have a conversation with him about the appeal of vintage cars. He believes that it is all about the craftsmanship and the beauty of the bodywork. He shows you an article featuring the top five British vintage cars.

5

4

3

2

1

**Top five British classic cars of all time**

[...] British manufacturers have produced some of the most beautiful and exciting cars in history. [...] Here is our list of the five best British classic cars of all time. [...]

**5. McLaren F1**

The ultimate British sportscar. With a top speed of 231 mph and a design that wouldn't look out of place in the RAF, it was originally created to be the ultimate road car. [...] If you do find one of these cars available, you will be very lucky, as only 102 were ever made. Twenty-five years after its first debut, it is still one of the fastest cars you can legally drive on the road. A truly astonishing feat of British engineering.

**4. Aston Martin DB5**

The story of the Aston Martin DB5 is always going to be tied to that other icon of British culture – James Bond. [...] Demand for the car rose significantly after the film's premiere, with many seeking to drive the same car as the super-suave secret agent. [...]

**3. Land Rover Series I**

Inspired by the Jeep used by American GIs in World War Two, the Land Rover Series I was built to be a workhorse utility vehicle that would help post-war Britain get back onto its feet. Who would have thought this car with humble origins would go on to become such an icon? Part of the car's big success is how well-built the original models were. [...]

**2. The Original Mini**

20　Just narrowly missing out on top spot, the Mini is perhaps the car most closely associated with the idea of a British classic car. The second car on this list designed by Alec Issigonis, the car wasn't built with lofty ambitions of longevity or celebrity. Built to be a small, economical car, its quirky design made it an instant icon, influencing a whole generation of car makers. […]

**1. Jaguar E-Type**

25　If there's a man who knows cars, it's Enzo Ferrari, founder of the eponymous car company that has produced many of the most beautiful, desirable classic cars of all time. He was also a proud man, quick to boast about his products and show his disdain for cars from other companies. So for Enzo Ferrari to
30　describe a car, a British car, as anything other than ordinary, would be almost unthinkable. "The most beautiful car ever made." That was Enzo's reaction after he first saw the Jaguar E-type. That should give you an idea of just how special this car is. […]

(414 words)

James Dwyer, *Creditplus*, 2017

**RAF** (*short for:* Royal Air Force) – Britische Luftwaffe; **GI** – US-Soldat; **eponymous** – gleichnamig

### Step 1

Read the article and talk to a partner. Do you agree with the article? Why/why not? Are there any cars in the "Top 5" that you don't like?

### Step 2

Go online and find out more about vintage cars. Find three more vintage cars that are not mentioned in the article.

### Step 3 → Grammar 4

Write a short summary about each of the cars you found during your research.

### Step 4

Choose your favourite vintage car from the article and your research.
Create a poster about your car. Make sure you include:

- a picture of the car
- some general information (e.g. when and where it was made)
- any special features

### Step 5

Present your poster to the class. After everyone has presented, take a vote on which vintage car is the best.

# 9 Customer service

## Roadside assistance

The work of a car mechanic also includes customer service. In this area it is important to be friendly and patient. If customers have a positive experience at the workshop, they are more likely to come back.

**At the end of this module, you will be able to:**
- deal with a breakdown
- assess repair costs
- inform customers about upgrading options
- talk about the digital repair process

### 1 Areas of customer service → ○ 1, p. 159
List the different aspects of customer service.

1

2

3

4

5

6

**Starting point 9**

👥 **2** Discuss with a partner how customer service is provided in your workshop. How are you involved in customer service?

A28 🔊  **3 Dealing with a breakdown**
D9 📄
Ben, the apprentice at *KFZ Hoffmann*, receives a call from a driver. His company car has broken down and he needs help. Listen to the phone call and complete the customer service sheet in German.

*KFZ Hoffmann*

**Gesprächsnotiz – Pannenhilfe**

- Datum: …
- Anrufer/-in: …
- Telefonnummer: …
- Grund des Anrufs: …
- Ort: …
- Maßnahmen vor Ort: …
- Details zum Fahrzeug: …
- weitere Informationen: …

A29 🔊 **4** At the workshop, the driver talks to Ben. Listen to their conversation and answer the questions in German. → ◯ 4, p. 160

1. What if it's the driver's fault?
2. What is the procedure at *ABC Software*?
3. What help is available to the customer?

> **Words**
>
> **to recommend** – *empfehlen*  |  **on the spot** – *an Ort und Stelle*
> **to tow** – *abschleppen*  |  **reliable** – *zuverlässig*  |  **contract** – *der Vertrag*

👥 **5 In your workshop**

What can you do to give customers an excellent experience at your workshop? Work with a partner. Do some research and find videos to help you. Consider the following questions.

- How do you make sure the car stays clean and does not get scratched while you are working on it?
- How can you keep up to date with modern car technology?
- How do you make sure the customer is happy with the repair work?
- What should you tell the customer about the condition of the car once it has been repaired?

## 9 Basic

## Repair costs

### Situation

The cylinder head gasket of Mr Wouters' company car is faulty. The manager of *KFZ Hoffmann* is considering the fastest way to get a replacement. Ben has been asked to do some research for him and call the customer's company.

### Information

When repairing a vehicle, car mechanics either use OEM (original equipment manufacturer) parts or aftermarket parts, which are based on the OEM part designs. These can be vehicle replacement parts, accessories, tools, equipment, or services. The idea is to offer lower prices to customers.

### 1 OEM or aftermarket parts?

Decide if the following statements are true for OEMs or aftermarket parts.
Then compare and discuss your answers with a partner.

1. same design specifications for manufacturing and spare parts
2. generally have a warranty
3. comparable quality to original car parts
4. more difficult to get
5. you always know what you are getting
6. same level of performance and quality as your car
7. normally less expensive
8. quality can differ depending on manufacturer

### Words

**cylinder head gasket** – *die Zylinderkopfdichtung*
**replacement part / spare part** – *das Ersatzteil*
**original equipment manufacturer (OEM)** – *der Erstausrüster*
**warranty** – *die Garantie*

### 2 Over to you Working out costs

To inform a customer about upcoming repair costs, a mechanic needs to create a cost estimate. Work out the cost of buying and installing the new cylinder head gasket:

- Choose a vehicle type.
- Research the material cost of a new cylinder head gasket.
- How many working hours are needed to exchange the part?
- What does your workshop charge per working hour?
- Now work out the total cost. Compare and discuss your results with a partner.

Basic 9

**3** Ben calls *ABC Software* to discuss the faulty car.
D15  Work with a partner and act out the dialogue between Ben and an *ABC* employee.

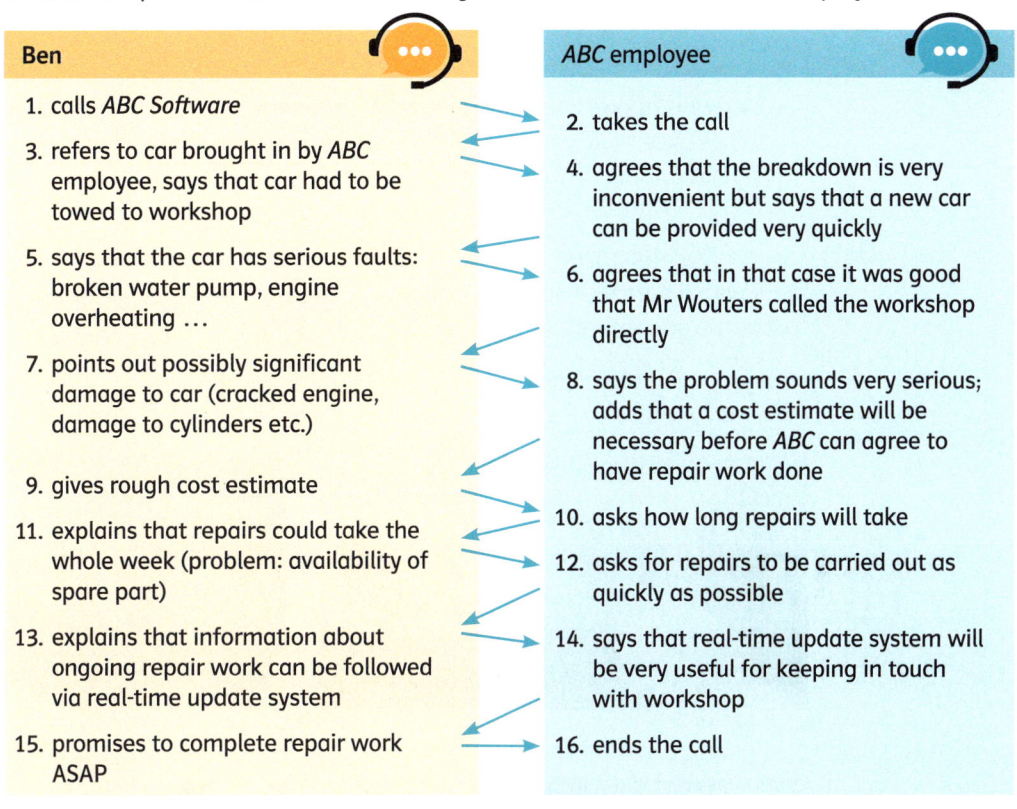

| Ben | ABC employee |
|---|---|
| 1. calls *ABC Software* | 2. takes the call |
| 3. refers to car brought in by *ABC* employee, says that car had to be towed to workshop | 4. agrees that the breakdown is very inconvenient but says that a new car can be provided very quickly |
| 5. says that the car has serious faults: broken water pump, engine overheating … | 6. agrees that in that case it was good that Mr Wouters called the workshop directly |
| 7. points out possibly significant damage to car (cracked engine, damage to cylinders etc.) | 8. says the problem sounds very serious; adds that a cost estimate will be necessary before *ABC* can agree to have repair work done |
| 9. gives rough cost estimate | 10. asks how long repairs will take |
| 11. explains that repairs could take the whole week (problem: availability of spare part) | 12. asks for repairs to be carried out as quickly as possible |
| 13. explains that information about ongoing repair work can be followed via real-time update system | 14. says that real-time update system will be very useful for keeping in touch with workshop |
| 15. promises to complete repair work ASAP | 16. ends the call |

### Words

**inconvenient** – *unangenehm* | **rough** – *grob/ungefähr*
**ASAP (as soon as possible)** – *so bald wie möglich*

**4** **Over to you** Day-to-day tasks of a mechanic

1. Discuss with a partner how day-to-day tasks in your workshop are organised.
2. Think about the work you have done in your workshop recently. Create a list of your own typical day-to-day tasks, including how much time you spend on each of them. Include the following tasks:

- changing oil
- changing tyres (summer to winter)
- changing tyres (worn tread to new)
- checking vehicle lights

### Phrases

One of my typical day-to-day tasks is changing … / doing maintenance work / …
At least once a week …
Replacing … / Performing … takes about …
… takes a whole working day.

# 9 Basic

## Upgrading a car

> **Situation**
>
> During his apprenticeship, Ben learns about all the different options for upgrading cars offered by *KFZ Hoffmann*. He has found a short English text about upgrading cars which he wants to share with his boss.

### 1 Upgrading options

Work with a partner. Look at the photos showing different options for upgrading a car. Match the photos with the words.

cruise control | infotainment system | sunroof | navigation system | trailer coupling
ambient lighting

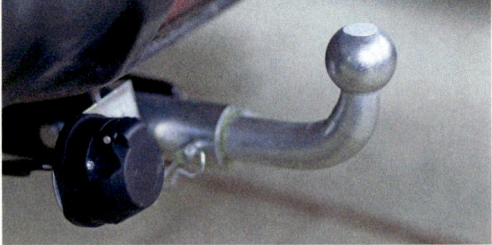

1
2
3
4
5
6

### 2 Put the upgrading options from the previous exercise into the following categories.
Think of two more options for each category. → ○ 2, p. 160 → ● 2, p. 164

| Safety | Comfort | Entertainment |
|---|---|---|
| … | … | … |

### 3 How to upgrade cars with driver assistance systems

Read the text and list the three ways for upgrading cars with driver assistance systems.

To install a driver assistance system, it is often unnecessary to make any changes to the car itself. The required sensors can often already be found in the car, meaning that a driver assistance system can simply be installed via a software update or by activating functions which are already present in the car, but which have not been unlocked.

The workshop can activate the functions once the customer has bought the update and acquired a product key.

Customers who have registered on their car manufacturer's website and have a corresponding contract can also carry out the activation process themselves via the website or an app.

Last but not least, driver assistance system technology and diagnostic software can also be bought and installed by independent third-party providers.

(127 words)

### 4 Over to you  Modifying my dream car

Talk to a partner. What would be your dream car? What would you modify or change about it? Think about what you would use it for, what it would look like, and what features it would have.

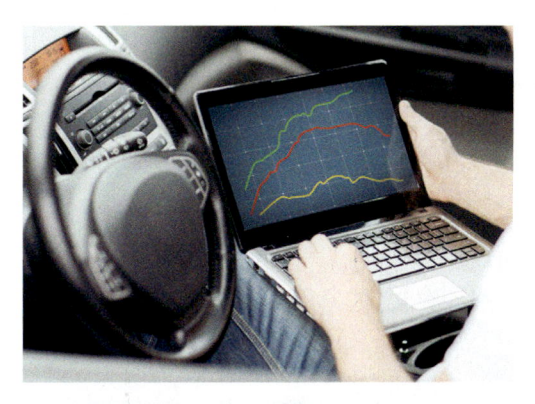

# 9 Advanced

## Digital vehicle inspection

### Situation
*KFZ Hoffmann* wants to introduce new automotive management software to automate administrative processes and improve the customer experience.
Ben has been asked to support this process and gather some information.

### Information
In the past, car mechanics always contacted customers directly. These days, many customers prefer a contactless experience wherever possible. Workshops can now share digital images and information with customers to show them what maintenance, repair, inspection, and diagnostic work needs to be carried out. It is also important to explain to customers why any additional work is necessary, and to make this information clear on the invoice.

### What is Digital Vehicle Inspection?

A common topic in the automotive industry and auto shops is digitalisation, and you've likely heard the term "Digital Vehicle Inspection" or "DVI". [...]
Say a customer left their car at the garage and went to work. Their car needs attention and requires repairs to fix the ailing brake. The technician inspects the vehicle and completes a DVI including a video clip of how bad the rotors work including many other inspection points supported by photos and video clips with recommendations included in the report. The customer reviews the recommendations and gives his approval to repair the issues. Usually, nine out of 10 times customers' responses are fast and the recommendations are carried out the same day.

Let's summarize what Digital Vehicle Inspection is
– DVI is software where the vehicle inspections are recorded electronically.
– DVI replaces the traditional method of using paper inspection sheets, clipboards with smartphones or tablets.
– Technician reports are supported with photos and videos to enable a clear understanding of the problem.

– Your client receives instant, clear and concise information of the vehicle's overall health on their device.
DVI gives your customer a tangible approach providing transparencies of work carried out and most importantly, it is stored in the customer's profile for future references. [...]

**Custom reports**
Digital inspections are enhancing every phase of the vehicle inspection process. Workshops can now create a full multi-point inspection template which provides consistent quality reports enabling technicians to improve productivity.

**Pictures and videos**
[...] Digital images and high-resolution videos completely change the customer experience and reduce the customer time in the shop. Once a customer reviews the recommendations through a video clip they then give their approval to carry out the repair work. Photos and videos provide transparency and boost customers confidence.

**Easy navigation**
A workshop can build their own inspection reports by using simple built-in templates

which provide consistent, professional quality checklists that are easy to understand and navigate.
DVI software highlights the critical repairs that require immediate attention as standard in the digital inspection process.
The report generates a higher level of <u>engagement</u> with the customer.

**Text messages or email**
The completed reports are then sent to the customers via email or text message along with estimates and recommendations. Yes, vehicle owners won't need to visit the auto shop to approve the repairs as they can complete the process digitally as the photos and videos are attached in the report.

This technology keeps the customer engaged and allows the owner to make informed decisions regarding their vehicle repairs. [...] (422 words)

*FiiviQ (5iQ) Pvt Ltd.*, 2021

### Words

**approval** – *die Zustimmung* | **recorded** – *aufgenommen* | **to enable** – *ermöglichen*
**concise** – *präzise* | **tangible** – *greifbar* | **stored** – *gespeichert*
**engagement** – *die aktive Beteiligung*

## 1 Digital vehicle inspection → ○ 1, p. 160
Find verbs in the text that go with these nouns.

1. … the traditional method
2. … information
3. … transparency
4. … a template
5. … the customer experience
6. … confidence
7. … attention
8. … engagement
9. … the repairs
10. … the process

## 2 Use the information given in the text to complete the sentences. → ○ 2, p. 160

1. Instead of using paper, DVI uses —.
2. The information the client receives is —.
3. For future reference, information about the vehicle's health is stored in the —.
4. Digital images and videos can reduce —.
5. After seeing what repairs are recommended, the customer gives —.
6. Quality checklists are provided by — that are created by the workshop.
7. — that require immediate attention are highlighted.
8. The customer is sent — via text or email.

## 3 Over to you  Digitalisation of customer service
Work with a partner and discuss the level of digitalised customer service at your workshop.

- Are you happy with the level of digitalisation of customer service at your workshop?
- What advantages/problems do you see with using digital vehicle inspections?
- What positive/negative experiences have you had with digitalised customer service?

# 9 Task

## Dealing with a complaint

### Situation

*ABC Software* has written a letter of complaint because they have not been satisfied with the workshop's service recently. As the company is a regular and valuable customer, *KFZ Hoffmann* does not want to lose them.
Frank Hoffmann shows the email to Ben and the other mechanics. He asks them to create a list of measures for keeping customers satisfied.

### Step 1

Work in a small group. Read the examples of actions that could lead to mistrust between a customer and a workshop. Rank the examples from most serious (1) to least serious (11).

- recommending unnecessary repairs
- charging more than the original cost estimate
- quality of work not as high as expected
- no transparency about costs
- workshop not well equipped
- repairs take a long time
- no communication about stages / timeframe of repair work
- vehicle has to be brought back again after repairs have been carried out
- poor customer service
- workshop does not accept warranty claims
- car not clean when it is picked up

## Step 2

Read the email from *ABC* and summarise their complaints.

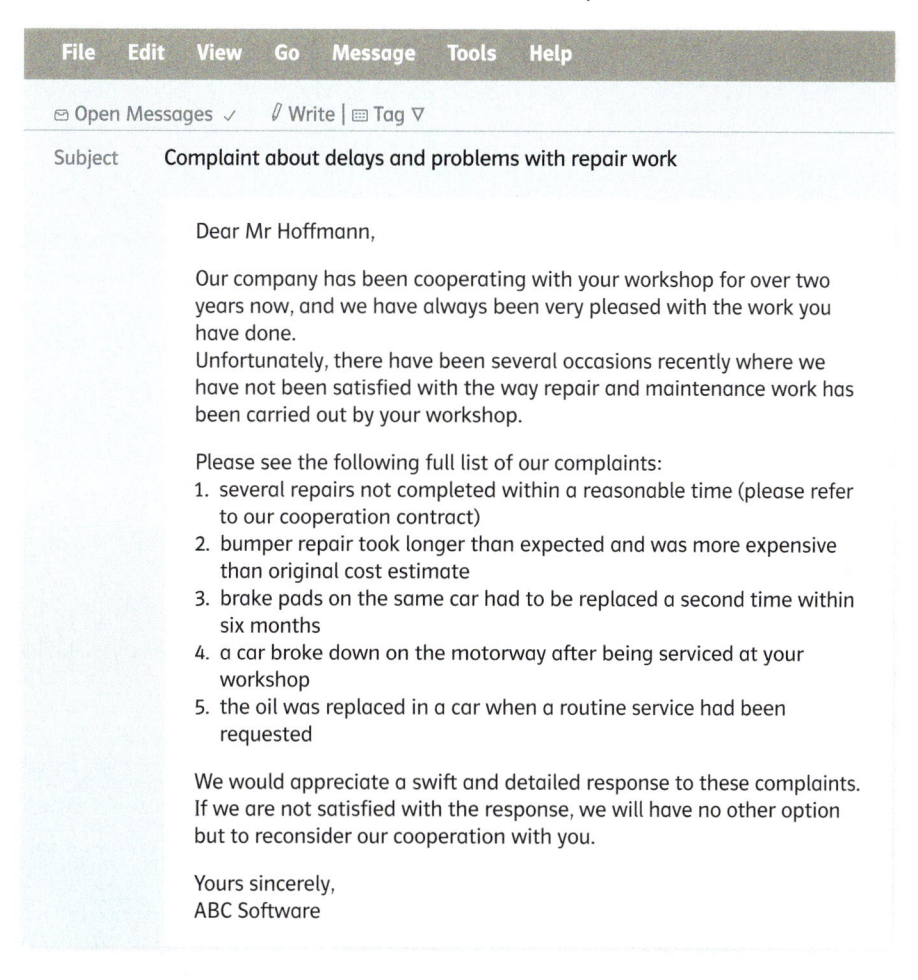

---

**File    Edit    View    Go    Message    Tools    Help**

✉ Open Messages ✓    ✏ Write | 🏷 Tag ▽

Subject    **Complaint about delays and problems with repair work**

Dear Mr Hoffmann,

Our company has been cooperating with your workshop for over two years now, and we have always been very pleased with the work you have done.
Unfortunately, there have been several occasions recently where we have not been satisfied with the way repair and maintenance work has been carried out by your workshop.

Please see the following full list of our complaints:
1. several repairs not completed within a reasonable time (please refer to our cooperation contract)
2. bumper repair took longer than expected and was more expensive than original cost estimate
3. brake pads on the same car had to be replaced a second time within six months
4. a car broke down on the motorway after being serviced at your workshop
5. the oil was replaced in a car when a routine service had been requested

We would appreciate a swift and detailed response to these complaints. If we are not satisfied with the response, we will have no other option but to reconsider our cooperation with you.

Yours sincerely,
ABC Software

---

## Step 3 → Grammar 2

Try to think of possible reasons for the issues mentioned in the email.

## Step 4 → Grammar 8

Agree on steps workshops can take to avoid problems and make sure customers are satisfied.

# 10 Electric vehicles

## Modern driving systems

The number of electric vehicles (EVs) on our streets is growing. To work safely and productively on EVs, mechanics have to make sure that they stay informed about the latest developments in this innovative technology. It is also important that they can talk about the benefits, risks and disadvantages of these cars, and advise customers on whether they should buy an EV.

At the end of this module, you will be able to:
- talk about EVs and their parts
- explain how to handle EVs and prepare a workstation
- talk about advanced driver-assistance systems and sensors in EVs

### 1 At the service station
Work with a partner. Look at the four pictures and discuss what they have in common and what differences you can find.

1

2

3

4

### 2 Match the descriptions with the pictures.

petrol station | charging station | natural gas filling station | hydrogen refuelling station

3 Work in small groups. Discuss what you already know about the four types of fuel.

> **Phrases**
>
> This kind of fuel powers …
> … is a liquid / gas …
> I have already repaired a car that uses … / is powered by …
> … is good for … because …
> Only very few cars use … because …
> … require less / more repairs.

4 Listen to the radio show and complete the sentences. → ○ 4, p. 161

1. Almost — % of all cars sold in Germany in 2023 have an electric motor.
2. Electric car sales are divided into three categories: all-electric vehicles account for — % of sales, — account for 21.8 %, and — account for — %.
3. Hybrid cars cannot be charged at a charging station. Instead, they are charged either while —, which is known as recuperation, or by the combustion engine.
4. The battery in a plug-in hybrid car is usually — than the battery in a hybrid and can be charged using a —.
5. The battery in an — is very big. It can be as heavy as — in a larger car.

5 Answer the following questions.

1. Which type of car had the highest sales figures in Germany in 2023?
2. Are the batteries in electric vehicles, hybrids and plug-in hybrids all the same?
3. What was the most popular type of car with an electric motor in Germany in 2023?

6 In your workshop → Grammar 1.1

Write a short text about your own experiences of EVs or hybrid cars. How often do you work with these types of cars in your workshop? Which models does your company repair? Do you like driving and travelling in EVs? Why / why not?

> **Phrases**
>
> In my workshop, there is / are …
> The company I work for sells / repairs …
> I like / don't like EVs because …
> We often / sometimes repair …
> I did drive a … and it was …

# 10 Basic

## How to handle EVs

### Situation

Felix has just finished training to become a car mechanic. During his training, he learned a lot about how to handle EVs. Now his boss has asked him to put together some information about EVs for the new apprentice at the company. The information should be in English, since the apprentice is not yet fluent in German, and should help her to understand how electric vehicles work and what rules she must follow when working with them.

**1 Parts of the electrical drive** → Vocabulary

Look at the parts of an electrical drive and match the words with the correct labels.

onboard charger | charge port | electric motor | DC/DC converter
power electronics controller | battery pack | thermal system | transmission

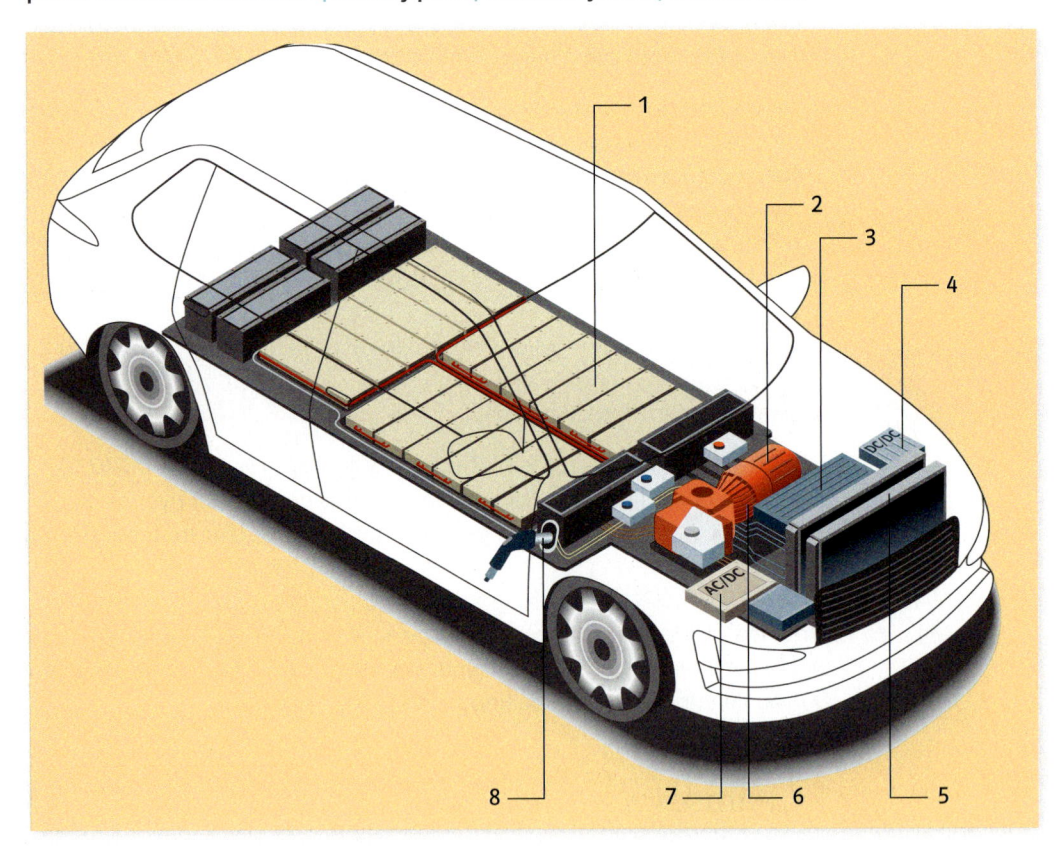

**2** Put the words from the previous exercise into the three categories.

| | |
|---|---|
| 1. Energy supply | ... |
| 2. Powertrain | ... |
| 3. Electric charging and managing parts | ... |

124

## Basic 10

**3** Work with a partner. Take turns to explain the purpose of each of the charging and managing parts. Use the *Phrases* to help you. → ○ 3, p. 161

> **Phrases**
>
> This part manages / contains / charges / makes sure that …
> This is the main operator of …
> The cable … is plugged into …
> … the voltage of the battery pack is converted to …
> … runs on 12V. / heats or cools … / supplies … with …

A32
D13

### Working with electric and hybrid vehicles: The hazards you need to be aware of

As environmental awareness continues to grow, the use of electric and hybrid vehicles (EVs and HVs) is steadily increasing. People working in the motor vehicle repair and recovery industry are now more likely than ever before to come across these vehicles. Therefore, they need to be aware of the additional hazards they may be exposed to as a result. To run a garage or a recovery service safely, workers […] will need to develop a wider range of skills and knowledge, as well as having access to special tools and equipment. […]

Garages and recovery services will be familiar with vehicles having 12- or 24-volt electrical circuits, but EVs and HVs use significantly higher currents. They operate at up to 800 volts DC (direct current). DC voltages above 120 volts can be lethal, as can AC voltages above 50 volts. Therefore, there is a real risk of electrocution […]. The battery systems store significant amounts of energy […]. Should this power system be short-circuited or suddenly released, it could cause dangerous fires. […]

**Risks of working with EVs and HVs**

EVs and HVs introduce hazards into the workplace in addition to those normally associated with the repair and maintenance of vehicles. These include:

- High voltage components and cables capable of delivering a fatal electric shock.
- Stored electrical energy with the potential to cause […] fire.
- Components that can hold a dangerous voltage even when vehicles are "off". […]
- Electric vehicles are silent when operated. There's a risk that people would be unaware of planned or unexpected movements. […]

**Safe working with EVs and HVs**

As you can see, additional skills and training will be necessary for people to work safely with EVs and HVs. The skill level of the worker will vary based on the type of work that they're expected to do. An awareness of additional risks is likely to be all that is required for people who undertake vehicle sales […]. However, those involved in repair and maintenance are likely to need a much greater level of competence to safely work with EVs and HVs. […]

(352 words)
*Peninsula Group, Manchester, UK, 2023*

## 10 Basic

**4 Handling EVs in the workshop** → ○ 4, p. 162
Find synonyms in the text for the following words and phrases.
Then translate them into German.

1. danger
2. to be unprotected
3. towing service
4. circles
5. much more electric energy
6. injury or death caused by electricity
7. when the positive pole of a battery touches the negative pole
8. connected to
9. quiet
10. to differ

D7 **5** Write a short text about the hazards associated with electric vehicles.
You can write about things you have experienced, heard about or read about.

**6** Look at the special warning signs that are used when working with EVs.
Do you know what they mean? Write down the purpose of each sign. Use the
*Phrases* to help you.

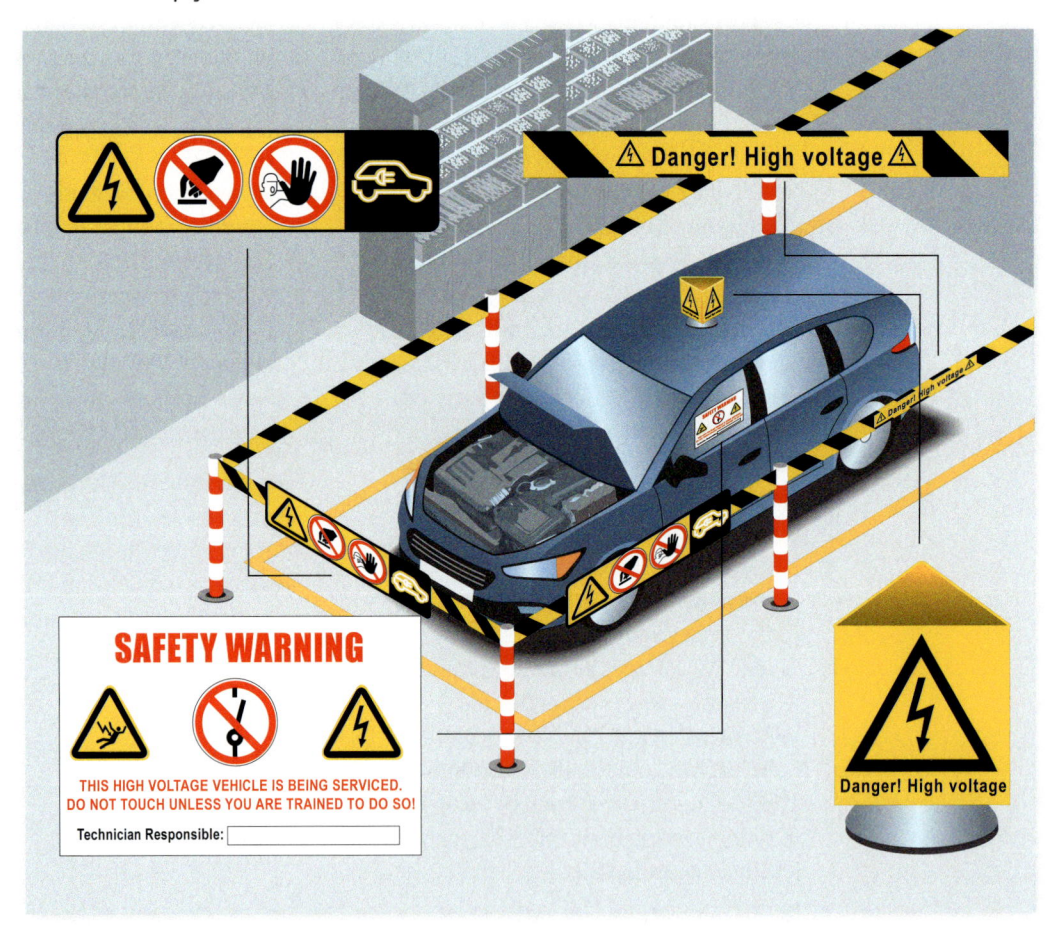

Basic 10

**7** Work in a group. Discuss why warning signs are important.

> **Phrases**
>
> The barrier goes around / in front of …
> I think this warning sign is to warn …
> You need … to …
> … is to prevent people from …
> You need … to warn people that …
> … is important to get … attention.

> **Information**
>
> The rules for working with and around EVs are similar in most countries. Workshops and mechanics in Germany must follow the guidelines of the German Accident Insurance Society (*Deutsche Gesetzliche Unfallversicherung DGUV*) to prevent dangerous accidents.
> Always look up the current safety rules and regulations! They may have changed recently.

D3 **8 Rules and guidelines**

Match the English phrases below with the corresponding levels of qualification (S, 1S, 2S and 3S) provided by the *DGUV*.

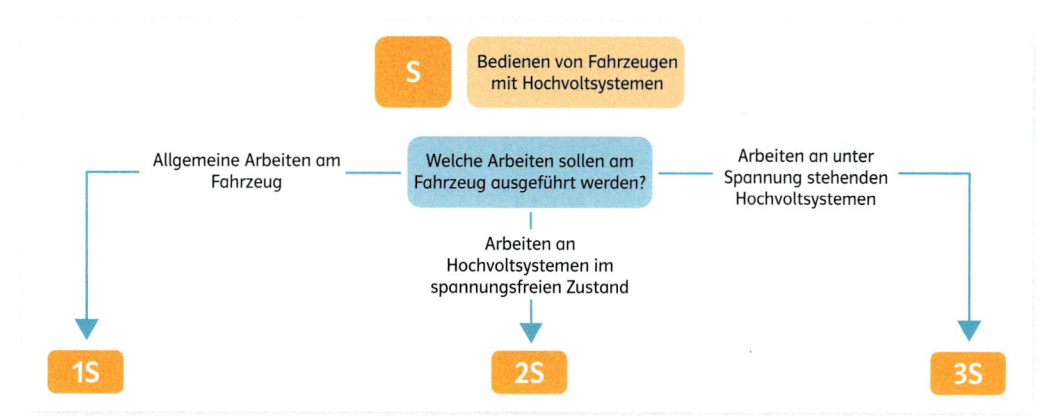

**S** — Bedienen von Fahrzeugen mit Hochvoltsystemen

Welche Arbeiten sollen am Fahrzeug ausgeführt werden?

- Allgemeine Arbeiten am Fahrzeug → **1S**
- Arbeiten an Hochvoltsystemen im spannungsfreien Zustand → **2S**
- Arbeiten an unter Spannung stehenden Hochvoltsystemen → **3S**

A  Measuring and testing parts of an EV while it is turned on
B  Adjusting the radio stations in an EV
C  Bringing an EV into the garage
D  Working on parts of an EV which are not part of the high voltage system
E  Working on parts of the high voltage system while it is deactivated

127

## Qualifizierung für Arbeiten an Serienfahrzeugen mit Hochvoltsystemen

### Qualifikation Stufe S:
### Sensibilisierte Person

Für das Bedienen von HV-Fahrzeugen ist es ausreichend, die Beschäftigten auf den bestimmungsgemäßen Gebrauch hinzuweisen und zu den dabei zu beachtenden Besonderheiten zu unterweisen. Zum Bedienen zählen auch Servicearbeiten, deren elektrische Gefährdung mit dem Bedienen durch den Fahrer oder die Fahrerin vergleichbar ist, zum Beispiel:
- Wechseln der Scheibenwischerblätter, Auffüllen von Wischwasser [...]
- Nutzen bekannter Befüllanschlüsse (z. B. für Motoröl, Kühlwasser)
- Benutzen von Bedienelementen mit neuen Symbolen und Gefahrenkennzeichnungen oder neuen Anschlüssen (z. B. Ladevorrichtung am Fahrzeug)

Zum Bedienen der Fahrzeuge gehört auch die Innen- und Außenreinigung. [...] Bei unsachgemäßer Reinigung mit hohem Wasserdruck besteht die Gefahr der Beschädigung von HV-Komponenten. Dabei sind immer die Herstellervorgaben zu beachten. [...]

Sensibilisierungen können von der Unternehmerin oder vom Unternehmer oder von einer geeigneten Person, z. B. einer Fachkundig unterwiesenen Person (FuP), durchgeführt werden.

### Qualifikation Stufe 1S:
### Fachkundig unterwiesene Person (FuP)

Fachkundig unterwiesene Personen dürfen allgemeine Arbeiten am Fahrzeug, die nicht unmittelbar das HV-System betreffen, durchführen. Dazu zählen zum Beispiel Karosseriearbeiten, Öl- und Radwechsel, Arbeiten an der konventionellen Bremsanlage [...], Arbeiten neben den HV-Leitungen an der Lenkung, dem Verbrennungsmotor, den Achsen usw. sowie Arbeiten am konventionellen Bordnetz (bis 30 V AC und 60 V DC). [...] Beschäftigte müssen zu den Gefährdungen, den Schutzmaßnahmen und Verhaltensregeln von Fachkundigen Personen (FHV) unterwiesen werden. [...]

Die unterwiesenen Personen müssen beim Umgang mit Werkzeugen und Hilfsmitteln in der Nähe des HV-Systems auf die möglichen Gefahren hingewiesen werden. Sie müssen mit den Kennzeichnungen der Komponenten vertraut sein. [...] Versehentliches Beschädigen [...] von HV-Leitungen ist der zuständigen Fachkundigen Person zu melden. [...] Die Unterweisung muss dokumentiert werden. [...]

### Qualifikation Stufe 2S:
### Fachkundige Person (FHV)

Die erfolgreiche Qualifizierung nach dieser Stufe befähigt die Fachkundigen, an Hochvoltsystemen selbstständig und sicher zu arbeiten. Alle Arbeiten an spannungsfreien HV-Systemen und -Komponenten oder in deren Gefährdungsbereich, z. B. Messen von Isolationswiderständen, Instandsetzen, Auswechseln, Ändern und Prüfen, zählen zu Arbeiten an Hochvoltsystemen im spannungsfreien Zustand. [...] Die FHV muss in der Lage sein, den spannungsfreien Zustand entsprechend den „Fünf Sicherheitsregeln" und den Herstellerangaben herzustellen.

Arbeiten an HV-Systemen im spannungsfreien Zustand dürfen nur von Fachkundigen Personen (FHV) oder unter Leitung und Aufsicht einer FHV durchgeführt werden! [...] In den Ausbildungsberufen der Kfz-Branche werden [...] elektrotechnische Grundkenntnisse sowohl im theoretischen als auch im praktischen Teil vermittelt. Darüber hinaus werden das Messen elektrischer Größen und das Arbeiten an elektrischen Aggregaten [...] in der betrieblichen Ausbildung praktisch vermittelt. [...] Personen, die die Ausbildung im Bereich Kfz-Mechatronik [...] erfolgreich abgeschlossen haben, besitzen die Fachkunde nach Stufe 2S. [...]

## Basic 10

**Qualifikation Stufe 3S:**
**Fachkundige Person für Arbeiten an unter Spannung stehenden HV-Systemen**
Mit der Qualifikation für Arbeiten an unter Spannung stehenden HV-Systemen kann die Fehlersuche an unter Spannung stehenden HV-Komponenten durchgeführt werden, wenn das Fahrzeug nicht spannungsfrei geschaltet oder die Spannungsfreiheit nicht festgestellt werden kann. [...]

Arbeiten an unter Spannung stehenden HV-Systemen bedeuten für die Beschäftigten ein Gefährdungspotenzial, das höher ist als das bei Arbeiten im spannungsfreien Zustand. Um diese Arbeiten sicher durchführen zu können, ist eine weitergehende Qualifizierung erforderlich. [...]

(477 Wörter)
*DGUV Deutsche Gesetzliche Unfallversicherung*, 2021

**D4  9** Answer the following questions about working on EVs in a workshop.
Write full sentences and use the DGUV guidelines to explain your answers.

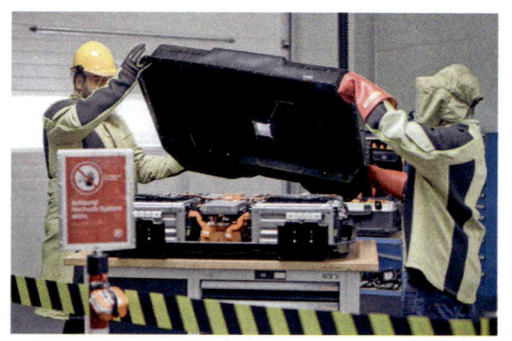

1. If a colleague tells you to drive an EV, are you allowed to do so?
2. What are you allowed to do without any special training relating to EVs?
3. What kinds of tasks are you allowed to do with the qualification *Stufe 1S*?
4. How do you get the qualification *Stufe 1S*?
5. What should you do if you see that a high voltage cable is damaged?
6. Explain the main differences between *Stufe 1S* and *Stufe 2S*.
7. How do you qualify for *Stufe 2S*?
8. What is the highest level of qualification and what can you do with it?

### 10 Over to you Working on EVs in your workshop

Answer the following questions and share your experiences with a partner.

1. Are you allowed to operate EVs at your company?
2. Are you allowed to work on EVs in your workshop?
3. Which level of qualification do you have at the moment?
4. Do you want to have special training so that you can reach a higher level?
5. Do you have any colleagues who are EV specialists?

## 10 Advanced

# Advanced driver-assistance system (ADAS)

### Situation

Besides their superior drivetrain technology, electric vehicles have another advantage: they make it easier to implement systems to support the driver and increase safety on the road. Felix wants to include these systems in the information he is putting together for the new apprentice.

### Information

An advanced driver-assistance system (ADAS) includes technologies that help drivers with the safe handling of a vehicle. ADAS uses automated technology such as sensors and cameras to discover nearby obstacles or driver errors and react accordingly.

**1 Levels of ADAS**

Work with a partner. Copy and complete the table. Add any other systems you know in German, along with their English translations and short forms.

| ADAS List German | English | short forms |
|---|---|---|
| ESP, Elektronisches Stabilitätsprogramm | Electronic Stability Control | ESC |
| BAS, Bremsassistent | … | … |
| Adaptive Geschwindigkeitsregelanlage | … | … |
| Spurhalteassistent | … | … |
| Verkehrszeichenerkennung | … | … |
| … | … | … |

**2** There are six levels of autonomous driving. Match the English terms with their German translations.

**Level 0:** no automation
**Level 1:** driver assistance
**Level 2:** partial automation
**Level 3:** conditional automation
**Level 4:** high automation
**Level 5:** full automation

A hochautomatisiertes Fahren
B autonomes Fahren
C assistiertes Fahren
D vollautomatisiertes Fahren
E kein assistiertes Fahren
F teilautomatisiertes Fahren

Advanced 10

3 Work in small groups and find out more about the different levels of automation. Write down the missing English or German explanations and add the right level of automation. The *Words* can help you. → ○ 3, p. 162

| | Explanation English/German | Level |
|---|---|---|
| A | **English:** The car is manually controlled. The driver is responsible for braking, steering, accelerating etc. → **German:** Der Mensch übernimmt alle Aktionen während des Fahrens. | 0 |
| B | **English:** — → **German:** Das Fahrzeug kann vollautomatisch auf alle Ereignisse in einem Gebiet oder auf einer gewissen Strecke reagieren. Der Fahrer ist hierbei nur noch Passagier. Diese Form des autonomen Fahrens wird in naher Zukunft angestrebt. | — |
| C | **English:** Fully automated driving is possible and humans can simply be passengers on all types of road. → **German:** — | — |
| D | **English:** The vehicle can drive on its own in some situations, for example on the motorway. This is made possible by combining cruise control with lane assistance. The driver is still responsible in all situations and should always be focusing on the road. → **German:** — | — |
| E | **English:** Cars with this level of automation can adapt to their environment. For example, they can adjust to speed limits. Fully automated driving is possible in certain situations. The driver only has to take over if alerted by the system. On a motorway with no obstructions, the driver becomes a passenger. This is currently the highest level of automation on European and American roads. → **German:** — | — |
| F | **English:** — → **German:** Das Fahrzeug kann automatisch die Spur halten oder die Geschwindigkeit anpassen. Der Fahrer bleibt in der vollen Verantwortung und darf seine Hände nicht vom Lenkrad nehmen. | — |

## Words

**manually** – *von Hand* | **to accelerate** – *beschleunigen*
**passenger** – *der/die Passagier/-in* | **cruise control** – *der Geschwindigkeitsregler*
**lane assistance** – *der Spurhalteassistent* | **to focus on sth** – *sich auf etw. konzentrieren*
**to adapt to sth** – *sich an etw. anpassen* | **environment** – *die Umgebung*
**to adjust to sth** – *sich auf etw. einstellen* | **to alert** – *alarmieren*
**obstruction** – *das Hindernis*

## 10 Advanced

## Sensors in EVs

### Situation
Felix has a heavily damaged EV coming into his workshop. He and his colleagues are trying to find out how the accident happened and whether it could have been prevented.

**D3** **1 Sensors for level 3 automation and higher**
Look at the graphics and complete the sentences. The *Words* can help you.

400 m | expensive | laser | RADAR | sensors | short | time | travels back | ideal

1. The — sensor sends out a beam (radio wave) that can travel up to —. The beam is reflected by objects and — to the sensor. By measuring the — it takes for the beam to travel back, the sensor can detect how far away objects are.
2. They work in quite similar ways, but instead of radio waves, LiDAR sends out — waves. The sensors work from a distance of a few centimetres up to 250 m. These sensors are very —. LiDAR systems can take very precise measurements of distance and position, making them — for self-driving cars.
3. PDC — use ultrasound technology. They work in a similar way to RADAR systems, but only over — distances of 2.5 m.

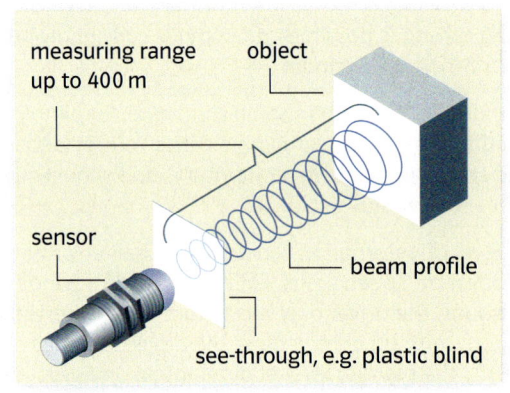

1  RADAR stands for *radio detection and ranging*.

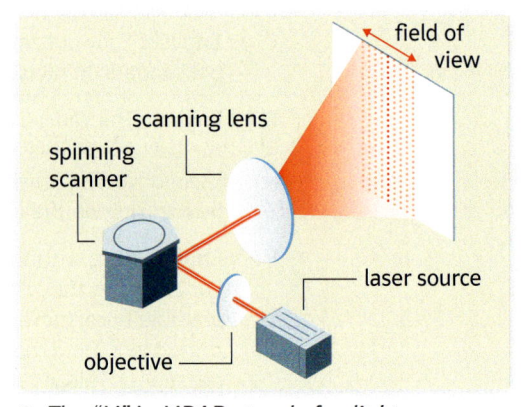

2  The "Li" in LiDAR stands for *light*.

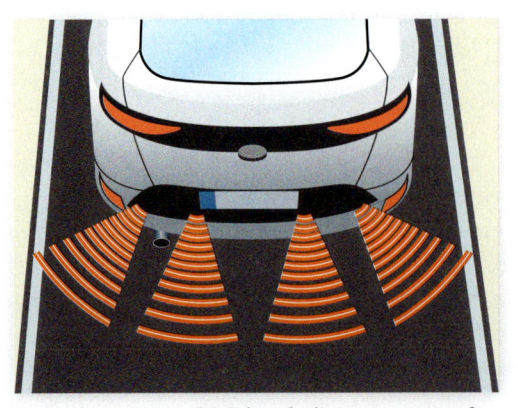

3  Park assist or PDC (*park distance control*).

### Words
**detection** – *die Erkennung, die Ortung*
**to detect** – *ermitteln, feststellen*
**beam** – *der Strahl*
**radio wave** – *die Radiowelle*
**to reflect** – *reflektieren*
**ultrasound** – *der Ultraschall*

## 2 Problems with automation today

Even with very high automation, accidents still happen. Talk to a partner about the reasons for that.

### Technical malfunction or human error?

Evidence shows that the car was in "autopilot" mode while driving on the motorway. The driver's attention must have been elsewhere, because he failed to notice the large truck with its long trailer slowly crossing the road. The part of the motorway where the accident took place was completely straight, with no changes in the elevation of the road. The EV did not brake and passed underneath the trailer at very high speed. Due to the height of the trailer, the roof and windscreen of the EV were pushed in. The car continued to travel for around 400m and drove through two fences before hitting a pole and coming to a stop.

The driver of the truck said afterwards: "He went under the trailer so fast I didn't even see him."

The camera in the EV didn't detect the white trailer because the sun was shining right into the lens. The manufacturer later gave a statement that these types of cameras, which use computers to process images, are designed for rear-end collisions and not for situations where there is an obstacle in front of the vehicle. In cases like these where the cameras are ineffective, the RADAR sensors have to do most of the work. However, the RADAR sensors recognised the elevated white surface of the trailer as a road sign. Therefore, no warning was given by the RADAR sensors either.

The statement given by the manufacturer emphasised that "autopilot" mode still requires the full attention of the driver and demands immediate action if there is a warning from the system. The driver should have their hands on the steering wheel at all times. If they do not, the system will issue a warning, slow the car down and, if there is still no response from the driver, stop the car in a safe place by the side of the road.

The US National Highway Traffic Safety Administration (NHTSA) has now started an investigation into the case. Several other public authorities are also investigating whether advertising the system as "autopilot" mode is misleading. Did the driver have his hands on the steering wheel and did the system give him any warning? We will probably never know. But this case shows that the potential malfunctioning of cameras and sensors and the risks of automated driving exist. However, technology in smart cars can also save lives. There are hundreds of videos of smart cars preventing collisions. Nevertheless, for this kind of technology to become more widely used, the systems need to be optimised and the risks greatly reduced.

(431 words)

## 3 Read the text and summarise how the accident happened. → ○ 3, p. 162

## 4 Write a text about the dangers and benefits of automation in its current state.
Use the information you have learned so far, including information from the text.

# 10 Task

## Electric vehicle or petrol car?

### Situation

Your British aunt is moving to Germany in a few months. She will be selling her right-hand drive vehicle and has asked for your advice on what kind of car she should buy once she has moved. She is wondering if she should buy another petrol or diesel car or if she should buy an EV instead. To help her decide, you do some research and share your findings with her.

### Step 1

Work with a partner. Discuss the following questions:

- What should you consider before you decide what kind of car you want to buy?
- Have you ever thought about buying an electric car? Why/why not?
- What kind of car would you like to have in the future? Why?

A33
D9

### Step 2

Listen to the podcast and make a list of the pros and cons of buying an EV.

Task 10

### Step 3

Your aunt has told you that she is thinking about buying an EV because she does not usually drive long distances and could charge her car at home.
However, she is still concerned about the environment and is not sure if a car with a battery is the right choice.
Work in pairs. One partner does research on the risks of battery production for humans and the environment, the other one looks up problems of the production of petrol/diesel cars.

### Step 4

Exchange the information you found and write a short paragraph to give your aunt an idea about the eco-friendliness of the different technologies.

D7
D8

### Step 5

Using your notes from steps 1 to 4, write down the advice you would give to your aunt. Explain in detail why you would advise her to choose a particular vehicle.

# KMK-Prüfungsvorbereitung

## Informationen zur KMK-Prüfung

Das Fremdsprachenzertifikat der Kultusministerkonferenz (kurz: KMK) ist eine freiwillige Zusatzqualifikation, die nur an beruflichen Schulen erworben werden kann. Im Rahmen einer KMK-Prüfung werden berufstypische Fremdsprachenkompetenzen unabhängig von schulischen Noten überprüft und bescheinigt.

### Die Kompetenzbereiche

Im Rahmen des KMK-Fremdsprachenzertifikats werden vier Kompetenzbereiche abgefragt. Alle Aufgabenstellungen weisen immer einen thematischen Bezug zur jeweiligen Berufswelt auf.

**Rezeption**

Hier werden englischsprachigen Texten relevante Informationen entnommen und auf Deutsch korrekt wiedergegeben. Rezeptionsaufgaben bestehen aus einem Hörverstehen und einem Leseverstehen. In der Regel dürfen Hörtexte im Rahmen der Prüfung zwei Mal angehört werden.

**Produktion**

Produktionsaufgaben zielen auf das Verfassen eines berufstypischen Schriftstücks auf Englisch ab. Bei der Bewertung spielen inhaltliche Richtigkeit und sprachlicher Ausdruck eine Rolle.

**Mediation**

Ziel einer Mediation ist es, relevante Inhalte von der einen in die andere Sprache zu übertragen. Innerhalb der vorliegenden KMK-Prüfungssätze werden Mediationsaufgaben sowohl in der Richtung Deutsch – Englisch als auch in der Richtung Englisch – Deutsch bereitgestellt.

**Interaktion**

Im mündlichen Teil wird abgeprüft, ob in beruflichen Situationen sicher auf Englisch ein Gespräch geführt werden kann. Dieser Prüfungsteil wird in Gruppen von mindestens zwei Personen durchgeführt.

# KMK-Prüfungsvorbereitung

## Details zur Prüfung

Zum Erhalt des KMK-Fremdsprachenzertifikats muss eine schriftliche und eine mündliche Prüfung abgelegt werden. Die **Punkteverteilung** orientiert sich an den vier Kompetenzbereichen:

| Schriftliche Prüfung | Mündliche Prüfung |
| --- | --- |
| Rezeption:<br>Hörverstehen – 20 Punkte*<br>Leseverstehen – 20 Punkte* | Interaktion – 30 Punkte |
| Produktion – 30 Punkte* | |
| Mediation – 30 Punkte* | |
| **Summe** – 100 Punkte | **Summe** – 30 Punkte |

\* Bei der schriftlichen Prüfung ist eine leicht veränderte Gewichtung der Kompetenzbereiche möglich.

Um das KMK-Fremdsprachenzertifikat zu erhalten, muss in beiden Prüfungsteilen mindestens die Hälfte der möglichen Punkte erreicht werden. Es ist nicht möglich, schlechte Leistungen in einem Bereich durch gute Leistungen im anderen Bereich auszugleichen. Im Zertifikat werden nur die Punktezahlen angegeben, Noten gibt es keine.

Die **Prüfungszeiten** sind an das jeweilige Anforderungsniveau angepasst:

| Niveaustufe | Schriftliche Prüfung | Mündliche Prüfung |
| --- | --- | --- |
| A2 | 75 Minuten | 15 Minuten* |
| B1 | 90 Minuten | 20 Minuten* |
| B2 | 120 Minuten | 25 Minuten* |
| C1 | 150 Minuten | 30 Minuten* |

\*Der Richtwert orientiert sich an einer Prüfung mit zwei Prüflingen.

Für die mündliche Prüfung gibt es eine angemessene Vorbereitungszeit. Manche schriftlichen Aufgaben können mit Stichwortantworten gelöst werden, aber in der Regel ist eine Beantwortung in ganzen Sätzen erwünscht. In beiden Prüfungsteilen darf ein allgemeinsprachliches, zweisprachiges Wörterbuch verwendet werden.

KMK-Prüfungsvorbereitung

# Niveau A2

A34 🔊
D16 📄

**1** `Rezeption` **Hörverstehen (20 Punkte)**

Sie interessieren sich für Rennsport. Und Bremsen haben Sie wegen des hohen Anspruchs an die Sicherheit schon immer fasziniert. Auch im Werkstattbereich werden Bremsen für Sie in Kürze wichtig werden. Sie sollen bei den nächsten Inspektionen erstmals selbstständig die Bremsen überprüfen. Informieren Sie sich mit Hilfe des folgenden Podcasts über das Thema.

Hören Sie sich das Interview mit der Expertin Laura Mitchell zweimal an und beantworten Sie dann die folgenden Fragen in ganzen deutschen Sätzen.

1. Berichtigen Sie die Aussage:
   Das übliche Bremssystem in PKWs funktioniert mit Hilfe von Bewegungsenergie.
2. Vervollständigen Sie die Auflistung der genannten Teile von Scheibenbremsen: Kolben, …
3. Warum stellt die Reibung bei Bremsen ein Sicherheitsproblem dar?
4. Welche Möglichkeiten, Bremsen zu kühlen, werden genannt?
5. Wählen Sie die zwei genannten Anzeichen, dass eine Bremse ausgetauscht werden muss, aus.
   A Vibration                C Zug auf eine Seite
   B Kreischendes Geräusch    D Verzögerte Bremswirkung
6. Vervollständigen Sie die Tabelle über die genannten visuellen Veränderungen von Bremsen:

| Teil der Bremse | Bremsscheibe | Bremsbeläge |
|---|---|---|
| Veränderung | … | … |

7. Notieren Sie die genannte Website.

**2** `Rezeption` **Leseverstehen (20 Punkte)**

Lesen Sie den Text und beantworten Sie anschließend die Fragen in ganzen Sätzen auf Deutsch.

### Electric Vehicle Technology

Today's drivers are looking for ways to use the Earth's energy resources better. This is why Electric Vehicles (EVs) are on the rise.
⁵ Technically speaking, EVs run on an electric motor, while gasoline-powered cars run on an engine powered by the combustion of a fuel-air-mixture. There are three major types of EVs:
¹⁰ **Battery electric vehicles** (BEVs) only use electricity saved in an internal battery pack. You can charge the battery with a wallbox at home or at a public charging station. BEVs have one or more electric motors and do not need a traditional internal combustion engine (ICE). That is why BEVs are also called "pure EVs". ¹⁵
**Plug-in hybrid vehicles** (PHEVs) work with both a battery-powered electric motor and a conventional gasoline engine. The battery gets charged externally or through ²⁰ regenerative braking. Regenerative braking, also called recuperation, uses the energy from braking and converts it into electrical power.
The system switches from battery to ²⁵ gasoline power when the battery pack is

empty. It can also use the regular engine when the battery is not strong enough to speed up the car. In some plug-in hybrid cars, the drivers can choose between electricity or gas, depending on what they prefer.

**Hybrid electric vehicles** (HEVs) also combine a gasoline engine and an electric motor. However, the battery cannot be charged externally. The vehicle's driving energy comes only from fuel. The power for the electric motor is generated with the help of regenerative braking. The electric and the conventional drive system work in combination most of the time. For shorter distances or in low power mode, the car can run on electricity alone.

(282 words)

1. An welchen zwei Orten kann die Batterie eines BEVs aufgeladen werden?
2. Warum werden BEVs auch als „reine Elektrofahrzeuge" bezeichnet?
3. Berichtigen Sie die Aussage:
   Bei der Rekuperation wird der Motor durch den Generator im Motorraum angetrieben.
4. Ergänzen Sie die Übersicht, wann das System eines PHEVs vom elektrischen Motor auf den Verbrennungsmotor umschaltet:
   Die Batterie ist leer, ...
5. Berichtigen Sie die Aussage:
   HEVs werden ausschließlich von Strom angetrieben.
6. Wählen Sie die Situationen aus, in denen ein HEV nur mit Elektroantrieb fahren kann.
   A  Bergab
   B  Bei kurzen Strecken
   C  Im Sparmodus
   D  Bei konstanter Geschwindigkeit

## 3 Produktion (30 Punkte)

Ihr Betrieb bildet zum ersten Mal auch Auszubildende aus dem Ausland aus. Diese Auszubildenden kommen immer wieder mit Fragen zu den Motorölen, die in der Werkstatt verwendet werden, auf Sie zu. Um Fehler beim Ölwechsel zu vermeiden, sollen Sie nun ein englisches Merkblatt zum Thema Motoröle erstellen.

Verfassen Sie das Merkblatt in ganzen englischen Sätzen. Erwähnen Sie dabei die folgenden Punkte:

**Klassifikation**
- Motoröle sind unterschiedlich zähflüssig/viskos. Dies wird mit Hilfe von Zahlen beschrieben:
  - Hohe Zahlen = dickflüssiges/hochviskoses Öl
  - Niedrige Zahlen = dünnflüssiges/niedrigviskoses Öl
- Die Viskosität verändert sich mit der Temperatur.
- Auf Motorölbehältern findet man eine Kombination von Zahlen und Nummern, die „SAE-viscosity classes". Dieser Code gibt die Viskosität des Motoröls bei Kälte und bei Hitze an.

**Ölwechsel**
- Nur das Motoröl benutzen, das der Hersteller für das Fahrzeug angibt.
  Die SAE-Klasse des Öls steht in der Bedienungsanleitung oder im Serviceheft.
- Motoröle für Verbrenner und Motoröle für Dieselmotoren nicht mischen.
- Motoröle für Viertaktmotoren nicht mit Motorölen für Zweitaktmotoren mischen.
- Ölwechsel sollten etwa alle zwei Jahre durchgeführt werden.
- Beim Ölwechsel auch den Ölfilter kontrollieren und wechseln.

## 4 Mediation Englisch – Deutsch (30 Punkte)

In der Onlinereparaturanleitung für einen neuen Wagen ist bisher nur ein englischer Artikel zum Thema Klimaanlagen vorhanden. Ihr Chef bittet Sie, eine Übersicht über die am häufigsten vorkommenden Probleme und deren Behandlung zu erstellen.

Lesen Sie den Text und fassen Sie die Inhalte auf Deutsch und in einer Tabelle zusammen.

### A/C problems

A leak will slowly reduce the amount of refrigerant and the A/C will no longer be able to cool down the car properly. Look for leaks and check the hoses and the sealing rings. These rubber parts can be replaced. Holes in the condenser can make the system lose refrigerant. It needs to be replaced.

The condenser could also be blocked by dirt, dust, insects or other small particles from the road. This problem can be fixed by cleaning the car grille. The car's cabin filter can be dirty. Such a filter will not allow the cooled air into the cabin. Replace the filter.

The cooling fand can also have an electrical problem, such as a failed switch or a blown fuse. Make sure to look for broken wires and inspect the control module, which could be defective. Replace these parts if necessary.

Strange noises can be a sign that a broken compressor stops the A/C from cooling the cabin. Various components of the compressor can fail, often as a result of a lack of lubricant in the refrigerant and the damage this does to the metal parts. Either repair or replace the compressor.

(198 words)

## 5 Mediation Deutsch – Englisch (30 Punkte)

Ihre Ausbildung findet in einem kleinen Kfz-Betrieb statt. Häufig kommen ausländische Kunden und Kundinnen vorbei, um sich nach Elektrofahrzeugen zu erkundigen. Da Ihr Chef wenig Zeit hat, sollen Sie sich nun um diese Anfragen kümmern. Bereiten Sie sich auf die zukünftigen Beratungsgespräche mit Hilfe des Texts vor.

Fassen Sie die Vorteile von Elektrofahrzeugen in ganzen englischen Sätzen zusammen. Beachten Sie folgende Kategorien:

- Emissionen
- Kosten
- Fahrverbote
- Parksituation
- Energieeffizienz

## Elektroauto: Die Vor- und Nachteile

[…] Der Aufruf nach mehr Umweltschutz wird immer größer. Dementsprechend ist auch die Nachfrage an Elektroautos in den letzten Jahren gestiegen. Denn im Vergleich zum Verbrennungsmotor benötigt der Antrieb dieser Autos keinen fossilen Brennstoff. Somit produziert das Elektroauto auch kein umweltschädigendes $CO_2$ (Kohlenstoffdioxid) beim Fahren. […]

[…] Ein Elektroauto ist in der Anschaffung sicherlich teurer als ein herkömmliches Fahrzeug. Allerdings solltest du hierbei die Unterhaltungskosten beider Autos gegenüberstellen. Für eine „Tankfüllung" Strom für circa 100 Kilometer müsstest du nur halb so tief in die Tasche greifen, als würdest du die gleiche Strecke mit einem benzinbetriebenen Auto fahren. […]

[…] Der Beitrag, den Elektrofahrzeuge zur Energiewende leisten, ist dem Staat von großem Wert. Daher kommt er den Fahrern von diesen Autos im Alltag mit vielerlei Privilegien entgegen. So sind batteriebetriebene Fahrzeuge von deutlich weniger Fahrverboten betroffen als herkömmliche Verbrenner. Denn sie dürfen auch in Lärmschutz- und Umweltzonen fahren. Ebenso stehen Elektrofahrzeugen eigene Parkplätze inklusive Ladestation zur Verfügung, während alle übrigen Abstellmöglichkeiten mit verringerten Parkgebühren einhergehen. […]

[…] Ein weiterer Vorzug zeigt sich in heimischen Ladestationen (Photovoltaikanlage), denn mit diesen kannst du die benötigte Energie obendrein noch selbst erzeugen. […]

(189 Wörter)
Ricardo Izzi, 2022

## 6 Interaktion (30 Punkte)

Führen Sie mit Hilfe der Rollenkarten ein Gespräch auf Englisch.

### Auszubildender/Auszubildende A

Ein Auszubildender/eine Auszubildende aus den Niederlanden fängt in Ihrer Ausbildungswerkstatt neu an. Sie kümmern sich gerne um seine/ihre Fragen.
Die Gespräche finden auf Englisch statt, da er/sie gerade erst anfängt, Deutsch zu lernen.
Der/Die neue Auszubildende beginnt das Gespräch und möchte von Ihnen wissen, ob er/sie bald bei den Hauptuntersuchungen (HU, *general vehicle inspections*) helfen kann.
Die Frage überrascht Sie, da in Deutschland die HU normalerweise durch bestimmte Organisationen (z. B. TÜV oder Dekra) durchgeführt wird. Sie kommen ins Gespräch.

Vergleichen Sie in Ihrer freien Unterhaltung die deutsche und niederländische HU für PKWs. Reagieren Sie auf die Fragen und Hinweise, die im Gespräch aufkommen.

Sie interessieren sich ganz besonders für die folgenden Punkte:

- Wie oft finden die HU in den Niederlanden statt?
- Was kostet eine HU?
- Wird auch eine Abgasuntersuchung (AU, *emissions test*) durchgeführt?
- Was wird bei der Reifenprüfung beachtet?
- Wird die Klimaanlage kontrolliert?

# KMK-Prüfungsvorbereitung

Die Fragen, die Ihnen gestellt werden, können Sie mit Hilfe der folgenden Tabelle beantworten:

**HU PKW (Deutschland)**

| | |
|---|---|
| Zeitabstände | 3 Jahre nach Zulassung des PKW, dann alle zwei Jahre. Ablesbar an der TÜV-Plakette *(inspection sticker)* am Nummernschild. |
| Umfang | HU (AU ist die Voraussetzung für HU) |
| Kosten | ca. 140 € (HU und AU) |
| Kontrolle der Lichtanlage | ✓ |
| Kontrolle der Bremsen | ✓ |
| Kontrolle der Klimaanlage | – |
| Kontrolle der Scheiben und Spiegel | Frontscheibe, Rückspiegel, Scheibenwischer |
| Kontrolle der Reifen | ✓ Profiltiefe muss mindestens 1,6 mm betragen |
| Kontrolle der Lenkung | ✓ |
| Nachweis | Sticker fürs Nummernschild |

Diskutieren Sie kurz, ob Sie die deutsche oder die niederländische Form der HU bevorzugen. Sie beenden das Gespräch.

**Auszubildender/Auszubildende B**
Sie sind ein neuer Auszubildender / eine neue Auszubildende in einer deutschen Kfz-Werkstatt. Sie kommen aus den Niederlanden und lernen gerade erst Deutsch. Aus diesem Grund verständigen Sie sich im Ausbildungsbetrieb noch auf Englisch.
Sie beginnen ein Gespräch mit einem/einer hilfsbereiten Auszubildenden. Sie fragen, ob Sie bald bei Hauptuntersuchungen (HU, *general vehicle inspections*) behilflich sein können. Diese HU gehören in den Niederlanden zur Routine in jeder Werkstatt. Sie wollen auf diesem Weg sämtliche Autoteile kennenlernen. Die Antwort überrascht Sie.

Sie führen eine freie Unterhaltung über die deutsche und niederländische HU für PKWs. Reagieren Sie auf die Fragen und Hinweise, die im Gespräch aufkommen.

Sie interessieren sich ganz besonders für die folgenden Punkte:

- Was kostet eine HU in Deutschland?
- Was ist bei der Reifenprüfung wichtig?
- Was sind drei Beispiele für Fahrzeugkomponenten, die kontrolliert werden müssen?
- Wie kann man wissen, wann das Auto wieder zur HU muss?
- Wird die Innenausstattung auch kontrolliert?

Die Fragen, die Ihnen gestellt werden, können Sie mit Hilfe der folgenden Tabelle beantworten:

**HU PKW (Niederlande)**

| Zeitabstände | 4 Jahre nach Zulassung des PKW, dann alle zwei Jahre. Der Fahrzeughalter erhält eine schriftliche Nachricht, wenn es Zeit für die Hauptuntersuchung ist. |
|---|---|
| Umfang | HU und AU (Abgasuntersuchung, *emissions test*) |
| Kosten | kein einheitlicher Preis, abhängig von der Werkstatt (ca. 20 € bis 75 €) |
| Kontrolle der Lichtanlage | ✓ |
| Kontrolle der Bremsen | ✓ |
| Kontrolle der Klimaanlage | ✓ |
| Kontrolle der Innenausstattung | – |
| Kontrolle der Reifen | ✓ Profiltiefe muss mindestens 4,0 mm betragen |
| Kontrolle der Lenkung | ✓ |
| Nachweis | Onlineformular mit Unterschrift der Werkstatt |

Diskutieren Sie kurz, ob Sie die deutsche oder die niederländische Form der HU bevorzugen. Azubi A beendet das Gespräch.

KMK-Prüfungsvorbereitung

## Niveau B1

A35 🔊 **1** Rezeption **Hörverstehen (20 Punkte)**
D17 📄

Ein Kunde plant die Neuanschaffung eines PKWs. Da er in Erwägung zieht, von einem Verbrenner auf ein Elektrofahrzeug umzusteigen, hat er sich bereits über die Vorteile der Elektromobilität informiert. Nun möchte er auch die Risiken abschätzen. Um den Kunden kompetent beraten zu können, sammeln Sie mit Hilfe eines Podcasts Informationen zum Thema.

Hören Sie das Interview mit der Autojournalistin Joanna Rashford zwei Mal an und beantworten Sie dann die folgenden Fragen in ganzen deutschen Sätzen.

1. Ergänzen Sie die Tabelle über die genannten Vorteile von Elektroautos:

| Bereich | Vorteil |
| --- | --- |
| Verbrauch | … |
| Wartung | … |
| Stabilität der Ausgaben | … |
| Fahrerlebnis | … |

2. Berichtigen Sie die Aussage:
   Joanna sieht ein Problem bei der Anschaffung von Elektroautos darin, dass nur wenige Hersteller Elektroautos produzieren.
3. Wählen Sie die zwei genannten Gründe aus, die das Aufladen der Elektroauto-Batterie erschweren.
   A Lange Wartezeiten    C Zahlung funktioniert nicht
   B Defekte Ladesäulen    D Langsame Aufladegeschwindigkeit
4. Geben sie die genannte Reichweite einer Aufladung an.
5. Warum ist es ein Nachteil, mit einem Elektroauto in den Urlaub zu fahren?
6. Berichtigen Sie die Aussage:
   Müssen Elektroautos gewartet werden, dann stellt das Finden geeigneter Werkzeuge, fehlende Reparaturanleitungen und die lange Bearbeitungszeit eine Schwierigkeit dar.
7. Über welche Probleme beschweren sich die Besitzer/Besitzerinnen von Elektroautos im Winter?

## 2 Rezeption · Leseverstehen (20 Punkte)

Lesen Sie den Text und beantworten Sie anschließend die Fragen in ganzen Sätzen auf Deutsch.

### V2X explained [...]

[...] Vehicle-to-everything systems are essentially a combination of two other vehicular communication systems – vehicle-to-vehicle (V2V) and vehicle-to-infrastructure (V2I). In the case of the former, it involves cars 'talking' to each other, while the latter system involves cars communicating with things such as traffic lights, buildings, and so on. [...]

[...] Say you're driving a car with V2X [...] and you encounter a broken down car on the side of the road, or you have to make an emergency stop for whatever reason. The car, recognising this, will then send out an alert to other cars nearby that also have a V2X system, and a message will flash up on the dashboard to alert the drivers of other cars of what's coming up, and how far away it is. Furthermore, emergency services vehicles equipped with V2X capability can also automatically alert drivers of their approach from behind or positioning ahead, allowing drivers to move over safely and promptly.

However, that's only the V2V element of this two-part system, as V2X also includes V2I functionality. [...] This involves the infrastructure around you talking to your car to alert you of things such as the timing of traffic lights – allowing you to adjust your speed to sail through green lights rather than getting stuck at a red – as well as pedestrian and cyclist activity at intersections based off information collected by sensors [...].

[...] All V2X-equipped vehicles will be fitted with a wireless local area network (WLAN) transmitter that uses a standardised language to enable communication between cars of all brands, and infrastructure in any location. [...] Developed specifically for spontaneous, local communication between vehicles, it operates without the need for a connection to a 5G mobile phone network.

Volkswagen developer Thomas Biehle, speaking of the standardised system, notes that, "Consequently, it works across EU countries and provides blanket coverage within the limits of the system. Vehicles equipped with the associated hardware modules – in our examples this also includes the emergency services vehicle – directly exchange positioning data and information using Wi-Fi. This is potentially possible within a radius of up to 800 metres and within a matter of milliseconds. The data is not saved anywhere and thus data privacy is maintained." [...]

German automobile association ADAC, which has also independently tested the system, described it as a "technological milestone" after it passed eight tests it put it through, including detecting a broken down car positioned behind a tight corner at 100km/h from 300 metres away, and detecting a trailer indicating a blocked carriageway as part of roadworks and a strongly braking vehicle ahead, among others.

[...] With more vehicles and more infrastructure able to communicate more information between each other, it means a greater number of drivers will be better prepared for incidents. [...]

(467 words)
Patrick Jackson, 2020

## KMK-Prüfungsvorbereitung

1. Vervollständigen Sie die Tabelle über das Konzept V2X.

| System | Kommunikation zwischen ... |
|---|---|
| V2V | ... |
| V2I | ... |

2. Wie kommunizieren zwei Fahrzeuge miteinander, sobald sich eine gefährliche Situation ergibt?
3. Berichtigen Sie die Aussage:
   Rettungsfahrzeuge nutzen die V2X Systeme, um Fahrer über aktuelle Unfälle und Alternativrouten zu informieren.
4. Wovor kann ein V2I System warnen?
5. Vervollständigen Sie die Aussage:
   Die WLAN-Verbindung der V2X Systeme ermöglicht eine Kommunikation ...
6. Vervollständigen Sie die Tabelle über die Aussagen von Thomas Biehle zur Leistungsfähigkeit des Systems.

| Bereich | Leistung V2X |
|---|---|
| Einsatzbereich | ... |
| Radius | ... |
| Geschwindigkeit | ... |
| Datensicherheit | ... |

7. Beschreiben Sie einen der drei genannten ADAC-Praxistests, den das System erfolgreich bestanden hat.

## 3 Produktion (30 Punkte)

Sie sind als Kfz-Mechatroniker/Mechatronikerin bei einem Betrieb tätig und haben vor Kurzem das Fahrzeug eines Kunden repariert. Leider bleibt die Beschwerde bestehen.
Sie stellen nun fest, dass die Ursache auf Werkstattebene nicht weiter erforscht werden kann. Wenden Sie sich an die europäische Zentrale des japanischen Herstellers des Fahrzeugs.

Verfassen Sie eine englische E-Mail an die Zentrale. Erwähnen Sie dabei die folgenden Punkte:

- Bitten Sie um Hilfe bei einem Problem, das die Elektronik des PKWs eines Kunden betrifft (Modell Sonic, Baujahr 2016).
- Trotz Verriegelung des Fahrzeugs bleibt die Fahrzeugelektronik aktiviert.
- Der Sleep-Modus tritt nicht ein, so dass ein zu hoher Strom fließt. Dieser entleert langsam die Batterie, so dass nach zwei Tagen kein elektrischer Verbraucher (z. B. die Zentralverriegelung) mehr funktioniert.
- Beschädigte Kabel konnten nicht festgestellt werden.
- Ein Austausch der Steuergeräte hat in der Werkstatt bereits stattgefunden.
- Die Vermutung liegt nahe, dass ein Bus Controller defekt ist.
- Das Problem kann in der Werkstatt nicht behoben werden.

KMK-Prüfungsvorbereitung

- Bitten Sie darum, dass sich ein Experte online in das Fahrzeug einschaltet.
- Alternativ könnten Sie das Fahrzeug zu einem Herstellerzentrum bringen lassen.
- Schließen Sie die E-Mail angemessen ab.

## 4 Mediation Englisch – Deutsch (30 Punkte)

Im Rahmen Ihrer Ausbildung werden Sie in Kürze beim Einbau von Abstandsregeltempomaten behilflich sein. Da die Erfassung vorausfahrender Fahrzeuge auf verschiedene Arten stattfinden kann, informieren Sie sich sowohl über LIDAR- als auch über RADAR-Sensoren.

Stellen Sie auf der Grundlage des folgenden Artikels Notizen in vollständigen Sätzen auf Deutsch zusammen. Beachten Sie insbesondere folgende Punkte:

- Funktionsweisen beider Systeme
- Vergleich der zwei Sensorenkategorien

### [...] What is the difference between LIDAR and RADAR?

[...] LIDAR [...] is used to measure the distance between the sensor and objects in the surrounding environment. Typically, a LIDAR sensor sends pulses of light waves into the environment. The pulses will reflect off objects and surfaces in the surrounding area, and a sensor will detect the returning light. The sensor will calculate the time taken for the pulse to return to the sensor, and from this calculate the distance to the object [...]
[...] There are two primary methods of measuring distance using radar. The first is known as the direct propagation method, and measures the delay associated with reception of the reflected signal, which can be correlated to the distance of the reflecting object [...].For indirect propagation, a modulated frequency is sent and received, the difference in the frequency can be used to directly determine the distance as well as the relative speed of the object. [...]
[...] Level of precision is the key advantage of LIDAR over RADAR, but there are three advantages that RADAR systems enjoy over LIDAR systems. The first is range, with RADAR systems effectively 'seeing' further than LIDAR systems. This is particularly important for larger commercial vehicles, which will often require more advance notice in order to be able to slow sufficiently to avoid a collision. [...] Secondly, as they often involve more moving parts, LIDAR scanners are less reliable over time than RADAR sensors. [...] Lastly, RADAR sensors are significantly less costly than their LIDAR alternatives.

(247 words)
*Oponeo*, 2021

## 5 Mediation Deutsch – Englisch (30 Punkte)

Eine gute englischsprachige Kundin Ihres Unternehmens glaubt, dass jedes Elektroauto autonom fahren kann. Ihr Meister gibt Ihnen die Aufgabe, dieser Kundin die Unterschiede genauer zu erklären.

Fassen Sie die wichtigsten Informationen zu den Stufen des autonomen Fahrens in ganzen englischen Sätzen zusammen, um einen guten Überblick für das Gespräch mit der Kundin zu haben. Gehen Sie dabei auf die Rolle des Systems und die Rolle des Fahrers ein.

## Autonomes Fahren [...]

**[...] Level 1: Assistiertes Fahren**
[...] Die Fahrer beherrschen hier entweder dauerhaft die Quer- oder Längsführung. Die jeweils andere Fahrzeugführung kontrolliert das System in gewissen Grenzen. Dabei müssen die Fahrer den Verkehr und das System ständig im Blick behalten und jederzeit die Kontrolle übernehmen können.[...]

**Level 2: Teilautomatisiertes Fahren**
Das System übernimmt Quer- und Längsführung für einen gewissen Zeitraum und/oder in spezifischen Situationen. Die Fahrer müssen Verkehr und System ständig im Blick behalten und ihm jederzeit das Steuer wieder entreißen können. Unter definierten Bedingungen (etwa auf der Autobahn oder beim Parken) führt der Autopilot Fahrmanöver ohne menschlichen Eingriff aus. [...]

**Level 3: Hochautomatisiertes Fahren**
Bei Level 3 des autonomen Fahrens übernimmt das System Fahraufgaben selbstständig und ohne menschlichen Eingriff für einen gewissen Zeitraum und in spezifischen Situationen. Die Fahrer dürfen sich vorübergehend vom Fahren und dem Verkehr abwenden. Auf Anforderung müssen sie das Steuer mit ausreichender Zeitreserve übernehmen können. [...]

**Level 4: Vollautomatisiertes Fahren**
[...] Das System übernimmt die komplette Fahrzeugführung; die Fahrer sind lediglich Passagiere. Das Fahrzeug bewältigt Strecken komplett selbstständig, etwa auf der Autobahn oder im Parkhaus, und darf dort auch ohne Passagiere fahren. [...] Das System erkennt seine Grenzen so rechtzeitig, dass es regelkonform einen sicheren Zustand erreichen kann [...].

**Level 5: Autonomes Fahren**
[...] Das meint die komplette dauerhafte Fahrzeugführung des Systems. Selbst komplexe Situationen an Kreuzungen oder Übergängen meistert das Fahrzeug selbstständig. Es gibt nur noch Passagiere. Fahrten ohne Insassen sind ebenso möglich.

(233 words)
Raimund Schesswendter, 2021

## 6 Interaktion (30 Punkte)

Führen Sie mit Hilfe der Rollenkarten ein Gespräch auf Englisch.

**Situation:**
Verständigen Sie sich telefonisch mit Ihrem Kollegen / Ihrer Kollegin über die Auswahl eines Reifengroßhändlers, der Ihre Berliner Kfz-Werkstatt (Privatfahrzeuge) in Zukunft beliefern soll. Das Angebotsmaterial zweier Großhändler liegt Ihnen beiden gleichermaßen vor.

**Kollege/Kollegin A**
Sie rufen Ihren neuen Kollegen / Ihre neue Kollegin an und halten kurz Small Talk. Sie sind beide Formel 1-Fans und der Saisonbeginn steht vor der Tür.

Nennen Sie den Grund des Anrufs: Bitte um Unterstützung bei der Auswahl eines neuen Reifengroßhändlers. Fragen Sie, ob das Informationsmaterial per E-Mail angekommen ist. Ihnen ist die steigende Nachfrage nach Ganzjahresreifen bewusst. Sie betonen die Fahrsicherheit, die Kostensituation und die schnelle Lieferung der Reifen.

Diskutieren Sie die Möglichkeiten und wählen Sie zusammen einen Großhändler aus.
Sie lassen das Gespräch von Ihrem Kollegen / Ihrer Kollegin beenden und reagieren erfreut auf den Vorschlag, der Ihnen gemacht wird.
Kollege/Kollegin A beendet das Gespräch.

## KMK-Prüfungsvorbereitung

**Kollege/Kollegin B**

Sie kommen aus Schottland und arbeiten seit kurzem in einer Kfz-Werkstatt in Berlin. Ihr Kollege / Ihre Kollegin ruft Sie an. Der anfängliche Small Talk bezieht sich auf das gemeinsame Interesse an der Formel 1 und den bevorstehenden Saisonbeginn.

Sie sollen mit Hilfe des Informationsmaterials, das Sie gestern per E-Mail erhalten haben, die Liefererauswahl unterstützen. Sie tun dies sehr gerne! Ihnen ist die Fahrsicherheit, Hersteller- und Preisvielfalt des Reifenangebots besonders wichtig.

Diskutieren Sie die Möglichkeiten und wählen Sie zusammen einen Großhändler aus.
Sie beenden das Gespräch. Kündigen Sie an, ab Montag wieder in der Werkstatt zu sein. Sie schlagen vor, Ende nächster Woche die erste Bestellung zusammen aufzugeben.

**Portfolio Ganzjahresreifen**
*GRIP Reifen GmbH*, Leipzig

| Hersteller | Artikel | Nasshaftung laut EU-Label | Preis pro Reifen |
|---|---|---|---|
| Monumental | 4xSeason | B | 85 € |
| Next Year | AllSeason2 | B–C | 75 € |
| Deferrall | 365-Universal | D | 48 € |

- auch erhältlich: Sommer- und Winterreifen; SUV- und LKW-Reifen; Felgen und Kompletträder
- Premium- und Budgetreifen
- Lieferung am nächsten Werktag bei Bestellung bis 18:00 Uhr; garantierte Verfügbarkeit
- frachtfrei ab zehn Reifen im Bundesgebiet

**Portfolio Ganzjahresreifen**
*Reifen Wolf*, Berlin

| Hersteller | Artikel | Nasshaftung laut EU-Label | Preis pro Reifen |
|---|---|---|---|
| Monumental | 4xSeason | B | 90 € |
| Firestorm | Canyon4 | B | 80 € |
| Bridgeport | 24-7-4 | B | 79 € |

- auch erhältlich: PKW- und SUV-Reifen; nicht im Sortiment: Felgen und Kompletträder
- nur Premiummarken

# Helping hand

## 1 You and your company

### Presenting yourself

2 Match each statement with the jumbled question.

| | |
|---|---|
| 1 "I live in a shared apartment in the city centre." | A are \| from \| you \| where \| ? |
| 2 "Hello! I'm Karin." | B hobbies \| are \| what \| your \| ? |
| 3 "I love wildlife photography. I spend a lot of time outdoors." | C where \| live \| do \| you \| ? |
| 4 "I'm from Portugal. My family lives in Lisbon." | D doing \| which \| apprenticeship \| are \| you \| ? |
| 5 "I'm doing an apprenticeship in IT in systems integration." | E what \| name \| is \| your \| ? |

### The company and its people

5 Complete the sentences to describe the infographic.

benefits | nice place to be | working models | heading | comfortable | illustrations | bonuses

1. Each section has a main — and small — giving more detail on the topic.
2. Some advantages are financial — , things which provide flexibility to make workers' lives easier and things which make a workplace a nice, — place to work.
3. The company offers — and a pension scheme and gives public transport subsidies. A variety of — and child-care facilities are available.
4. Modern sites and equipment, recreational facilities and a company canteen with a variety of options make the workplace modern and a — .

# Helping hand

## 2 Your place of work

### Different workplaces

3 What are the risks and dangers of each workplace? How might they be reduced? Using the words and phrases, share ideas with a partner before discussing them in class.

1. fast-moving, sharp parts | to get hot | training | health-and-safety rules protective clothing
2. loose tools and equipment | to fall | secured | licence and qualifications | to drive safely
3. hazardous substances | protective clothing | secure position | toxic fumes
4. layout | to trip | to fall | evacuation | loose or trailing cables | appliances safety standards

### Data protection

4 Follow the steps to prepare for the presentation.

1. Come up with a short introduction saying what you are going to present and why.
2. Look back at the email. Write down the key points Louis' colleagues need to know about.
3. Use keywords and phrases to summarise each point as precisely as possible. Keep your language and sentence structure simple and leave out unnecessary details (e.g. dates, times, repeated information).
4. Prepare a brief closing section – summarise the key points to be taken away from the presentation and ask if anybody has any questions.
5. Create presentation cards. Note down the points from steps 1 to 4 with keywords and phrases to prompt you when giving the presentation.
6. Using your cards, practise your presentation out loud. You can practise alone or with a classmate, friend or family member.
7. Go back to any points where you felt unsure and write down additional notes or words which can help you. Practise them again before repeating the presentation.

# Helping hand

## 3 Tasks and responsibilities

### Tasks, responsibilities and expectations

A5 🔊 **2** Listen to the first part of the podcast. Choose the correct definition for each phrase.

| | | |
|---|---|---|
| 1 | hands-on experience | A making sure that your company acts responsibly |
| | | B values that influence how well and why you do your work |
| | | C when you do something rather than hearing or reading about it |
| 2 | work ethic | D how much a company spends on its production processes |
| | | E learning about work that is done by people and not by machines |
| 3 | cheap labour | F when people are not paid or treated fairly for their work |

### Conflicts and issues at work

A7 🔊 **3** Listen to the people talking about work-related problems. Match the expressions with their German equivalents.

| | | | |
|---|---|---|---|
| 1 | to think twice | A | zuerst an sich selbst denken |
| 2 | supposedly | B | sich etwas zweimal überlegen |
| 3 | left out | C | jemanden nicht Ernst nehmen |
| 4 | to not take somebody seriously | D | belasten |
| 5 | to jump in | E | jemanden enttäuschen |
| 6 | to join in | F | ausgeschlossen |
| 7 | to put a strain on something | G | einspringen |
| 8 | to put yourself first | H | angeblich |
| 9 | to let someone down | I | teilnehmen, mitreden |

A7 🔊 **5** Decide which category from the diagram best fits each problem described in the audio. More than one option may be possible.

1. Julian
   A structural conflict     B value conflict     C external conflict

2. Erika
   A relationship conflict     B conflict of interest     C data conflict

3. Luis
   A external conflict     B relationship conflict     C value conflict

# Helping hand

## 4 Working in a global world

### Intercultural awareness

**8** Match the small talk example situations with the possible opening sentence.

| | | | |
|---|---|---|---|
| 1 | meeting someone at an international conference | A | "There are so many to choose from. Do you have as many flavours in your country?" |
| 2 | picking up a visitor from the airport | B | "Thank goodness English is so widely spoken here. I've been brushing up my vocabulary!" |
| 3 | visiting a foreign country | C | "Excuse me … I think I remember you from last time?" |
| 4 | tea break with an English-speaking colleague | D | "How was your journey? You must be tired." |

### A project abroad

**2** Complete the sentences summarising the most important points from the text.

**valuable metals | recycling technologies | local communities and authorities
their CV and a covering letter | the next four weeks | local technicians
mechanics and electricians | hazardous components | e-waste recycling facilities**

1. The *Green Horizons* project aims to set up — in India, designing and implementing an advanced recycling process made specifically for the market.
2. The goals of the project are to maximise the extraction of — from e-waste and develop effective methods for the safe disposal or recycling of —.
3. The project team will train — and collaborate with — in India.
4. The project is especially suitable for — who want to develop their skills, are good at solving problems and have a good understanding of —.
5. Applicants are invited to hand in — via the company website within —.

**4** Write a covering letter for the *Green Horizons* project. Explain why you would like to be part of the team going to India and why you would be a suitable candidate. The following sentence starters can help you.

- I am very excited about the chance to …
- I am very interested in …
- I want to help create safe ways to …
- I look forward to working with people in India to …
- I am interested in learning more about …
- I know a lot about recycling technology and I think that …
- I'm ready for a challenge that will …
- I want to be part of the *Green Horizons* project because …

Helping hand

## 5 Communication

### Media and methods

**5** Complete the text describing the graph about a survey on workplace communication.

The graph presents ten different — such as email, video call and letters. For each one, it shows the — of people surveyed who — it at work. Messaging apps were the — popular medium, with 56 % of people asked using them. Emails, text messages and phone calls were also popular. — was the least popular medium, with only 5 % of people asked using it. — people used letters and project management software.

### Company communication

**4** Think about the communication options used at your company. Make notes to answer the following questions:

- Which communication tools do you use the most? When and why?
- How do you access them? Do you have one central device, workspace or platform? Can you access them when you are working offsite?
- Are any of the tools linked?
- Have you had any problems with any of the tools? Which of them do you avoid and why?

Share your notes with a partner. Together, discuss which of the following suggestions could be relevant for their company's communication tools.

- Employees and teams could receive training on how to use the tools more effectively.
- There could be one central platform where all the information is available.
- Data could be synchronised between different tools and programs and could be updated automatically when connected to the internet.
- It could be made possible to access communication tools and programs remotely.
- Extras (e.g. translation function, dictionary of company words and phrases, notes) could be built into the program.

### Instructions

**5** Work in pairs. Use the cards to perform a role play about how to use the drill.

## Helping hand

**Supervisor**

Explain the electric drill and describe its features and functions.
- Adjust the chuck like this.
- Press the speed trigger gently
- Set the torque for the material.

Make sure that they have understood.
- Do you understand how to change the drill bit?
- Any questions on adjusting the chuck?
- Are you comfortable with controlling the speed?
- Do you know how to set the right torque?

Answer their questions, offer tips and explain how to use the drill safely.

**Apprentice**

Listen to the supervisor's explanations and show interest. Ask questions to deepen your understanding and clarify information.
- Is the chuck tight enough now?
- How fast should I drill?
- Is my grip correct?
- Which torque setting is for wood/metal/plastic?
- How do I change the speed?
- What do I do if the drill bit gets stuck?
- How do I know if I'm applying too much pressure?
- Can we practise on different materials?

### Telephone communication

**3** For each challenge, choose the most suitable options for dealing with the situation.

1. lack of knowledge or information
    A  be honest that she can't answer the question
    B  promise to ask her supervisor about it
    C  guess an answer or solution
    D  get back to the caller once the information has been found
    E  tell the caller that it's not important

2. caller is rude or unfriendly
    A  ask the caller to call back later
    B  remain polite
    C  make sure the caller understands she is listening to them
    D  keep the interaction brief
    E  inform her supervisor about the caller's behaviour

3. poor signal or internet connection
    A  ask the caller to call back later
    B  apologise for the situation
    C  try another device or advise the caller to do the same
    D  if nothing works, write an email to arrange another time to speak
    E  tell the caller how unhappy the company is with the internet or phone provider

4. difficulty understanding the caller due to language
    A  be honest about the situation
    B  ask the caller to use a translator
    C  tell the caller she can't deal with their enquiry
    D  ask the caller to speak more slowly or to rephrase sentences she doesn't understand
    E  ask for explanations of words or phrases she doesn't know

# Helping hand

## 6 In the workshop

### Safety measures

**6** Match the words from the text with the right categories.

fluids | skin burns | workshop floor | vehicle falling on top of the mechanic
flammable/combustible fluids | engine | electrical issues | tool | customized uniform
clutter | chemical spills | repair shop | exhaust system | tool cabinet | fire | toolbox
radiator coolant | office | fire extinguisher | workplace | manifold | ear protection
gas | goggles | protective gear | loose/ripped/torn clothing | equipment
unacceptable attire | work apparel | walkway | damage | gloves | hot ash | oil
radiator | chemical and fire resistant clothing | workbench

| Car parts | Areas and equipment in a workshop | Safety attire and equipment | Safety risks and possible accidents |
|---|---|---|---|
| … | … | … | … |

### Transporting a vehicle

**1** Which type of vehicle matches each of the following descriptions?

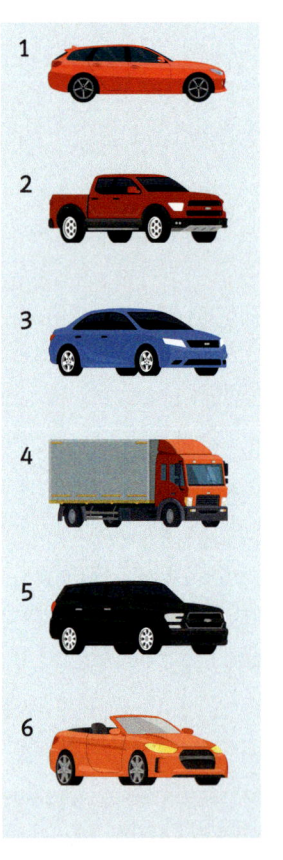

1.
2.
3.
4.
5.
6.

A This type of car comes with a hard or soft top that can be removed or folded down.

B This vehicle has a lot of space behind the back seat. It also has an extra door at the back for transporting large items.

C This type of vehicle is for transporting goods.

D Many drivers like this type of car because of its high driver's seat and off-road capabilities.

E Surprisingly, this standard four-door car with extra space for luggage is popular among millennials.

F This car often has a driver's cabin and an open cargo bed.

# Helping hand

**5** Put the following steps explaining how to jump-start a car in the correct order.

- Check that all clips are securely attached.
- Do not connect the other black clamp to the dead battery. The cable must be grounded. Make sure the clip is not near the battery.
- Park the car with the working battery next to the vehicle with the dead battery and open the hoods of both cars.
- Try to start the car with the dead battery.
- Start the car with the working battery and leave it running for a few minutes.
- Leave the car running for at least 30 minutes to let the battery recharge.
- Connect the positive terminals of the dead and the working battery with a red clamp.
- Then connect one black cable to the negative terminal of the working battery.
- Remove the leads in the reverse order of how you had attached them.

## 7 Maintenance and repair work

### The main inspection

A19 🔊 **2** Aylin's boss wants to know what she discussed with Mr Singh. Complete the table in German.

| Autoteil | vereinbartes Vorgehen |
|---|---|
| Katalysator | — |
| — | aufziehen |
| Linker Blinker | — |
| — | auffüllen |
| Kostenvoranschlag | — |

### Brakes

**6** Put the steps for changing brake rotors and brake pads into the correct order. Compare your results with a partner.

- Remove the brake rotor.
- Clean the brake rotor mounting surface.
- Raise the vehicle.
1. Check the brake fluid level.
- Install the wheel.
- Slide the brake pads out of the brake assembly.
- Install the new brake rotor, clips and pads.
- Check the brake fluid again.
- Lower the car and pump the brake pedal.
- Inspect the brake caliper, then compress and install it.
- Remove the wheel, bolts and caliper.

# Helping hand

## Diagnostic tools in the workshop

**1** Read the text and complete the sentences with the the correct verbs.

categorised | corresponds | covers | decoded | depend | identify | notify

1. The system uses codes to — the mechanic about an issue.
2. A code — to a fault with the car.
3. The code helps the mechanic to — the issue.
4. The codes are — into four different systems.
5. Each category — certain functions of the car.
6. Some digits — on the system that is being used.
7. Some codes are — automatically and some are not.

## 8 Servicing a vintage car

### Planning repairs

**1** Match the German keywords with their English counterparts from the text.

| | | | |
|---|---|---|---|
| 1 | Batterieleitung | A | chassis |
| 2 | Herauslaufen | B | suppressor |
| 3 | abtrennen | C | battery leads |
| 4 | Entstörer | D | disconnect |
| 5 | Mutter | E | spring washers |
| 6 | Federring | F | mounting bracket |
| 7 | Befestigungsteil | G | siphoning |
| 8 | Fahrgestell | H | transmission |
| 9 | Übertragung | I | nut |

### Ordering a spare part

A26 **2** Listen to the voicemail and put these words in the order in which you hear them.

in stock | working days | payment | extra cost | delivery

**4** The following words and phrases are common in customer reviews.
Match them with their German counterparts.

| | | | |
|---|---|---|---|
| 1 | I highly recommend this business. | A | Ihr Kundendienst ist unübertroffen. |
| 2 | Their customer service is second to none. | B | Ich empfehle diesen Betrieb wärmstens. |
| 3 | Their service is consistently outstanding. | C | Ihr Service ist durchweg herausragend. |
| 4 | Efficiency and punctuality are hallmarks of their service. | D | Ich war von ihrem Service beeindruckt. |
| 5 | I was impressed with their service. | E | Die Mitarbeiter sind nicht nur freundlich, sondern auch hochqualifiziert. |
| 6 | Their staff is not only friendly but also highly skilled. | F | Effizienz und Pünktlichkeit sind Markenzeichen von ihrem Service. |

Helping hand

## 9 Customer service

### Roadside assistance

1 Choose the correct aspect of customer service for each picture.

1
- A Roadside assistance
- B Estimating and figuring out repair costs
- C Giving advice and discussing what repair work will be necessary

2
- A Preparing to hand over the car
- B Estimating and figuring out repair costs
- C Giving advice and discussing what repair work will be necessary

3
- A Preparing to hand over the car
- B Handling customer complaints
- C Roadside assistance

4
- A Giving advice and discussing what repair work will be necessary
- B Preparing to hand over the car
- C Handling customer complaints

5
- A Roadside assistance
- B Handling customer complaints
- C Estimating and figuring out repair costs

159

# Helping hand

A29 🔊 **4** At the workshop, the driver talks to Ben. Listen to their conversation and choose the correct German answer.

1. What if it's the driver's fault?
   A Dann übernimmt die Firma einen Teil der Kosten.
   B Dann muss der Kunde die Rechnung bezahlen.

2. What is the procedure at *ABC*?
   A Zunächst wird dem Kunden nichts berechnet. Danach meldet sich *ABC*, falls doch Kosten anfallen.
   B Der Kunde bezahlt die Rechnung zuerst selbst. Dann meldet sich *ABC* mit der Erstattung.

3. What help is available to the customer?
   A Ein Ersatzwagen, wenn er verfügbar ist.
   B Eine gratis Taxifahrt zum Ziel.

## Upgrading a car

**2** Choose the right category for the following upgrading options.

**heated seat covers** | **onboard wifi** | **cold air intake system** | **blind spot alerst system** **car amplifier** | **window tint**

| Safety | Comfort | Entertainment |
| --- | --- | --- |
| … | … | … |

## Digital vehicle inspection

**1** Choose the correct verbs from the text for each noun.

1. **replace** | **complete** the traditional method
2. **boost** | **receive** information
3. **provide** | **receive** transparency
4. **create** | **generate** a template
5. **change** | **replace** the customer experience
6. **approve** | **boost** confidence
7. **create** | **require** attention
8. **change** | **generate** engagement
9. **approve** | **provide** the repairs
10. **complete** | **require** the process

**2** Use the information given in the text to complete the sentences.

**built-in templates** | **completed reports, estimates and recommendations** | **critical repairs** **customer's profile** | **instant, clear and concise** | **the time the customer spends in the shop** **their approval to carry out the repair work** | **smartphones or tablets**

1. Instead of using paper, DVI uses — .
2. The information the client receives is — .
3. For future reference, information about the vehicle's health is stored in the — .
4. Digital images and videos can reduce — .
5. After seeing what repairs are recommended, the customer gives — .
6. Quality checklists are provided by — that are created by the workshop.
7. — that require immediate attention are highlighted.
8. The customer is sent — via text or email.

Helping hand

## 10 Electric vehicles

### Modern driving systems

A31 🔊 **4** Listen to the radio show. Choose the correct words to complete the sentences.

Almost **70%** | **60%** | **50%** of all cars sold in Germany in 2023 have an electric motor. Electric car sales are divided into three categories: all-electric vehicles account for **20%** | **40%** | **30%** of sales, **(all-)electric vehicle** | **plug-in hybrid cars** | **hybrid cars** account for 21.8%, and **(all-)electric vehicle** | **plug-in hybrid cars** | **hybrid cars** account for 5.9%. Hybrid cars cannot be charged at a charging station. Instead, they are charged either while **driving** | **parking** | **braking**, which is known as recuperation, or by the combustion engine. The battery in a plug-in hybrid car is usually **bigger than** | **smaller than** | **as big as** the battery in a hybrid and can be charged using a socket or a special charger. The battery in an **hybrid cars** | **(all-)electric vehicle** | **plug-in hybrid cars** is very big. It can be as heavy as **600 kg** | **800 kg** | **700 kg** in a larger car.

### How to handle EVs

**3** Choose the correct charging and managing parts for each purpose.

1. This makes sure that the voltage of the battery pack (400 V) is converted to 12 V. This is important because other electronic components in the car such as the radio run on 12 V.
   A onboard charger
   B DC/DC converter

2. This charges the battery pack. The electric energy can travel through various connectors and therefore supply different amounts of energy.
   A onboard charger
   B power electronics controller

3. This is similar to the air conditioning units in cars with combustion engines. It heats or cools the battery pack so that it can work at maximum efficiency.
   A charge port
   B thermal system

4. This is where the cable from the charging station is plugged into.
   A charge port
   B thermal system

5. This manages all the activities and tasks of the DC/DC converter and the onboard charger. It also contains the inverter, which is used to change AC to DC and vice versa. It is the main operator of the electric system.
   A power electronics controller
   B DC/DC converter

## Helping hand

**4** Match the words and phrases with their synonyms from the text.

1 danger
2 to be unprotected
3 towing service
4 circles
5 much more electric energy
6 injury or death caused by electricity
7 when the positive pole of a battery touches the negative pole
8 connected to
9 quiet
10 to differ

A to vary
B hazard
C short-circuited
D recovery service
E electrocution
F significantly higher currents
G circuits
H silent
I associated with
J to be exposed to

### Advanced driver-assistance system (ADAS)

**3** Mediate the English explanations into German.

- **Level 0:** The car is manually controlled. The driver is responsible for braking, steering, accelerating, etc.
- **Level 1:** This level of automation includes basic features like lane assistance or cruise control. The driver cannot take their hands off the steering wheel.
- **Level 2:** The vehicle can drive on its own in some situations, for example on the motorway. This is made possible by combining cruise control with lane assistance. The driver remains responsible in all situations and should always be focusing on the road.
- **Level 3:** Cars with this level of automation can adapt to their environment. For example, they can adjust to speed limits. Fully automated driving is possible in certain situations. The driver only has to take over if alerted by the system. On a motorway with no obstructions, the driver becomes a passenger. This is currently the highest level of automation on European and American roads.
- **Level 4:** The car does not need a human driver in most situations. The driver can be a passenger on certain routes or in certain areas. Engineers around the world are working to achieve this level of automation.
- **Level 5:** Fully automated driving is possible and humans can simply be passengers on all types of road.

### Sensors in EVs

**3** Choose the correct statement for each part of the text.
1. A The accident happened in a sharp bend.
   B The accident happened on a straight part of the road.
2. A The car crashed into a pole with full speed.
   B The car stopped abruptly right on the road.
3. A The camera failed to detect the trailer because of the sun.
   B The camera failed to detect the trailer because it was driving too fast.
4. A The RADAR sensor detected the trailer correctly but sent no signal.
   B The RADAR sensor incorrectly detected the trailer as a road sign.
5. A The autopilot system should have been able to react to the danger by itself.
   B Even with autopilot activated, the driver still had to pay attention to the road.

# More

## 2 Your place of work

### Data security

2 Explain the following data security terms in your own words.

1. encryption
2. firewall
3. malware
4. phishing
5. two-factor authentication
6. data breach
7. spyware

## 3 Tasks and responsibilities

### Tasks, responsibilities and expectations

A6 🔊 5 Listen again. For each of the apprentices interviewed, write a short description of their job and daily tasks.

## 4 Working in a global world

### Meeting international business partners

3 Create an organigram of your department or company. Present it to your partner and explain the hierarchical levels and who reports to whom.

More

## 7 Maintenance and repair work

### The main inspection

A19 🔊 **1** Listen to Aylin's phone conversation with Mr Singh. Note down any additional comments about the car parts.

1. tyres   2. indicators   3. oil

**4** A car mechanic is telling an English-speaking customer about the main inspection in Germany. Write a dialogue using the prompts below.

| Customer's questions | Car mechanic's answers |
|---|---|
| • purpose of main inspection and exhaust emissions test?<br>• only one organisation that carries out main inspections and exhaust emissions tests?<br>• when to show main inspection report? | • car safe to drive<br>• no, several organisations: …<br>• when registering a vehicle |

### Brakes

**3** Write a small text explaining the differences between hydraulic brakes and regenerative brakes in German.

## 8 Servicing a vintage car

### Researching fuel system problems

**2** Summarise the most important points from each paragraph of the text.

### Planning repairs

**3** What is your opinion on environmental guidelines? Are they very important for your day-to-day work or do you find them annoying and time-consuming?

## 9 Customer service

### Upgrading a car

**2** Explain the advantage of each upgrading option.

1. navigation system   3. cruise control       5. ambient lighting
2. sunroof             4. infotainment system  6. trailer coupling

# Grammar files

## G1 Tenses

### G1.1 Simple present

| Positive sentences | Negative sentences | Questions |
|---|---|---|
| I use social media.<br>You use social media.<br>He/she/it uses social media.<br>We use social media.<br>You use social media.<br>They use social media. | I don't use social media.<br>You don't use social media.<br>He/she/it doesn't use social media.<br>We don't use social media.<br>You don't use social media.<br>They don't use social media. | Do I use social media?<br>Do you use social media?<br>Does he/she/it use social media?<br>Do we use social media?<br>Do you use social media?<br>Do they use social media?<br><br>Questions with a question word:<br>Why do I use social media?<br>Why do you use social media?<br>Why does he/she/it use social media?<br>Why do we use social media?<br>Why do you use social media?<br>Why do they use social media? |

> **!** Be careful with these verbs: to be, to have.

**Examples of typical use:**
- Facts and general statements:
  The cartoon shows a family.
- Everyday activities or habits:
  Justin listens to podcasts on the bus.
  Tense markers:
  always, often, sometimes, never, usually, every day/week/month/year, on Mondays/Tuesdays..., at 7 o'clock / 11 o'clock ...
- A set sequence of events or actions:
  Young people spend too much time on their phones, get very little sleep and are tired the next day at school.
- For scheduled future events with an adverbial phrase of time:
  The programme finishes at ten o'clock.

## Grammar files

### G1.2 Present progressive

| Positive sentences | Negative sentences | Questions |
|---|---|---|
| I am studying.<br>You are studying.<br>He/she/it is studying.<br>We are studying.<br>You are studying.<br>They are studying. | I'm not studying.<br>You aren't studying.<br>He/she/it isn't studying.<br>We aren't studying.<br>You aren't studying.<br>They aren't studying. | Am I studying?<br>Are you studying?<br>Is he/she/it studying?<br>Are we studying?<br>Are you studying?<br>Are they studying?<br><br>Questions with a question word:<br>What am I studying?<br>What are you studying?<br>What is he/she/it studying?<br>What are we studying?<br>What are you studying?<br>What are they studying? |

> **!** Some verbs are never used in the progressive form, especially those which express feelings or a belief: to believe, to love, to hate, to seem, to have (in the sense of own), can, to mean, to want to, to feel, to notice, to realise.

**Examples of typical use:**
- An activity that is going on right now and will continue for a limited period of time:
  Reese is giving an interview (now).
  Tense markers:
  now, just now, at the moment
- Planned future events with an adverbial phrase of time:
  Reese is flying to London next week.

### G1.3 Simple past

| Positive sentences | Negative sentences | Questions |
|---|---|---|
| I played a video game.<br>You played a video game.<br>He/she/it played a video game.<br>We played a video game.<br>You played a video game.<br>They played a video game. | I didn't play a video game.<br>You didn't play a video game.<br>He/she/it didn't play a video game.<br>We didn't play a video game.<br>You didn't play a video game.<br>They didn't play a video game. | Did I play a video game?<br>Did you play a video game?<br>Did he/she/it play a video game?<br>Did we play a video game?<br>Did you play a video game?<br>Did they play a video game?<br><br>Questions with a question word:<br>Why did I play a video game?<br>Why did you play a video game?<br>Why did he/she/it play a video game?<br>Why did we play a video game?<br>Why did you play a video game?<br>Why did they play a video game? |

## Grammar files

> ! **Be careful with irregular verbs.**

**Examples of typical use:**
- For activities that began and ended at a specific time in the past:
  The technical team tested the device **last week**.
  Tense markers:
  yesterday, ago, last week/month/year, in 2017/on Tuesday/...
- For a series of events in the past, as in a story, often called the 'narrative past':
  As Kate didn't have a job, she went to Australia. Her aunt found her a job there and one thing led to another. After six months, Kate had a permanent job.

### G1.4 Past progressive

| Positive sentences | Negative sentences | Questions |
| --- | --- | --- |
| I was thinking.<br>You were thinking.<br>He/she/it was thinking.<br>We were thinking.<br>You were thinking.<br>They were thinking. | I wasn't thinking.<br>You weren't thinking.<br>He/she/it wasn't thinking.<br>We weren't thinking.<br>You weren't thinking.<br>They weren't thinking. | Was I thinking?<br>Were you thinking?<br>Was he/she/it thinking?<br>Were we thinking?<br>Were you thinking?<br>Were they thinking?<br><br>Questions with a question word:<br>What was I thinking?<br>What were you thinking?<br>What was he/she/it thinking?<br>What were we thinking?<br>What were you thinking?<br>What were they thinking? |

**Examples of typical use:**
- An activity in the past that was already in progress when something else happened:
  Kate was working in a bar **when** she heard about the job in a bank.
- Several activities or events that were happening at the same time in the past:
  **While** Kate was living in England, she only had temporary jobs.

## Grammar files

### G1.5 Present perfect simple

| Positive sentences | Negative sentences | Questions |
|---|---|---|
| I have finished.<br>You have finished.<br>He/she/it has finished.<br>We have finished.<br>You have finished.<br>They have finished. | I haven't finished.<br>You haven't finished.<br>He/she/it hasn't finished.<br>We haven't finished.<br>You haven't finished.<br>They haven't finished. | Have I finished?<br>Have you finished?<br>Has he/she/it finished?<br>Have we finished?<br>Have you finished?<br>Have they finished?<br><br>Questions with a question word:<br>What have I finished?<br>What have you finished?<br>What has he/she/it finished?<br>What have we finished?<br>What have you finished?<br>What have they finished? |

> ! Be careful with irregular verbs.
> With the present perfect simple, the result of the action is usually more important than the action itself. Never use the present perfect with adverbs of past time, e.g. yesterday, last week, three years ago, in 2017 …

Examples of typical use:
- Activities that happened recently and whose effects are still being felt in the present:
  Kate has moved to Australia and she is still getting used to the different accent there.
- With certain adverbs, such as just, so far, ever, never, recently, lately, today, this week, already, (not) yet:
  He has listed all his work experience so far. – Has he ever worked abroad?
- With 'for' and 'since', for activities that started in the past and are continuing:
  Lisa hasn't checked her emails for two days. – She has received 20 emails since Tuesday.

### G1.6 Present perfect progressive

| Positive sentences | Negative sentences | Questions |
|---|---|---|
| I have been waiting.<br>You have been waiting.<br>He/she/it has been waiting.<br>We have been waiting.<br>You have been waiting.<br>They have been waiting. | I haven't been waiting.<br>You haven't been waiting.<br>He/she/it hasn't been waiting.<br>We haven't been waiting.<br>You haven't been waiting.<br>They haven't been waiting. | Have I been waiting?<br>Have you been waiting?<br>Has he/she/it been waiting?<br>Have we been waiting?<br>Have you been waiting?<br>Have they been waiting?<br><br>Questions with a question word:<br>Why have I been waiting?<br>Why have you been waiting?<br>Why has he/she/it been waiting?<br>Why have we been waiting?<br>Why have you been waiting?<br>Why have they been waiting? |

**Examples of typical use:**
- Activities that have been going on either continuously or at intervals up to the present, often with adverbials of time such as all day, for a week, etc.:
  We have been looking at job adverts all evening.
- There is no mention of time but the activity has taken place very recently and the result is still visible:
  It has been raining.

## G1.7 Past perfect simple

| Positive sentences | Negative sentences | Questions |
|---|---|---|
| I had finished.<br>You had finished.<br>He/she/it had finished.<br>We had finished.<br>You had finished.<br>They had finished. | I hadn't finished.<br>You hadn't finished.<br>He/she/it hadn't finished.<br>We hadn't finished.<br>You hadn't finished.<br>They hadn't finished. | Had I finished?<br>Had you finished?<br>Had he/she/it finished?<br>Had we finished?<br>Had you finished?<br>Had they finished?<br><br>Questions with a question word:<br>What had I finished?<br>What had you finished?<br>What had he/she/it finished?<br>What had we finished?<br>What had you finished?<br>What had they finished? |

> ! Be careful with irregular verbs.

**Examples of typical use:**
- An activity that happened before another activity in the past, showing the connection between the two activities:
  When I arrived at college, the lesson had already started.
  After I had finished my homework, I decided to go out.
- In reported speech, when the original statement is in the past or present perfect:
  Jane said that she had forgotten to do her homework.

# Grammar files

## G1.8 Past perfect progressive

| Positive sentences | Negative sentences | Questions |
|---|---|---|
| I had been waiting.<br>You had been waiting.<br>He/she/it had been waiting.<br>We had been waiting.<br>You had been waiting.<br>They had been waiting. | I hadn't been waiting.<br>You hadn't been waiting.<br>He/she/it hadn't been waiting.<br>We hadn't been waiting.<br>You hadn't been waiting.<br>They hadn't been waiting. | Had I been waiting?<br>Had you been waiting?<br>Had he/she/it been waiting?<br>Had we been waiting?<br>Had you been waiting?<br>Had they been waiting?<br><br>Questions with a question word:<br>Why had I been waiting?<br>Why had you been waiting?<br>Why had he/she/it been waiting?<br>Why had we been waiting?<br>Why had you been waiting?<br>Why had they been waiting? |

**Examples of typical use:**
- An activity that occurred over a period of time, and before another activity, in the past. The two activities are directly related:
  He was tired because he had been working so hard.
- In reported speech, when the original statement is in the present perfect progressive:
  He said that he had been working hard.

## G1.9 Going to-future

| Positive sentences | Negative sentences | Questions |
|---|---|---|
| I am going to leave early.<br>You are going to leave early.<br>He/she/it is going to leave early.<br><br>We are going to leave early<br>You are going to leave early.<br>They are going to leave early. | I'm not going to leave early.<br>You're not going to leave early.<br>He/she/it's not going to leave early.<br><br>We're not going to leave early.<br>You're not going to leave early.<br>They're not going to leave early. | Am I going to leave early?<br>Are you going to leave early?<br>Is he/she/it going to leave early?<br>Are we going to leave early?<br>Are you going to leave early?<br>Are they going to leave early? |

**Examples of typical use:**
- For an action in the future that has already been planned or prepared:
  They're going to buy new tablets for the whole school.
- For a prediction about the future, when you can see that something is about to happen:
  Look at those clouds. It's going to rain soon.

# Grammar files

## G1.10 Future simple (will-future)

| Positive sentences | Negative sentences | Questions |
|---|---|---|
| I will finish college.<br>You will finish college.<br>He/she/it will finish college.<br>We will finish college.<br>You will finish college.<br>They will finish college. | I won't finish college.<br>You won't finish college.<br>He/she/it won't finish college.<br>We won't finish college.<br>You won't finish college.<br>They won't finish college. | Will I finish college?<br>Will you finish college?<br>Will he/she/it finish college?<br>Will we finish college?<br>Will you finish college?<br>Will they finish college?<br><br>Questions with a question word:<br>When will I finish college?<br>When will you finish college?<br>When will he/she/it finish college?<br>When will we finish college?<br>When will you finish college?<br>When will they finish college? |

> **!** English will = German werden
> English want = German wollen

**Examples of typical use:**
- Things that are likely to happen at a defined or undefined time in the future:
  You'll be a great business person one day.
- For forecasts, such as the weather forecast:
  On Saturday, it will rain for most of the day.
- In if-clauses type 1 – future situations that are probable/possible:
  If the weather is nice, I'll revise for my test in the park.

## G1.11 Future progressive

| Positive sentences | Negative sentences | Questions |
|---|---|---|
| I will be learning.<br>You will be learning.<br>He/she/it will be learning.<br>We will be learning.<br>You will be learning.<br>They will be learning. | I won't be learning.<br>You won't be learning.<br>He/she/it won't be learning.<br>We won't be learning.<br>You won't be learning.<br>They won't be learning. | Will I be learning?<br>Will you be learning?<br>Will he/she/it be learning?<br>Will we be learning?<br>Will you be learning?<br>Will they be learning?<br><br>Questions with a question word:<br>What will I be learning?<br>What will you be learning?<br>What will he/she/it be learning?<br>What will we be learning?<br>What will you be learning?<br>What will they be learning? |

# Grammar files

**Examples of typical use:**
- Events – which are often planned – that will be going on at a certain time in the future when another event occurs:
  You will be sleeping by the time I get home.

## G1.12 Future perfect simple

| Positive sentences | Negative sentences | Questions |
|---|---|---|
| I will have finished.<br>You will have finished.<br>He/she/it will have finished.<br>We will have finished.<br>You will have finished.<br>They will have finished. | I won't have finished.<br>You won't have finished.<br>He/she/it won't have finished.<br>We won't have finished.<br>You won't have finished.<br>They won't have finished. | Will I have finished?<br>Will you have finished?<br>Will he/she/it have finished?<br>Will we have finished?<br>Will you have finished?<br>Will they have finished?<br><br>Questions with a question word:<br>When will I have finished?<br>When will you have finished?<br>When will he/she/it have finished?<br>When will we have finished?<br>When will you have finished?<br>When will they have finished? |

> **!** Be careful with irregular verbs.

**Examples of typical use:**
- For an activity in the future that takes place before a second activity, to show the relation between them. The second activity is in the present tense:
  Joanna will have finished the college course by the time she is 20.

## G1.13 Future perfect progressive

| Positive sentences | Negative sentences | Questions |
|---|---|---|
| I will have been waiting.<br>You will have been waiting.<br>He/she/it will have been waiting.<br>We will have been waiting.<br>You will have been waiting.<br>They will have been waiting. | I won't have been waiting.<br>You won't have been waiting.<br>He/she/it won't have been waiting.<br>We won't have been waiting.<br>You won't have been waiting.<br>They won't have been waiting. | Will I have been waiting?<br>Will you have been waiting?<br>Will he/she/it have been waiting?<br>Will we have been waiting?<br>Will you have been waiting?<br>Will they have been waiting? |

**Examples of typical use:**
- Used in the same way as the future perfect simple, but it places more emphasis on the length of time the activity is expected to take:
  They will have been studying English for eight years by the time they take the exam.

# Grammar files

## G1.14 Conditional I

| Positive sentences | Negative sentences | Questions |
|---|---|---|
| I would take a gap year.<br>You would take a gap year.<br>He/she/it would take a gap year.<br>We would take a gap year.<br>You would take a gap year.<br>They would take a gap year. | I wouldn't take a gap year.<br>You wouldn't take a gap year.<br>He/she/it wouldn't take a gap year.<br>We wouldn't take a gap year.<br>You wouldn't take a gap year.<br>They wouldn't take a gap year. | Would I take a gap year?<br>Would you take a gap year?<br>Would he/she/it take a gap year?<br>Would we take a gap year?<br>Would you take a gap year?<br>Would they take a gap year?<br><br>Questions with a question word:<br>Why would I take a gap year?<br>Why would you take a gap year?<br>Why would he/she/it take a gap year?<br>Why would we take a gap year?<br>Why would you take a gap year?<br>Why would they take a gap year? |

**Examples of typical use:**
- For suggestions, polite questions and requests:
  Which country would you visit? – Well, I would visit Australia.
  Would you like a drink?
  Would you help me, please?
- In if-clauses type 2 – future situations that are improbable/unlikely:
  If I had enough money, I would start my own company.

## G1.15 Conditional II

| Positive sentences | Negative sentences | Questions |
|---|---|---|
| I would have applied for the job.<br>You would have applied for the job.<br>He/she/it would have applied for the job.<br>We would have applied for the job.<br>You would have applied for the job.<br>They would have applied for the job. | I wouldn't have applied for the job.<br>You wouldn't have applied for the job.<br>He/she/it wouldn't have applied for the job.<br>We wouldn't have applied for the job.<br>You wouldn't have applied for the job.<br>They wouldn't have applied for the job. | Would I have applied for the job?<br>Would you have applied for the job?<br>Would he/she/it have applied for the job?<br>Would we have applied for the job?<br>Would you have applied for the job?<br>Would they have applied for the job?<br><br>Questions with a question word:<br>Why would I have applied for the job?<br>Why would you have applied for the job?<br>Why would he/she/it have applied for the job?<br>Why would we have applied for the job?<br>Why would you have applied for the job?<br>Why would they have applied for the job? |

**!** Be careful with irregular verbs.

**Examples of typical use:**
- In if-clauses type 3 – past situations that are unreal/impossible/hypothetical:
  If you had prepared before the interview, they would have given you the job.

# Grammar files

## G2 If-clauses

There are three main types of if-clauses (or conditional sentences) in English. They are basically used in the same way as conditional sentences in German. You can put the if-clause at the beginning or at the end of the sentence.

### G2.1 Type 1 – Future situations (probable/possible)

1. if-clause: simple present – main clause: will-future
   **If** you **study** hard, you **will pass** the exam.
   *Wenn du fleißig lernst, wirst du die Prüfung bestehen.*
2. if-clause: present perfect – main clause: will-future
   **If** you **have studied** hard, you **will pass** the exam.
   *Wenn du fleißig gelernt hast, wirst du die Prüfung bestehen.*
3. if-clause: simple present – main clause: can + infinitive
   **If** you **study** hard, you **can pass** the exam.
   *Wenn du fleißig lernst, kannst du die Prüfung bestehen.*
4. if-clause: simple present – main clause: might + infinitive
   **If** you **study** hard, you **might pass** the exam.
   *Wenn du fleißig lernst, wirst du eventuell die Prüfung bestehen.*

### G2.2 Type 2 – Future situations (improbable/unlikely)

1. if-clause: simple past – main clause: conditional I (would + infinitive)
   **If** you **studied** hard, you **would pass** the exam.
   *Wenn du fleißig lernen würdest, würdest du die Prüfung bestehen.*
2. if-clause: simple past – main clause: could + infinitive
   **If** you **studied** hard, you **could pass** the exam.
   *Wenn du fleißig lernen würdest, könntest du die Prüfung bestehen.*

### G2.3 Type 3 – Past situations (unreal/impossible/hypothetical)

1. if-clause: past perfect – main clause: conditional II (would + have + past participle)
   **If** you **had studied** hard, you **would have passed** the exam.
   *Wenn du fleißig gelernt hättest, hättest du die Prüfung bestanden.*
2. if-clause: past perfect – main clause: could + have + past participle
   **If** you **had studied** hard, you **could have passed** the exam.
   *Wenn du fleißig gelernt hättest, hättest du die Prüfung bestehen können.*
3. if-clause: past perfect – main clause: might + have + past participle
   **If** you **had studied** hard, you **might have passed** the exam.
   *Wenn du fleißig gelernt hättest, hättest du eventuell die Prüfung bestanden.*

# Grammar files

> **!** Exception to the rules:
> - The present tense is used in both clauses in general statements and for repeated activities or habits:
>   If plants don't get enough water, they die. – If she has time, she goes to the gym.
> - For recommendations and advice use 'were' in the if-clause and conditional I in the main clause:
>   If I were you, I would study a bit harder.
> - 'If' can be left out when the order of the verb and subject are reversed:
>   Had I studied harder, I would have passed the exam.

> **!** Be careful:
> - If you start a sentence with an if-clause, use a comma. Don't use a comma if you start with the main clause:
>   If you study hard, you will pass the exam.
>   You will pass the exam if you study hard.
> - Don't use 'will' in the if-clause, except to express willingness:
>   You can have my car for the weekend if you'll pay for gas.
> - Don't use 'would' in the if-clause except when you are making a polite request:
>   I would be grateful if you would hand in your homework on time in future.

## G3 The passive

The passive is often used when the action is more important than who or what performed it. The passive is frequently used in scientific and technical writing. The passive can be formed with or without an 'agent'. The 'agent' is the person or thing that causes an action to occur.

Form the passive using a form of 'to be' + past participle (+ by + agent)
The Youth Agency carries out *research projects*.
*Research projects* are carried out by the Youth Agency.

| Simple present | Present progressive |
| --- | --- |
| I am invited for an interview. | I am being interviewed for a survey. |
| You are invited for an interview. | You are being interviewed for a survey. |
| He/she/it is invited for an interview. | He/she/it is being interviewed for a survey. |
| We are invited for an interview. | We are being interviewed for a survey. |
| You are invited for an interview. | You are being interviewed for a survey. |
| They are invited for an interview. | They are being interviewed for a survey. |

| Simple past | Past progressive |
| --- | --- |
| I was invited for an interview. | I was being interviewed for a survey. |
| You were invited for an interview. | You were being interviewed for a survey. |
| He/she/it was invited for an interview. | He/she/it was being interviewed for a survey. |
| We were invited for an interview. | We were being interviewed for a survey. |
| You were invited for an interview. | You were being interviewed for a survey. |
| They were invited for an interview. | They were being interviewed for a survey. |

# Grammar files

| Present perfect | Modal verbs |
|---|---|
| I have been invited for an interview.<br>You have been invited for an interview.<br>He/she/it has been invited for an interview.<br>We have been invited for an interview.<br>You have been invited for an interview.<br>They have been invited for an interview. | I can be contacted online.<br>You must be contacted online.<br>He/she/it mustn't be contacted online.<br>We needn't be contacted online.<br>You ought to be contacted online.<br>They should be contacted online. |

| Future | Future perfect |
|---|---|
| I will be invited for an interview.<br>You will be invited for an interview.<br>He/she/it will be invited for an interview.<br>We will be invited for an interview.<br>You will be invited for an interview.<br>They will be invited for an interview. | I will have been invited for an interview.<br>You will have been invited for an interview.<br>He/she/it will have been invited for an interview.<br>We will have been invited for an interview.<br>You will have been invited for an interview.<br>They will have been invited for an interview. |

> **!** Be careful with irregular verbs.

## G4 Relative clauses

Relative clauses are used to describe people or things. A relative clause usually begins with a relative pronoun.

| Relative pronoun | refers to |
|---|---|
| who | people (subject or object) |
| whom | people (object), formal English |
| which | things |
| that | people or things (subject or object) |
| whose | possessions |

### G4.1 Defining relative clauses

- A defining relative clause is important for the meaning of the sentence. Without the relative clause the sentence would not make any sense. Defining relative clauses are not separated from the rest of the sentence by commas:
  The text message that/which you sent me didn't arrive.
  This is the woman who(m) I emailed yesterday.
  This is the boy whose smartphone was stolen.
- The pronouns 'that', 'which' and 'who(m)' can be left out if the pronoun is the object of the relative clause. This type of relative clause is known as a 'contact' clause:
  The apps we use are all free.
  This is the woman I emailed yesterday.

## G4.2 Non-defining relative clause

- The information in non-defining relative clauses is additional and descriptive. Even without the relative clause the sentence is clear. Non-defining relative clauses are separated from the rest of the sentence by commas:
Aiden, who is still a teenager, runs a successful online business.

## G5 Adjectives

Adjectives describe people and things: the tall man – bright lights

- The present participle (-ing form) and past participle of verbs can often be used as adjectives:
an interesting book – the finished report
- Verbs are usually followed by adverbs, however some verbs are followed by adjectives:

| to be | The laptop is heavy. |
| to become | Anne became nervous before the interview. |
| to feel | Thomas felt excited about his new job. |
| to get | Her smartphone got broken. |
| to look | The office block looks modern. |
| to seem | My new colleagues seem nice. |

- Adjectives can be used as collective nouns. In such cases, the + adjective refers to a particular group of people as a whole:
It is important to help the unemployed to find work.
The very young and the very old are particularly at risk.
- The comparison of adjectives:

| Positive form | Comparative form | Superlative form |
| --- | --- | --- |
| cold | colder | the coldest |
| hot | hotter | the hottest |
| funny | funnier | the funniest |
| modern | more modern | the most modern |

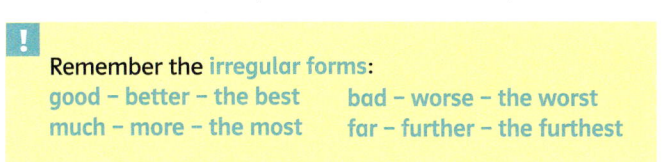

> **!** Remember the irregular forms:
> good – better – the best    bad – worse – the worst
> much – more – the most    far – further – the furthest

Use more / -er than, as … as and not as … as to make comparisons:
An email is more modern than a letter.
My smartphone is newer than yours.
Tablets are just as popular as laptops.
The internet at school is not as fast as the internet at home.

## Grammar files

## G6 Adverbs

Adverbs are formed by adding **-ly/-ily** to an adjective:

| Adjective | Adverb |
|---|---|
| safe | safely |
| happy | happily |
| real | really |
| reasonable | reasonably |

> **!** Remember the **irregular forms**:
> good – well
> fast – fast
> hard – hard

- Adverbs describe actions (verbs):
  He **walked quickly.** She **spoke slowly.**
- Adverbs before other adjectives:
  This is an **extremely good** essay.
- Adverbs before other adverbs:
  He was driving **incredibly fast.**
- Adverbs before past participles:
  Credit cards are **frequently accepted.**
- Some useful adverbs:
  always, usually, often, frequently, sometimes, seldom, rarely, never, recently, soon, lately, in the past, in the future, largely, for the most part, partly, probably, possibly, hardly, definitely, obviously, clearly, basically, consequently, as a result
- The comparison of adverbs:

| Positive form | Comparative form | Superlative form |
|---|---|---|
| fluently | more fluently | the most fluently |

> **!** Remember the **irregular forms**:
> well – better – the best
> badly – worse – the worst
> fast – faster – the fastest

# G7 Question tags

A question tag is added to the end of a sentence to turn it into a question.
In German you use expressions like '…, *nicht wahr?*' and '…, *oder?*' in a similar way.

- If the statement is positive, the question tag is negative:
  He **uses** social media, **doesn't** he?
- If the statement is negative, the question tag is positive:
  He **doesn't** use social media, **does** he?
- The subject of the sentence is also the subject of the question tag:
  Lisa never turns off her smartphone, **does she**?
- If the statement is in the simple present, the question tag is formed with 'is/are' or 'isn't/aren't', 'do/does' or 'don't/doesn't':
  He **likes** video games, **doesn't** he?
- For statements in the simple past, the question tag is formed with 'was/were' or 'wasn't/weren't' or 'did/didn't':
  He **took** a gap year, **didn't** he?
- If the statement uses an auxiliary verb (to be, to have, will, etc.) or a modal (can, must, etc.), use the modal or auxiliary verb in the same tense in the tag:
  Tom **is** here, **isn't** he?
  Roger **has bought** a new laptop, **hasn't** he?
  Jill **will be** at the interview, **won't** she?
  You **can** contact me by email, **can't** you?

# G8 Modal auxiliaries

Asking someone to do something:

- will/would/can/could/may
  **Will/Would/Can/Could** you do me a favour?
  Asking for permission / giving permission:
  **May** I use your phone? – Yes, of course, you **may**.
  Talking about abilities:
  She **can** speak English.

- must/mustn't/needn't
  Instructing someone to do something or not to do something:
  You **must** prepare before an interview.
  You **mustn't** tell lies at an interview.
  Talking about a necessity or duty:
  I **must** send in my job application by Friday.
  You **needn't** be nervous before the interview.

- may/might/could/must/will
  Expressing a possibility or probability:
  It **may/might/could/will** rain.
  You **must** be Mr Jones.
  Making a suggestion:
  We **could** look for typical interview questions online.

## Grammar files

- should/ought to/shouldn't/ought not to
  Giving advice:
  You **should/ought to** use a dictionary.
  You **shouldn't/ought not to** arrive late for the interview.
- Modal auxiliaries only have a present and/or past tense form. Substitutes are used for other tenses:

| Modal auxiliary | Substitutes | Examples |
| --- | --- | --- |
| can/could | to be able to | He **won't be able to** work under pressure. |
| may/mustn't | to be allowed to<br>to not be allowed to | We **were allowed to** use our smartphones in class.<br>We **weren't allowed to** play music. |
| must/needn't | to have to<br>to not have to | She **will have to** work this weekend.<br>We **didn't have to** work late. |

## G9  -ing forms

An -ing form can be either a present participle or a gerund.

### G9.1  The present participle

- The present participle is used in the progressive tenses (present progressive, past progressive, etc.):
  Mary **is checking** her emails. – The class **was discussing** the topic 'Take a gap year or find a job?'.
- The present participle can be used as an adjective: the **winning** party – a **growing** child
- The present participle can be used to shorten clauses, often after a conjunction, e.g:
  after, while, before, when:
  I was riding my bike to work when I saw her. → **While riding** my bike to work, I saw her.
  The class listened to the entrepreneur who was talking about start-ups.
  → The class listened to the entrepreneur **talking** about start-ups.
  After we had collected ideas in a word web, we discussed them.
  → **After collecting** ideas in a word web we discussed them.
  Read the text before you answer the questions. → Read the text **before answering** the questions.

## G9.2 The gerund

- The gerund is used after prepositions: You're very good at speaking English.
- The gerund is often used after certain verbs: like, hate, enjoy, to love, to mind, to prefer
  I don't mind watching TV but I prefer reading and I also enjoy playing computer games.
- The gerund can be used as a noun: Laughing is good for you. – Studying is very important.
- Some verbs have the construction verb + preposition + gerund:
  to be afraid of, to look forward to, to feel like, to talk about, to insist on, to decide against, to think about/of, to succeed in, to apologise for
  I'm afraid of flying.
- When the following expressions are followed by a verb, use the gerund:
  - No point: There's no point in waiting any longer.
  - To not be worth: It's not worth going to see the new James Bond film.
  - A waste of money/time: It's a waste of time talking to you.
  - To spend / to waste time/money: He spends all of his time sitting in front of a computer.

## G10 Reported speech

Reported speech (or indirect speech) is used to report what someone has said without quoting them.

- Start the reported speech with a reporting verb:
  a) Statements: to say (that), to tell sb. (that), to answer, to mention, to explain, to reply, etc.
     "I'm tired." → She says (that) she's tired.
  b) Questions: ask, want to know
     "Are you hungry?" → She asks me if I'm hungry.
     "Where do you go to school?" → She wants to know where I go to school.
  c) Commands: tell sb. to + infinitive
     "Leave me alone!" → She told me to leave her alone.
- If the reporting verb is in the present, present perfect or future tense, the tense stays the same:
  "Spending hours on social media is bad for you".
  → Mr Jones says spending hours on social media is bad for you.
  → Mr Jones has said spending hours on social media is bad for you.
  → Mr Jones will say spending hours on social media is bad for you.

## Grammar files

- If the reporting verb is in the past tense, the tense of the reported speech changes:

| | |
|---|---|
| simple present<br>"I text my best friend every day." | simple past<br>She said she texted her best friend every day. |
| present progressive<br>"I am texting my best friend." | past progressive<br>She said she was texting her best friend. |
| simple past<br>"I texted my best friend last night." | past perfect<br>She said she had texted her best friend the night before. |
| past progressive<br>"I was texting my best friend." | past perfect progressive<br>She said she had been texting her best friend. |
| present perfect<br>"I have texted my best friend." | past perfect<br>She said she had texted her best friend. |
| present perfect progressive<br>"I have been texting my best friend." | past perfect progressive<br>She said she had been texting her best friend. |
| past perfect<br>"I had texted my best friend." | past perfect<br>She said she had texted her best friend. |
| past perfect progressive<br>"I had been texting my best friend." | past perfect progressive<br>She said she had been texting her best friend. |
| will-future<br>"I will text my best friend every day." | conditional I<br>She said she would text her best friend every day. |

- Some adverbs of time also change in reported speech, for example:
  now → then
  yesterday → the day before / the previous day
  here → there
  last year → the year before / the previous year
  today → that day
  tomorrow → the next day
- Statements involving truths and facts do not have to change in reported speech:
  "The novel is by Zadie Smith." → The teacher said that the novel is by Zadie Smith.

# G11 Word order

Generally, the word order in English sentences is subject – verb – object. This is the case in main clauses and subordinate clauses:
We live in a world that is heavily influenced by the media.
I like Las Vegas because it has something for everyone.

## G11.1 Statements

- Normally, place comes before time:
  I went to school yesterday.
  I've wanted to visit the UK for years.
- The adverbs in a sentence generally follow the sequence:
  adverb of manner – adverb of place – adverb of time:
  I was waiting patiently for tickets outside the stadium all morning.
  I will be working hard in London this summer.
- In English, adverbs of frequency (never, sometimes, often, always, etc.) are directly in front of the verb:
  I usually check my phone as soon as I wake up.
  I never leave home without my phone.

> **!** But be careful – there is an exception when you use the verb to be:
> I'm always in the gym on Fridays.

## G11.2 Questions

- Questions never begin with a main verb:
  Do you like British food?
  Did you get my message last night?

> **!** But be careful – there is an exception when you use the verb to be:
> Are you thinking of taking a gap year?
> Am I the first person to arrive?

- Negative questions do not end with a main verb like they do in German:
  Aren't you going to miss German food?

## G11.3 Negated statements

The negation of 'don't'/'doesn't' comes before the main verb, unlike in German:
- I don't have school on Friday afternoons.
- I don't use my mobile phone during lessons.

# Grammar files

## Grammatik-Erklärvideos ▷ und interaktive Übungen

Mit Hilfe von Grammatik-Erklärvideos und interaktiven Übungen können grammatische Phänomene wiederholt und gefestigt werden.

| | | |
|---|---|---|
| V1 ▷ I1<br>V2 ▷ I2 | Talking about the present | – simple present, present progressive<br>– questions and negative sentences |
| V3 ▷ I3 | Talking about the past | – simple past, past progressive |
| V4 ▷ I4<br>V5 ▷ I5 | Talking about the present perfect | – present perfect simple, present perfect progressive<br>– present perfect, simple past |
| V6 ▷ I6 | Talking about the future | – will-future, going to-future, present with future meaning |
| V7 ▷ I7 | Talking about quantities | – some, any, every, no and their compounds |
| V8 ▷ I8<br>V9 ▷ I9 | Talking about qualities | – adjectives, adverbs<br>– comparison of adjectives and adverbs, exceptions |
| V10 ▷ I10 | Talking about ability, permission and necessity | – modal auxiliaries and their substitutes |
| V11 ▷ I11 | Talking about describing people or things in more detail | – relative clauses: who, which, that, whose |
| V12 ▷ I12 | Talking about conditions | – if-clauses |
| V13 ▷ I13 | Talking about likes and dislikes | – the gerund |
| V14 ▷ I14 | Talking about processes | – the passive: present, past, future |
| V15 ▷ I15 | Talking about passing on information | – reported speech |

# Irregular verbs

| | |
|---|---|
| be, was/were, been | sein |
| beat, beat, beaten | schlagen |
| become, became, become | werden |
| begin, began, begun | anfangen |
| bite, bit, bitten | beißen |
| break, broke, broken | (zer)brechen |
| bring, brought, brought | (mit)bringen |
| build, built, built | bauen |
| buy, bought, bought | kaufen |
| catch, caught, caught | fangen |
| choose, chose, chosen | wählen |
| come, came, come | kommen |
| cost, cost, cost | kosten |
| cut, cut, cut | schneiden |
| deal, dealt, dealt | umgehen (mit) |
| do, did, done | tun, machen |
| draw, drew, drawn | zeichnen |
| drink, drank, drunk | trinken |
| drive, drove, driven | fahren |
| eat, ate, eaten | essen |
| fall, fell, fallen | fallen |
| feel, felt, felt | (sich) fühlen |
| fight, fought, fought | (be)kämpfen |
| find, found, found | finden |
| flee, fled, fled | fliehen |
| fly, flew, flown | fliegen |
| forbid, forbade, forbidden | verbieten |
| forget, forgot, forgotten | vergessen |
| freeze, froze, frozen | frieren |
| get, got, got | bekommen |
| give, gave, given | geben |
| go, went, gone | gehen, fahren |
| grow, grew, grown | wachsen |
| hang, hung, hung | hängen |
| have, had, had | haben |
| hear, heard, heard | hören |
| hide, hid, hidden | (sich) verstecken |
| hit, hit, hit | schlagen |
| hold, held, held | (fest)halten |
| hurt, hurt, hurt | (sich) wehtun |
| keep, kept, kept | aufbewahren |
| know, knew, known | wissen, kennen |
| lead, led, led | führen |
| learn, learnt, learnt | bemerken, herausfinden |
| leave, left, left | (ver)lassen |
| let, let, let | lassen |
| lie, lay, lain | liegen |
| lose, lost, lost | verlieren |
| make, made, made | machen |
| mean, meant, meant | meinen, bedeuten |
| meet, met, met | treffen |
| pay, paid, paid | bezahlen |
| quit, quit, quit | aufhören |
| read, read, read | lesen |
| ride, rode, ridden | reiten, fahren |
| ring, rang, rung | klingeln |
| rise, rose, risen | steigen |
| run, ran, run | laufen |
| say, said, said | sagen |
| see, saw, seen | sehen |
| seek, sought, sought | suchen |
| sell, sold, sold | verkaufen |
| send, sent, sent | senden |
| set, set, set | setzen |
| shed, shed, shed | etw ablegen, abnehmen |
| shoot, shot, shot | (er)schießen |
| show, showed, shown | zeigen |
| shut, shut, shut | schließen |
| sing, sang, sung | singen |
| sink, sank, sunk | sinken |
| sit, sat, sat | sitzen |
| sleep, slept, slept | schlafen |
| speak, spoke, spoken | sprechen |
| spend, spent, spent | ausgeben, verbringen |
| split, split, split | sich trennen |
| stand, stood, stood | stehen |
| steal, stole, stolen | stehlen |
| stick, stuck, stuck | stecken |
| strike, struck, stricken | beeindrucken, betreffen |
| strive, strove, striven | streben |
| swear, swore, sworn | fluchen |
| swim, swam, swum | schwimmen |
| take, took, taken | nehmen |
| teach, taught, taught | unterrichten |
| tear, tore, torn | zerreißen |
| tell, told, told | sagen, erzählen |
| think, thought, thought | denken |
| throw, threw, thrown | werfen |
| wake, woke, woken | aufwachen |
| wear, wore, worn | tragen |
| win, won, won | gewinnen |
| write, wrote, written | schreiben |

## List of operators

| | |
|---|---|
| act out | durchspielen, darstellen |
| add | ergänzen, hinzufügen |
| analyse | analysieren |
| answer | beantworten |
| arrange | anordnen |
| categorise | einstufen, kategorisieren |
| check | überprüfen, kontrollieren |
| choose | auswählen, wählen |
| collect | sammeln |
| come up with | sich etw. einfallen lassen, sich etw. ausdenken |
| comment | kommentieren |
| compare | vergleichen |
| complete | vervollständigen |
| contrast | vergleichen |
| convince | überzeugen |
| create | gestalten |
| decide | (sich) entscheiden |
| describe | beschreiben |
| design | gestalten, entwerfen |
| develop | entwickeln |
| discuss | diskutieren |
| divide | teilen, aufteilen, unterteilen |
| evaluate | bewerten, beurteilen |
| explain | erklären |
| form (an opinion) | (sich eine Meinung) bilden |
| gather | sammeln, erfassen, zusammentragen |
| group | gruppieren, in Gruppen einteilen |
| illustrate | veranschaulichen, darstellen |
| introduce (yourself/somebody) | (sich / jemanden) vorstellen |
| invent | erfinden |
| look up | aufschauen, nachschauen |
| match | zuordnen |
| mediate | vermitteln, sprachmitteln |
| mention | erwähnen |
| name | benennen |
| offer | anbieten |
| outline | umreißen, skizzieren |
| point out | zeigen, darauf hinweisen |
| practise | üben, trainieren |
| prepare | (sich) vorbereiten |
| produce | produzieren, erzeugen |
| present | vorstellen, präsentieren |
| record | erfassen, aufnehmen |
| report | berichten |
| research | recherchieren, erforschen, untersuchen |
| review | begutachten, überprüfen |
| search for | suchen nach |
| select | auswählen, aussuchen |
| share | teilen |
| state | darlegen, darstellen |
| suggest | vorschlagen, andeuten |
| summarise | zusammenfassen |
| tell | erzählen, sagen |
| translate | übersetzen |

# Word banks

## Job titles

### Automotive

| | |
|---|---|
| car salesperson | Automobilkaufmann/-frau |
| vehicle painter | Fahrzeuglackierer/-in |
| automotive body and vehicle construction mechanic | Karosserie- und Fahrzeugbaumechaniker/-in |
| automotive mechatronics technician | Kraftfahrzeugmechatroniker/-in |

### Electricity

| | |
|---|---|
| electrical fitter | Elektroanlagenmonteur/-in |
| electronics technician | Elektroniker/-in |
| – automation technology | – für Automatisierungstechnik |
| – industrial engineering | – für Betriebstechnik |
| – building and infrastructure systems | – für Gebäude- und Infrastruktursysteme |
| – equipment and systems | – für Geräte und Systeme |
| electrotechnician | Elektrotechniker/-in |
| electrotechnical assistant | Elektrotechnische/-r Assistent/-in |

### IT

| | |
|---|---|
| IT specialist | Fachinformatiker/-in |
| – software development | – Anwendungsentwicklung |
| – system integration | – Systemintegration |
| – data and process analysis | – Daten- und Prozessanalyse |
| – digital networking | – Digitale Vernetzung |
| IT systems (electronics) technician | IT-System-Elektroniker/-in |
| management assistant | Kaufmann/-frau |
| – for digitisation management | – für Digitalisierungsmanagement |
| – for IT systems | – für IT-System-Management |

### Mechatronics

| | |
|---|---|
| mechatronics technician | Mechatroniker/-in |
| operator | Bediener/-in; Arbeiter/-in |
| machinist | Maschinist/-in, Maschinenschlosser/-in |
| assembler | Montagearbeiter/-in |

### Metal

| | |
|---|---|
| plant mechanic | Anlagenmechaniker/-in |
| industrial mechanic | Industriemechaniker/-in |
| construction mechanic | Konstruktionsmechaniker/-in |
| machine and plant operator; metalworker | Maschinen- und Anlagenführer/-in; Metallbauer/-in |
| metal and bell founder | Metall- und Glockengießer/-in |
| technical product designer | Technische/-r Produktdesigner/-in |
| materials tester | Werkstoffprüfer/-in |
| toolmaker | Werkzeugmechaniker/-in |
| metal cutting mechanic | Zerspanungsmechaniker/-in |

# Word banks

## Education

### School forms

| | |
|---|---|
| part-time vocational school (dual system) | die Berufsschule (Duales System) |
| full-time vocational school | die Berufsfachschule |
| vocational college | das Berufskolleg |
| specialised upper secondary school | das Fachgymnasium, das Berufliche Gymnasium |
| upper secondary vocational school | die Fachoberschule |
| technical college | die Fachschule für technische Berufe |
| upper secondary school | die Oberschule |
| grammar school | das Gymnasium |
| comprehensive school | die Gesamtschule |
| intermediate secondary school | die Realschule |
| general secondary school | die Hauptschule |
| primary school | die Grundschule |

### Qualifications

| | |
|---|---|
| A level / high school diploma | das Abitur |
| advanced vocational certificate of education | das Fachabitur |
| secondary modern school qualification | der Hauptschulabschluss |
| secondary school leaving certificate | die Mittlere Reife |
| additional qualification | die Zusatzqualifikation |

## Workplaces and companies

| | |
|---|---|
| business, company, firm | das Geschäft, die Firma, das Unternehmen |
| construction site | die Baustelle |
| garage | die Autowerkstatt |
| (open-plan) office | das (Großraum-)Büro |
| offsite | von Extern |
| on the road | auf der Straße |
| plant, factory | das Werk, die Fabrik |
| production line | das Fließband, der Produktionsbereich |
| server room | der Serverraum |
| warehouse | das Lager, die Lagerhalle |
| workshop | die Werkstatt, die Werkhalle |

# Word banks

## Communication and project management

| | |
|---|---|
| AI chatbot | der KI Chatbot |
| email | die E-Mail |
| face-to-face conversation | das persönliche Gespräch |
| intranet | das Intranet |
| letter | der Brief |
| messaging app | die Kommunikations-App |
| phone call | der Telefonanruf |
| project management software | die Software zur Projektverwaltung |
| video call / video conferencing | der Videoanruf, die Videokonferenz |
| voice message | die Sprachnachricht |
| webinar | das Online-Seminar, das Webinar |

## Rules and regulations

| | |
|---|---|
| assembly point | der Sammelpunkt |
| danger, hazard | die Gefahr, das Risiko |
| emergency exit | der Notausgang |
| fire extinguisher | der Feuerlöscher |
| first-aid kit | der Erste-Hilfe-Kasten |
| high voltage | die Hochspannung |
| PPE (personal protective equipment) | die Sicherheitsausrüstung |
| | |
| to access | zugreifen auf, Zugang haben zu |
| to authorise | authorisieren, erlauben |
| to clamp | einspannen, befestigen |
| to deactivate | deaktivieren, abschalten |
| to forbid, to prohibit | verbieten |
| to keep clear | frei halten |
| to locate | lokalisieren, ausfindig machen |
| to protect | schützen, beschützen |
| to remove | wegräumen, entfernen, beseitigen |
| to replace | ersetzen |
| to slip | ausrutschen |
| to turn on/off | ein-/ausschalten |
| to warn | warnen |
| to wear | tragen |
| | |
| corrosive | ätzend |
| hazardous | gefährlich |
| insulating | isolierend |
| radioactive | radioaktiv |
| required | nötig, erforderlich |
| toxic | giftig |
| unauthorised | unerlaubt, unbefugt |
| worn | abgenutzt |

# Word banks

## Clothing | Protective workwear

**ear protection**
der Gehörschutz

**eye protection | goggles | safety glasses**
die Schutzbrille

**overalls**
der Overall

**high-visibility vest**
die Warnweste

**hard hat**
der (Schutz-)Helm

**protection mask**
der Gesichtsschutz

**protective footwear**
die Sicherheitsschuhe
**boots with steel toe cap**
die Sicherheitsschuhe mit Stahlkappen

**safety harness**
der Sicherheitsgurt

**protective gloves**
die Schutzhandschuhe

**respiratory protection**
der Atemschutz

## Data security

| | |
|---|---|
| authentication | die Authentifizierung |
| backup | die Sicherung, die Sicherungskopie |
| to block | blockieren |
| breach | der Bruch, die Verletzung |
| configuration | die Konfigurierung |
| cyberattack | der Cyberangriff |
| cybercrime | die Cyberkriminalität |
| cybersecurity | die Internetsicherheit |
| cyber/corporate espionage | die Unternehmensspionage |
| data protection | der Datenschutz |
| data recovery | die Datenwiederherstellung |
| encryption | die Verschlüsselung |
| GDPR (General Data Protection Regulation) | die DSGVO (Datenschutzgrundverordnung) |
| identification | die Identifizierung |
| identity theft | der Identitätsdiebstahl |
| insider threat | die Bedrohung durch eine interne Person |
| to lock | sperren |
| to log (in/out) | sich (ein-/aus-)loggen |
| permission | die Berechtigung |
| reconfiguration | die Neukonfigurierung |
| restriction | die Beschränkung, die Einschränkung |
| spyware | die Spionagesoftware |

# Word banks

## Vehicle parts

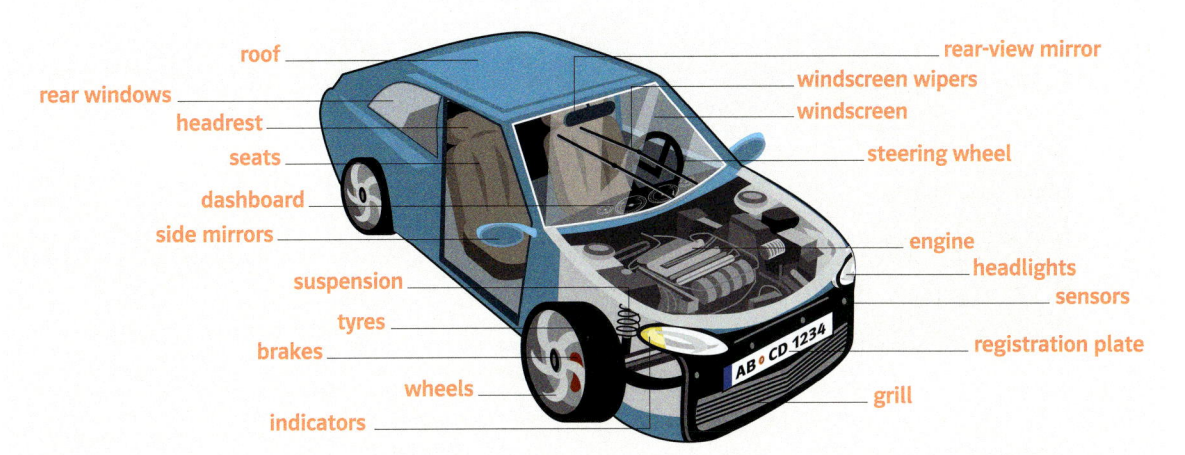

Labels on diagram:
- roof
- rear windows
- headrest
- seats
- dashboard
- side mirrors
- suspension
- tyres
- brakes
- wheels
- indicators
- rear-view mirror
- windscreen wipers
- windscreen
- steering wheel
- engine
- headlights
- sensors
- registration plate
- grill

|  |  |
|---|---|
| accelerator | das Fahrpedal |
| bonnet / hood | die Motorhaube |
| boot / trunk | der Kofferraum |
| brake | die Bremse |
| bumper | die Stoßstange |
| chassis | das Chassis / das Fahrgestell |
| dashboard | das Armaturenbrett |
| door handle | der Türgriff |
| engine | der Motor |
| exhaust / exhaust pipe | der Auspuff |
| grill / radiator grill | der Kühlergrill |
| headlight | der Scheinwerfer |
| headrest | die Kopfstütze |
| indicator | der Blinker |
| manifold | der Krümmer |
| radiator | der Kühler |
| rear-view mirror | der Rückspiegel |
| rear window | das Rückfenster |
| registration plate | das Autokennzeichen |
| roof | das Dach |
| seat | der Sitz |
| sensor | der Sensor |
| shock absorber | der Stoßdämpfer |
| side mirror / wing mirror | der Seitenspiegel |
| steering wheel | das Lenkrad |
| suspension | die Aufhängung |
| tyre | der Reifen |
| wheel | das Rad |
| windscreen | die Windschutzscheibe / die Frontscheibe |
| windscreen wiper | der Scheibenwischer |

# Word banks

## Dashboard

| | |
|---|---|
| button | die Taste |
| clutch | die Kupplung |
| gear stick | der Schalthebel |
| glove compartment / glove box | das Handschuhfach |
| hand brake | die Handbremse |
| heating and ventilation systems | die Heizung und die Belüftung |
| indicator lever | der Blinkerhebel |
| information systems, e.g. navigation system | das Fahrzeuginformationssystem, z.B. das Navigationssystem |
| left-/right-hand drive | die Links-/Rechtssteuerung |
| low beam / high beam | das Abblendlicht / das Fernlicht |
| rear-view camera | die Rückfahrkamera |
| reverse gear | der Rückwärtsgang |
| rocker switch | der Wippschalter |
| rotary switch | der Drehschalter |
| steering wheel | das Lenkrad |
| battery indicator | die Batterieanzeige |
| cruise control / speed control | der Geschwindigkeitsregler / der Tempomat |
| engine coolant temperature gauge | die Kühlflüssigkeitsanzeige |
| hazard lights | die Warnblinkanlage |
| lane assistance | der Fahrspurassistent |
| mileometer | der Kilometerzähler |
| oil level gauge | die Ölstandsanzeige |
| parc distance control | die Einparkhilfe |
| parking brake | die Feststellbremse |
| petrol / fuel gauge | die Tankanzeige |
| revolution counter | der Drehzahlmesser |
| seatbelt warning | der Gurtwarner |
| speedometer / tachometer | der Geschwindigkeitsmesser / der Tacho |

# Word banks

## In the workshop

**(pneumatic) car jack**
der (pneumatische) Wagenheber

**tyre balancing machine**
das Reifenauswuchtgerät

**fire extinguisher**
der Feuerlöscher

**grinding shop**
die Schleifwerkstatt

**waste and recycling bins**
der Abfall- und der Wertstoffbehälter

**workbench**
die Werkbank

**storage room**
das Lager / der Lagerraum

**reception area**
der Empfangsbereich

**spot welder**
das Punktschweißgerät

**inspection pit**
die Inspektionsgrube

**toolbox / ratchet box**
der Werkzeugkasten

**tool trolley**
der Werkzeugwagen

**car lift / car hoist**
die Hebebühne

**shelves**
die Regale

# Word banks

## Tools in a car workshop

**angle grinder**
der Winkelschleifer / die Flex

**bolt**
die Schraube / der Bolzen

**column drill**
die Standbohrmaschine

**combination pliers** *(pl)*
die Kombizange

**compressor**
der Kompressor

**diagnostic tester**
das Diagnosetestgerät

**file**
die Feile

**hacksaw**
die Bügelsäge

**hammer**
der Hammer

**(pneumatic) impact wrench**
der (Druckluft-)Schlagschrauber

**(outside) micrometer**
die Messschraube

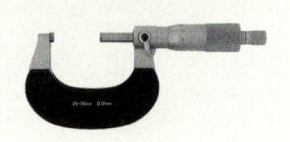

**dial gauge**
die Messuhr

**multimeter**
das Mehrfachmessgerät

**oscilloscope**
das Oszilloskop

**pliers** *(pl)*
die Zange

## Word banks

### Tools in a car workshop

**power drill**
die Bohrmaschine

**(cranked) ring spanner**
der (gekröpfte) Ringschlüssel

**screw**
die Schraube

**screwdriver**
der Schraubendreher

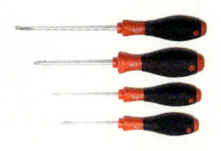

**socket wrench / socket spanner**
der Steckschlüssel

**square**
der Winkel

**torque wrench / torque spanner**
der Drehmomentschlüssel

**tyre inflator**
das Reifenfüllgerät

**tyre pressure gauge**
der Reifendruckmesser

**(bench) vice**
der (Bank-)Schraubstock

# Word banks

## Tyres

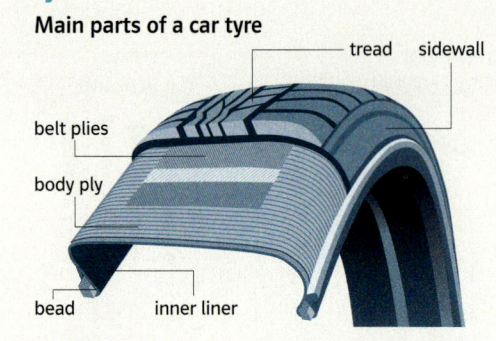

### Main parts of a car tyre

- tread
- sidewall
- belt plies
- body ply
- bead
- inner liner

### How to read a tyre

- tyre width (mm)
- height-width ratio (%)
- tyre construction (R=radial)
- wheel diameter (inches)
- speed rating
- load index
- rolling direction
- DOT number
- European certification mark

|  |  |
|---|---|
| bead | der Wulst |
| belt plies | die Gürtellagen |
| body ply | die Karkassenlage |
| inner liner | der Innerliner |
| sidewall | die Reifenflanke / die Seitenwand |
| tread | die Lauffläche / das Profil |
| tyre valve | das Reifenventil |
| DOT number | die DOT-Nummer / das Produktionsdatum |
| European certification mark | die Genehmigungskennzeichnung / das E-Prüfzeichen |
| height-width ratio | das Höhe-Breite-Verhältnis |
| load index | der Traglastindex |
| rolling direction | die Laufrichtung |
| speed rating | der Geschwindigkeitsindex |
| tyre construction | der Reifentyp |
| tyre width | die Reifenbreite |
| wheel diameter | der Felgendurchmesser |

# Word banks

## Brakes

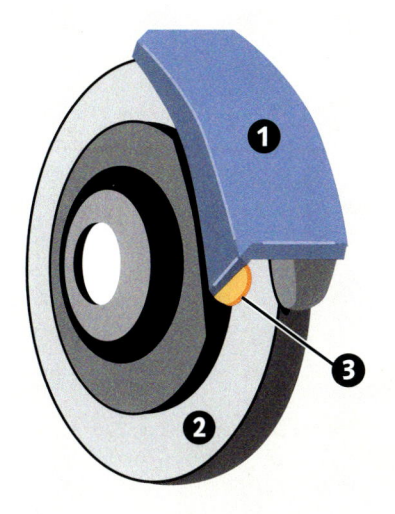

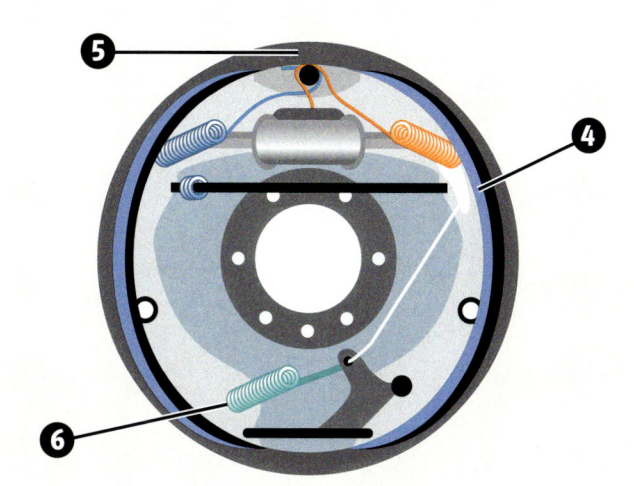

|  |  |
|---|---|
| backing plate ⑤ | die Trägerplatte |
| brake caliper ① | der Bremssattel |
| brake drum | die Bremstrommel |
| brake fluid | die Bremsflüssigkeit |
| brake pad ③ | der Bremsbelag |
| brake rotor / brake disc ② | die Bremsscheibe |
| brake shoe ④ | die Bremsbacke |
| disc brake | die Scheibenbremse |
| drum brake | die Trommelbremse |
| emergency brake | die Notbremse |
| piston | der Kolben |
| return spring ⑥ | die Rückholfeder |
| rim brake | die Felgenbremse |
| vacuum hose | der Vakuumschlauch |
| valve | das Ventil |

## Engine

|  |  |
|---|---|
| connecting rod | die Pleuelstange, der Pleuel |
| crank | die Kurbel |
| crankshaft | die Kurbelwelle |
| cylinder | der Zylinder |
| cylinder block | der Motorblock |
| exhaust manifold | der Abgaskrümmer / der Auspuffkrümmer |
| exhaust valve | das Auslassventil |
| inlet manifold | das Ansaugrohr |
| inlet valve | das Einlassventil |
| piston | der Kolben |
| spark plug | die Zündkerze |

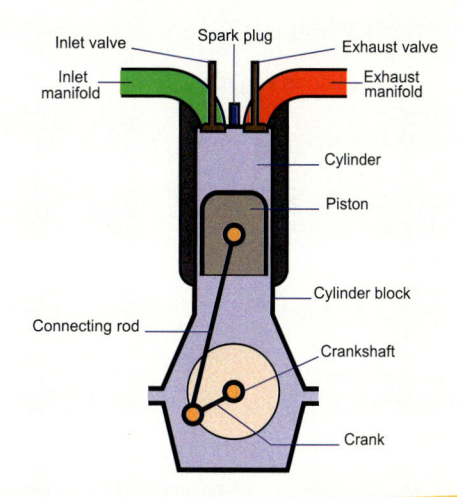

Inlet valve · Spark plug · Exhaust valve · Inlet manifold · Exhaust manifold · Cylinder · Piston · Cylinder block · Connecting rod · Crankshaft · Crank

# Word banks

## Electric and hybrid vehicles

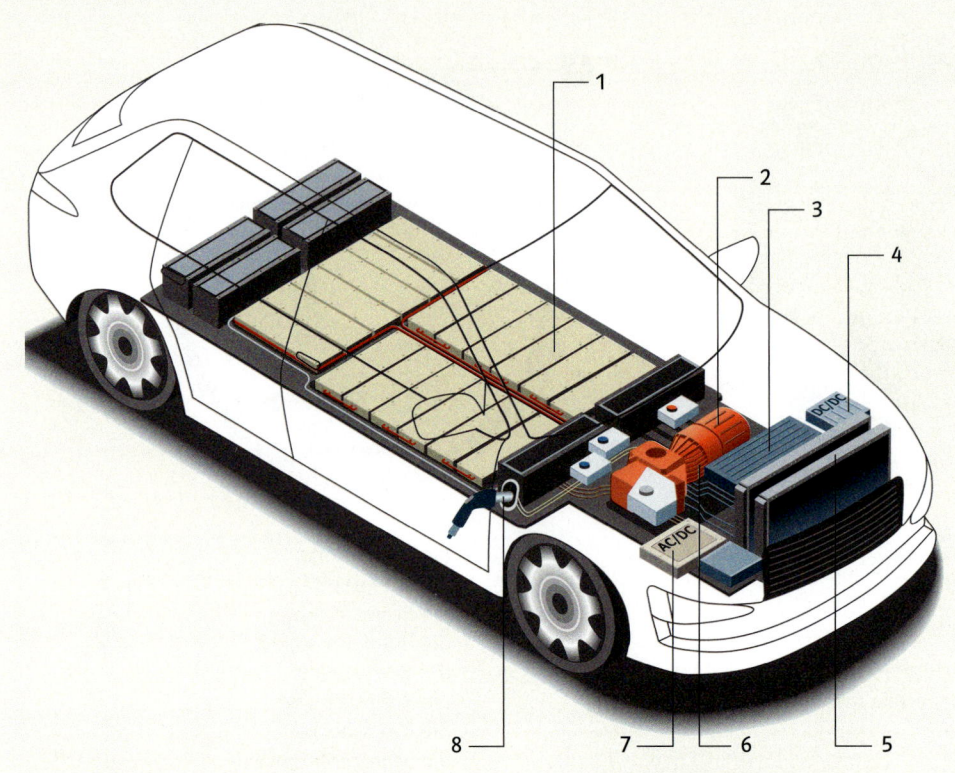

|  |  |
|---|---|
| advanced driver-assistance system | das Fahrerassistenzsystem |
| battery (1) | die Hochvoltbatterie |
| charge port (8) | der Ladeanschluss |
| charger | das Ladegerät / die Ladestation |
| connector | die Buchse / der Stecker / die Steckverbindung |
| DC/DC converter (4) | der Gleichspannungswandler |
| drivetrain | der Antrieb / der Antriebsstrang |
| electric drive / electric motor (2) | der Elektroantrieb / der Elektromotor |
| electric vehicle (EV) | das Elektrofahrzeug |
| energy supply | die Energieversorgung / -zufuhr |
| fuel | der Kraftstoff |
| fuel-cell technology | die Brennstoffzellentechnik |
| hybrid car | das Hybridauto |
| internal combustion engine | der Verbrennungsmotor |
| inverter | der Inverter / der Wechselrichter |
| onboard charger (7) | das Ladegerät (im Fahrzeug verbaut) |
| plug | der Stecker |
| power electronics controller (3) | die Leistungselektronik |
| power grid | das Stromnetz / das Energienetz |
| powertrain | der Antriebsstrang |
| recuperation | die Rekuperation / die Rückgewinnung |
| sensor | der Sensor |
| socket | die Steckdose |
| thermal system (5) | das Kühlsystem |
| transmission (6) | das Getriebe |
| voltage | die Spannung |

# Vocabulary

## Module 1  You and your company

### Important words

| | |
|---|---|
| apprenticeship; apprentice | die Ausbildung; der/die Auszubildende |
| client | der Kunde/die Kundin |
| colleague | der Kollege/die Kollegin |
| employment | die Anstellung, die Einstellung, die Beschäftigung |
| employee | der/die Arbeitnehmer/-in |
| to employ | einstellen, beschäftigen |
| headquarters (pl) | die Hauptgeschäftsstelle, die Zentrale |
| internship; intern | das Praktikum; der/die Praktikant/-in |
| maintenance; to maintain | die Instandhaltung; instandhalten |
| manufacturing | die Produktion |
| manufacturer | der/die Produzent/-in |
| to manufacture | produzieren, herstellen |
| provider | der/die Lieferant/-in, der/die Dienstleister/-in |
| to provide | liefern, bereitstellen |
| recruitment | die Anwerbung |
| recruiter | der/die Personalvermittler/-in |
| to recruit | einstellen, anwerben |
| to secure; secure; securely | (ab-)sichern; sicher; sicher |
| supervisor | der/die Betreuer/-in, der/die Abteilungsleiter/-in |
| supply | die Lieferung, das Angebot |
| supplier | der/die Lieferant/-in |
| to supply | liefern |
| workforce | die Belegschaft, die Arbeitskräfte |

### Company departments

| | |
|---|---|
| accounts | die Buchhaltung |
| customer service | die Kundenberatung |
| engineering | die Technik |
| finance | das Finanzwesen |
| human resources (HR) | die Personalabteilung |
| management | die Unternehmensleitung |
| purchasing | der Einkauf |
| quality control | die Qualitätssicherung |
| research and development (R&D) | die Forschung und Entwicklung |
| sales and marketing | der Vertrieb, der Verkauf |

### People and their companies

| | |
|---|---|
| garage | die Autowerkstatt |

### Presenting yourself

| | |
|---|---|
| round | die Runde |
| studies (pl) | das Studium, die Studien |
| to retrain | umschulen |
| from abroad | aus dem Ausland |
| rather | eher, lieber |

### The company and its departments

| | |
|---|---|
| based in | mit Sitz in |
| storage | die Lagerung, die Speicherung |
| operations process | der Betriebsprozess |
| efficiency | die Effizienz, die Leistungsfähigkeit |
| inactivity | die Untätigkeit, die Inaktivität |
| waste | die Verschwendung |
| immediately | sofort, gleich |
| to access | zugreifen auf |

## Vocabulary

| | |
|---|---|
| output | die Leistung |
| stock | der Bestand, das Lager |
| record | das Verzeichnis, der Bericht, die Dokumentation |
| capacity | die Kapazität, das Leistungsvermögen |
| data | die Daten (Pl.) |
| demand | die Nachfrage, die Anforderung |
| consumer | der/die Verbraucher/-in |
| timeframe | die Zeitspanne, der Zeitraum |
| personnel | das Personal |
| shortage | der Mangel |
| automated | automatisiert |
| relief | die Entlastung, die Erleichterung |
| overstretched | überfordert |
| misunderstanding | das Missverständnis |
| to manage | steuern, organisieren |
| everyday operations (pl) | der Alltagsbetrieb |
| to engage | einstellen |
| resource | die (finanziellen) Mittel, die Ressource, der Rohstoff |
| to advertise | anbieten, anpreisen, bewerben |
| to handle | umgehen mit, handhaben |
| functioning | funktionsfähig |
| mission | der Auftrag, die Mission |

### The company and its people

| | |
|---|---|
| range | das Spektrum, der Bereich |
| overall | insgesamt, Gesamt- |

| | |
|---|---|
| subsidies (pl) | die Subventionen, die Zuschüsse |
| recreational facilities (pl) | die Freizeiteinrichtungen, *hier:* der Pausenbereich |
| pension scheme | die Altersvorsorge |
| to regulate | steuern, regeln |
| sick leave | die krankheitsbedingte Abwesenheit |
| prevention | die Verhinderung, die Vermeidung |

### Securing skilled staff

| | |
|---|---|
| installation | die Montage, der Einbau, die Installation |
| representative | der/die Vertreter/-in, der/die Repräsentant/-in |
| to contribute (to) | beitragen (zu), mitwirken (an) |
| vacancy | die freie Stelle |
| knowledge | das Wissen, die Kenntnisse |
| state-of-the-art | hochmodern, auf dem neuesten Stand der Technik |
| tool | das Werkzeug, das Gerät |
| quarterly | vierteljährlich |
| competitive | konkurrenzfähig, wettbewerbsfähig |
| valuable | wertvoll |
| diversity | die Vielfalt |

### A recruitment campaign

| | |
|---|---|
| on behalf of | im Namen von, für |
| appearance | das Aussehen, die Erscheinung |
| suit | der Anzug, das Kostüm |

# Vocabulary

## Module 2  Your place of work

### Different workplaces

| | |
|---|---|
| measure | die Maßnahme |
| incident | der Vorfall, das Ereignis |
| policy | *hier:* die Richtlinie |
| sharp | scharf |
| trailer | der Anhänger |
| workshop | die Werkstatt, die Werkhalle |
| spare part | das Ersatzteil |
| to meet requirements | die Voraussetzungen erfüllen, den Voraussetzungen genügen |

### Safety at the workplace

| | |
|---|---|
| hazard | die Gefahr, das Risiko |
| to alter | ändern, verändern |
| switch | der Schalter |
| respiratory protection | der Atemschutz |
| protective | Schutz-, schützend |
| glove | der Handschuh |
| corrosive | ätzend |
| assembly point | der Sammelplatz |
| high-visibility vest | die Warnweste |
| eye protection | der Augenschutz |
| beam | der Strahl |
| first aid | die Erste Hilfe |
| to slip | ausrutschen |
| toxic | giftig, toxisch |
| access | der Zugang, der Zugriff |
| unauthorised | unbefugt, nicht autorisiert |
| ear protection | der Gehörschutz |
| automated | automatisiert |
| external | extern, Außen- |
| footwear *(no pl)* | die Schuhe, das Schuhwerk |
| warning | die Warnung |
| prohibition | das Verbot |
| to alert | benachrichtigen, alarmieren |
| mandatory | verpflichtend |
| construction site | die Baustelle |
| hazardous | gefährlich, riskant |
| authority | die Autorität |
| personal protective equipment (PPE) | die persönliche Schutzausrüstung (PSA) |
| hard hat | der Helm |
| safety harness | der Sicherheitsgurt |
| forklift truck | der Gabelstapler |
| load | die Last, die Ladung |
| horn | die Hupe |
| intersection *(AE)* | die Kreuzung |
| circuit | der Schaltkreis |
| plug | der Stecker |
| cord | das Kabel, die Schnur |
| extension wire | das Verlängerungskabel |
| outlet, socket | die Steckdose |
| loose | locker, lose |
| guideline | die Richtlinie |
| steel toe cap | die Stahlkappe |
| fire extinguisher | der Feuerlöscher |
| liquid | die Flüssigkeit |
| machinery | die Maschinen, die technischen Geräte |
| item | der Gegenstand, das Objekt |
| flammable | leicht entflammbar |
| poisonous | giftig |
| harmful | schädlich |
| to ensure | sicherstellen, gewährleisten |

### Data security

| | |
|---|---|
| to deny | verweigern |
| to expire | ablaufen, enden |
| to log onto | sich anmelden |
| to reconfigure | rekonfigurieren |

# Vocabulary

| | | | |
|---|---|---|---|
| to **fix** | reparieren | to **amend** | korrigieren, nachbessern |
| **attachment** | die Anlage, der Anhang | to **detect** | feststellen, ermitteln |
| **encryption** | die Verschlüsselung | to **contribute (to)** | beitragen (zu), mitwirken (an) |
| **malware** | die Schadsoftware | | |

## Mobile work

| | |
|---|---|
| **professional** | die Fachkraft, der Profi |
| to **involve** | verbunden sein mit, mit sich bringen |
| **reimbursement** | die Entschädigung |
| **expense** | die Kosten (Pl.), die Ausgaben (Pl.) |
| **operation** | der Betrieb |
| **shift** | die Schicht |
| **operator** | der/die Betreiber/-in |
| to **operate** | betreiben, bedienen |
| **physically** | körperlich, physisch |
| **facility** | die Anlage, die Einrichtung |
| to **assist** | helfen |
| **assistance** | die Hilfe |
| **towing** | das Abschleppen, Abschlepp- |
| **available** | erhältlich, verfügbar |
| **rota** | der Dienstplan |

| | |
|---|---|
| **authentication** | die Bestätigung, die Beglaubigung, die Authentifizierung |
| **breach** | der Verstoß, die Verletzung |
| **spyware** | die Spionagesoftware |
| **sensitive** | sensibel, heikel |
| **permission** | die Erlaubnis, die Genehmigung |
| to **pretend** | so tun als ob, vortäuschen |
| **trustworthy** | vertrauenswürdig |
| **identification** | die Identifikation |
| **unique** | einzigartig, einmalig |
| to **block** | blockieren, abblocken |
| to **harm** | schädigen, schaden |
| to **apply (to)** | anwenden (bei) |
| to **restrict** | einschränken, beschränken |
| **cyberattack** | der Cyberangriff |

## Data protection

| | |
|---|---|
| **privacy** | die Privatsphäre |
| **GDPR** (general data protection regulation) | die DSGVO (Datenschutzgrundverordnung) |
| to **resolve** | klären, lösen |
| **invoice** | die Rechnung |
| **approximately** | ungefähr, circa |
| to **encrypt** | verschlüsseln |
| to **lock** | sperren, abschließen |
| to **disable** | funktionsunfähig machen, ausschalten |
| to **encourage awareness** | sensibilisieren |
| **occurrence** | das Vorkommen, das Ereignis |

## Workplace of the year

| | |
|---|---|
| **involvement** | das Engagement, die Beteiligung |
| **sustainability** | die Nachhaltigkeit |
| **claim** | die Behauptung, der Anspruch |
| **contender** | der/die Bewerber/-in, der/die Kandidat/-in |
| to **set apart** | (sich) abheben |
| **retirement** | der Ruhestand |
| to **foster** | fördern, pflegen |
| to **extend** | (sich) ausdehnen, (sich) erstrecken |
| **beyond** | darüber hinaus, jenseits |

# Module 3  Tasks and responsibilities

### How people can be or feel

| | |
|---|---|
| confident | selbstsicher, selbstbewusst |
| creative | kreativ |
| demanding | anspruchsvoll, anstrengend, fordernd |
| desperate | verzweifelt |
| discriminated | diskriminiert, benachteiligt |
| eager | bestrebt, eifrig |
| engaged | eingebunden, beschäftigt, engagiert |
| exhausted | erschöpft |
| frustrated | frustriert, niedergeschlagen, enttäuscht |
| isolated | isoliert, einsam |
| keen | begeistert, leidenschaftlich |
| organised | organisiert |
| patient; impatient | geduldig; ungeduldig |
| satisfied | zufrieden |
| stressed | gestresst |
| supportive | unterstützend |
| useless | nutzlos, unnütz |
| valued | geschätzt |

### How things can be

| | |
|---|---|
| challenging | herausfordernd, schwierig |
| competitive | konkurrenzfähig, wettbewerbsfähig |
| confusing | verwirrend |
| enjoyable | angenehm, nett |
| essential | notwendig, wesentlich |
| manageable | kontrollierbar, beherrschbar |
| motivating | motivierend |
| necessary | nötig, erforderlich |
| overwhelming | überwältigend |
| repetitive | sich wiederholend, monoton |
| rewarding | lohnend |
| stimulating | stimulierend, anregend |
| stressful | stressig, anstrengend |

### First tasks

| | |
|---|---|
| to **balance** | ausgleichen, abwägen |
| to **succeed (in)** | Erfolg haben (in/bei/mit) |
| **prioritisation** | die Priorisierung |
| **obligation** | die Verpflichtung |
| **resolution** | die Klärung, die Lösung |
| **pace** | das Tempo, die Geschwindigkeit |
| **downside** | der Nachteil |
| **occasional** | gelegentlich |
| **despite** | trotz |

| | |
|---|---|
| **sheet metal** | das Blech |
| to **accompany** | begleiten |
| **construction site** | die Baustelle |
| **troubleshooting** | die Problem-/Fehlersuche und -behebung |
| **improvement** | die Verbesserung |
| **with regards to** | in Bezug auf, hinsichtlich |
| to **process** | verarbeiten, bearbeiten |
| **guidance** | die Anleitung, die Beratung |
| **encouragement** | die Ermutigung, die Unterstützung |

# Vocabulary

## Tasks, responsibilities and expectations

| | |
|---|---|
| insight | der Einblick |
| overlap | die Überlappung |
| hands-on experience | die praktische Erfahrung |
| profession | der Beruf |
| labour | die Arbeit, die Arbeitskräfte |
| long-term | langfristig |
| to contribute (to) | beitragen (zu), mitwirken (an) |
| work ethic | die Arbeitsmoral |
| to take the initiative | die Initiative ergreifen |
| networking | das Netzwerken |
| superior | der/die Vorgesetzte |
| environmental | Umwelt-, ökologisch |
| issue | das Thema, das Problem |
| to evolve | sich (weiter-)entwickeln |
| to adapt to | sich anpassen an |
| to prioritise | vorrangig behandeln, priorisieren |
| to run smoothly | funktionieren, reibungslos laufen |
| welding | das Schweißen |
| to customise | individuell anpassen |
| wiring | die Verkabelung |
| to diagnose | diagnostizieren |
| to encourage | ermutigen |

## Being organised, happy and healthy at work

| | |
|---|---|
| I don't mind. | Es ist mir egal. |
| to skip | überspringen, auslassen |
| commute | die Strecke zur Arbeit, die Pendelstrecke |

| | |
|---|---|
| to be a drag | nervig sein |
| confidence | das Vertrauen, die Zuversicht |
| to be based at | arbeiten in/bei |
| family-run | familiengeführt |
| purpose | das Ziel, die Absicht, der Zweck |
| to relate to | nachvollziehen, verstehen, sich identifizieren mit |

## Conflicts and issues at work

| | |
|---|---|
| dynamics | die Dynamik, das Kräftespiel |
| authority | die Autorität |
| to perceive | wahrnehmen |
| poor | hier: schlecht |
| clash | das Aufeinandertreffen, der Konflikt |
| pharmaceutical | arzneilich, pharmazeutisch |
| expertise | das Fachwissen, die Kompetenz |
| supposedly | vermutlich, angeblich |
| to solve | lösen |
| to hesitate | zögern |
| to assume | annehmen |
| strain | die Belastung, die Anstrengung |
| to split up | sich trennen |
| to let sb down | jdn. im Stich lassen, jdn. enttäuschen |
| to carry on | weitermachen, weitergehen |
| boundary | die Grenze |
| relief | die Entlastung, die Erleichterung |

## A welcome guide for apprentices

| | |
|---|---|
| curriculum | der Lehrplan |
| policy | hier: die Richtlinie |

# Vocabulary

## Module 4  Working in a global world

### Important words

| | |
|---|---|
| abroad | im/ins Ausland |
| accommodation; to accommodate | die Unterkunft; unterbringen, aufnehmen |
| agreement | die Vereinbarung |
| assignment; to assign | die Aufgabe, die Zuweisung; zuweisen, zuordnen |
| awareness; to be aware of | das Bewusstsein; sich bewusst sein |
| benefit | der Vorteil, der Nutzen |
| border crossing | der Grenzübertritt |
| challenge; challenging | die Herausforderung; herausfordernd, schwierig |
| custom; customary | der Brauch; üblich |
| to establish a relationship | eine Beziehung aufbauen |
| to generalise | verallgemeinern |
| to greet | grüßen, begrüßen |
| hospitality | die Gastfreundschaft |
| intercultural | interkulturell, zwischen den Kulturen |
| instruction; to instruct; instructional | die Anweisung; einweisen; Lehr- |
| to involve | einbeziehen, beteiligen |
| misunderstanding | das Missverständnis |
| offence | die Beleidigung, die Kränkung |
| residence permit | die Aufenthaltsgenehmigung |
| similarity | die Ähnlichkeit, die Gemeinsamkeit |
| sincere; insincere | aufrichtig, seriös; unehrlich |
| sign of appreciation | die Erkenntlichkeit, das Geschenk |
| to appreciate | wertschätzen, würdigen |
| toll road | die Mautstraße |
| trusting, trustworthy | vertrauensvoll, vertrauenswürdig |
| valid | gültig |
| visa | das Visum, die Einreisebewilligung |

### Hierarchical structures

| | |
|---|---|
| **Chief Executive Officer (CEO)** | der/die Vorstandsvorsitzende |
| **Chief Technology Officer (CTO)** | der Technikvorstand |
| **director** | der/die Direktor/-in |
| **executive** | der/die Geschäftsführer/-in |
| to align | ausrichten, anpassen |
| to be in charge of | verantwortlich sein für, betreuen |
| budget | der Etat, das Budget |
| to collaborate; collaborative | zusammenarbeiten; gemeinsam |
| corporation | das (große) Unternehmen |
| entry-level | Anfänger-, Einsteiger- |
| to manage | steuern, verwalten, organisieren |
| mid-level | mittlere/-r/-s |
| to operate | betreiben, bedienen |
| to oversee | betreuen, leiten |
| qualified | qualifiziert |
| to set targets | Ziele festlegen |

### Different locations

| | |
|---|---|
| **construction site** | die Baustelle |

| | |
|---|---|
| to **suppose** | vermuten, annehmen |
| **surveyor** | der/die Vemesser/-in |

## Vocabulary

| | |
|---|---|
| to **vary** | variieren, (sich) ändern |
| **male-dominated** | von Männern dominiert |
| **glazier** | der/die Glaser/-in |
| **roofer** | der/die Dachdecker/-in |
| **tiler** | der/die Fliesenleger/-in |
| **scaffolder** | der/die Gerüstbauer/-in |
| **bricklayer** | der/die Maurer/-in |
| **sense** | der Sinn, das Gespür |

### Intercultural awareness

| | |
|---|---|
| **domestic** | heimisch, inländisch |
| **branch** | die Zweigstelle |
| to **apply (to)** | anwenden (bei), zutreffen (auf) |
| **crucial** | entscheidend, äußerst wichtig |
| **patient** | geduldig |
| **outgoing** | aufgeschlossen |
| **essential** | notwendig, wesentlich |
| **interaction** | der Umgang, die Interaktion |
| **shy** | schüchtern |
| **anxious** | verängstigt, unsicher |
| **finances** (pl) | die Finanzen |
| **sensitive** | sensibel |
| to **compliment sb** | jdm. ein Kompliment machen |
| **appearance** | das Aussehen, die Erscheinung |
| to **bond** | eine Beziehung aufbauen |
| **embarrassment** | die Verlegenheit |
| **humour** | der Humor |

### Meeting international business partners

| | |
|---|---|
| to **accompany** | begleiten |
| to **display** | darstellen, ausstellen, zeigen |
| **expertise** | das Fachwissen |
| **objective** | das Ziel |
| **administrative** | Verwaltungs-, administrativ |
| **duty** | die Pflicht, die Verpflichtung |
| **capable of** | fähig zu, im Stande |
| to **relate to** | in Zusammenhang stehen, betreffen |
| **purpose** | das Ziel, die Absicht, der Zweck |
| **family-run** | familiengeführt |
| **it's a pleasure** | sehr erfreut, ich freue mich |
| **pleased** | froh, erfreut, zufrieden |
| **bow** | die Verbeugung |
| **handshake** | der Handschlag |

### Preparing for an international assignment

| | |
|---|---|
| to **specialise (in)** | sich spezialisieren (auf) |
| to **set up** | einrichten, aufbauen |
| to **adjust** | anpassen |
| to **calibrate** | eichen, kalibrieren |
| to **carry out** | durchführen, ausführen |
| **application** | die Anwendung |
| **manual** | die Gebrauchsanweisung |
| **phrasebook** | das Wörterbuch |
| to **facilitate** | erleichtern, ermöglichen |
| to **familiarise oneself with** | sich vertraut machen mit |

### A project abroad

| | |
|---|---|
| **e-waste** | der Elektromüll |
| **facility** | die Anlage, die Einrichtung |
| **sustainability** | die Nachhaltigkeit |
| **innovative** | innovativ, kreativ |
| **scalable** | skalierbar, anpassbar |
| **affordable** | bezahlbar, erschwinglich |
| **recovery** | die Rückgewinnung |
| **disposal** | die Entsorgung |
| **hazardous** | gefährlich, riskant |
| to **implement** | einführen, umsetzen |
| to **innovate** | Neuerungen einführen |
| **extraction** | die Gewinnung, die Förderung |
| **authorities** (pl) | die Behörden |
| **acceptability** | die Annehmbarkeit |
| **sustainable** | nachhaltig, umweltgerecht |
| to **dispose of sth** | etw. entsorgen, etw. beseitigen |
| **applicant** | der/die Bewerber/-in |

# Module 5 Communication

## Media and methods

| | |
|---|---|
| internal | intern, Innen- |
| to maintain | aufrechterhalten, beibehalten |
| to align with | anpassen an |
| external | extern, Außen- |
| to gain insight | einen Einblick gewinnen, verstehen |
| collaborative | gemeinsam |
| to receive | empfangen, bekommen, erhalten |
| hands-on approach | die praxisorientierte Herangehensweise |
| to confirm | bestätigen |
| appointment | der Termin, die Verabredung |
| trust | das Vertrauen |
| reminder | die Erinnerung, die Mahnung |
| to track | (nach-)verfolgen |
| request | die Bitte, die Anfrage |
| issue | das Thema, das Problem |
| invoice | die Rechnung |
| to document | dokumentieren, festhalten |
| face-to-face | persönlich |
| purpose | das Ziel, die Absicht, der Zweck |
| formal | formal, formell, förmlich |
| informal | informell, umgangssprachlich |
| mode of communication | die Kommunikationsweise |

## Company communication

| | |
|---|---|
| collaboration | die Zusammenarbeit |
| to enable | ermöglichen, befähigen |
| to schedule | planen, vereinbaren |
| to coordinate | aufeinander abstimmen, koordinieren |
| cost-effective | kostengünstig, wirtschaftlich |
| to invest | investieren |
| confidential | vertraulich, geheim |
| legal contract | der rechtsgültige Vertrag |
| signature | die Signatur, die Unterschrift |
| enquiry | die Anfrage |
| to access | zugreifen auf |
| occasionally | gelegentlich |

## Instructions

| | |
|---|---|
| sensitive | sensibel |
| sustainability | die Nachhaltigkeit |
| to monitor | überwachen, kontrollieren |
| charging station | die Ladestation |
| range indicator | die Reichweitenanzeige |
| to load | laden, beladen |
| to unload | ausladen |
| to secure | sichern, absichern, garantieren |
| to speed up | beschleunigen |
| to brake | bremsen |
| evenly | gleichmäßig |
| to distribute | verteilen |
| to strap | befestigen |
| residential area | das Wohngebiet |
| to approach | nähern, annähern |
| charger | das Ladegerät, die Ladestation |
| to attach | anbringen, befestigen, anhängen |
| to adjust | anpassen |
| to convert | umwandeln, umstellen |
| mains (pl) | das Stromnetz |
| safety goggles | die Schutzbrille |
| debris | die Teile |
| to clamp | festklemmen, einspannen |
| clutter | der Kram |
| lit | beleuchtet |
| hazard | die Gefahr, das Risiko |
| to deepen one's understanding | sein Verständnis vertiefen |
| to clarify | verdeutlichen, darlegen |

207

## Vocabulary

### Telephone communcation

| | |
|---|---|
| energy-efficient | energieeffizient |
| compatibility | die Kompatibilität |
| consumption | der Konsum, der Verbrauch |
| durability | die Haltbarkeit, die Lebensdauer |
| performance | die Leistung |
| output | die Leistung, der Ausstoß |
| bulb | die Lampe, die Glühbirne |
| voltage | die Spannung |
| DC (= direct current) | der Gleichstrom |
| lifespan | die Lebensdauer |
| certification | die Zertifizierung |
| compatible | kompatibel, passend |
| ability | die Fähigkeit, die Begabung |
| to fulfil | erfüllen |
| to greet | begrüßen, grüßen |
| to enquire about sth | sich nach etw. erkundigen |
| figure | die Ziffer, die Zahl |
| to place an order | einen Auftrag erteilen |
| quote | das Angebot |
| state-of-the-art | hochmodern, auf dem neuesten Stand der Technik |
| to consume | konsumieren, verbrauchen |
| estimate | die Schätzung |
| to assume | annehmen |
| party | die Partei, die Gruppe |

### Product development and communication

| | |
|---|---|
| connectivity | die Konnektivität, die Internetanbindung |
| resident | der/die Bewohner/-in, der/die Anwohner/-in |
| public services (pl) | die öffentlichen Versorgungsbetriebe |
| to impact | sich auswirken auf |
| assessment | die Einschätzung, die Beurteilung |
| implementation | die Einführung, die Umsetzung |
| core | Kern-, zentral |
| growth | das Wachstum |
| optimisation | die Optimierung |
| to involve | einbeziehen, beteiligen |
| stakeholder | der/die Interessenvertreter/-in |

# Vocabulary

## Module 6  In the workshop

### Important words

| | |
|---|---|
| break room | der Pausenraum |
| changing room | der Umkleideraum |
| spare parts and tyres store | das Ersatzteil- und Reifenlager |
| tyre balancing machine | die Auswuchtmaschine |
| tool trolley | der Werkzeugwagen |

### Car types

| | |
|---|---|
| convertible/cabriolet | das Cabrio |
| coupé | das Coupé |
| estate car / station wagon | der Kombi |
| hatchback/liftback | das Fließheck |
| lorry | der Lastwagen (Lkw) |
| pickup truck | der Pick-up |
| sedan/saloon | die Limousine |
| SUV | der SUV |

### Transporting cars

| | |
|---|---|
| to burn up the clutch | die Kupplung verschleißen |
| cable winch | die Seilwinde |
| chain | die Kette |
| (hauling) ramp | die Auffahrrampe |
| hydraulic lift (gate) | der hydraulische Aufzug |
| low clearance vehicle | das Fahrzeug mit geringer Bodenfreiheit |
| manoeuvring aid | die Rangierhilfe |
| nylon tie down | der Nylongurt |
| strap | der Gurt |
| trailer | der Anhänger, *hier:* Abschleppwagen |

### Working with electricity

| | |
|---|---|
| alternator | die Lichtmaschine |
| to conduct | leiten *(Strom)* |
| to connect; to disconnect | verbinden, anschließen; trennen |
| (frayed) cord | das (durchgescheuerte) Kabel |
| current | der Strom |
| electrical circuit | der Stromkreis |
| electrocution | der Tod durch Stromschlag |
| fuse | die Sicherung |
| ignition system | die Zündanlage, die Zündung |
| lighting system | die Lichtanlage |
| to insulate | isolieren |
| to plug; to unplug | einstecken; abstöpseln, entfernen |
| spark | der Zündfunke |

# Vocabulary

## A workshop tour

| | |
|---|---|
| essential | notwendig, wesentlich |
| inspection pit | die Wartungsgrube, die Inspektionsgrube |
| reception area | der Empfangsbereich |
| workbench | die Werkbank |
| car lift/hoist | die Hebebühne |
| storage room | der Lagerraum, das Lager |
| recycling bin | der Wertstoffbehälter |
| spot welder | das Punktschweißgerät |
| to involve | beinhalten |
| facilities (pl) | die Räumlichkeiten, die Anlage |
| invoice | die Rechnung |
| first-aid box/kit | der Erstehilfekasten |
| tech manual | das Handbuch |
| spray can | die Sprühdose |
| paint | die Farbe, der Lack |
| flammable | leicht entflammbar |
| to equip | ausstatten, ausrüsten |
| beside | neben |
| to store | lagern, aufbewahren |
| clutter | der Kram |
| screw | die Schraube |
| bolt | die Schraube, der Bolzen |
| torque wrench | der Drehmomentschlüssel |
| power drill | die Bohrmaschine |
| (pneumatic) impact wrench | der (Druckluft-)Schlagschrauber |
| multimeter | das Mehrfachmessgerät |
| toolbox | der Werkzeugkasten |
| tyre inflator | das Reifenfüllgerät |
| tyre pressure gauge | der Reifendruckmesser |

## Tools in a car workshop

| | |
|---|---|
| (outside) micrometer | die Messschraube |
| oscilloscope | das Oszilloskop |
| dial gauge | die Messuhr |
| (cranked) ring spanner | der (gekröpfte) Ringschlüssel |
| diagnostic tester | das Diagnosetestgerät |
| screwdriver | der Schraubendreher |
| ratchet | die Knarre |
| to measure | messen |
| pliers (pl) | die Zange |
| socket wrench | der Steckschlüssel |
| to disassemble | zerlegen |
| compressor | der Kompressor, der Verdichter |
| to fix | reparieren |
| dent | die Beule, die Delle |

## Safety measures

| | |
|---|---|
| measure | die Maßnahme |
| safety shoes | die Sicherheitsschuhe |
| safety goggles | die Schutzbrille |
| overall | der Overall |
| kneepad | der Knieschützer |
| protective mask | die Schutzmaske |
| protective gloves | die Schutzhandschuhe |
| flame-resistant | feuerfest |
| ear protection | der Gehörschutz |
| face shield | das Gesichtsvisier |
| safety helmet | der Schutzhelm |
| to be supposed to | sollen |
| trust | das Vertrauen |
| rubber grip | die gummierte Grifffläche |
| palm | die Handfläche |
| waterproof | wasserfest |
| hazard | die Gefahr, das Risiko |
| to grind | schleifen |
| to sand | schleifen, schmirgeln |
| sufficient | genug, genügend, ausreichend |
| combustible | brennbar |
| fluid | die Flüssigkeit |
| tool cabinet | der Werkzeugschrank |
| loose | locker, lose |

## Vocabulary

| | |
|---|---|
| ripped | zerrissen |
| attire (no pl) | die Kleidung |
| to customise | individuell anpassen |
| apparel (no pl) | die Bekleidung |
| gear (no pl) | die Ausrüstung |
| appropriate | geeignet, passend |
| fire extinguisher | der Feuerlöscher |
| to access | zugreifen auf |
| to charge | laden, aufladen, hier: befüllen |
| to verify | prüfen, bestätigen |
| stable | stabil, beständig |
| manifold | der Krümmer |
| coolant | das Kühlmittel, die Kühlflüssigkeit |
| to pressurize | unter Druck setzen |
| chemical spill | der Chemieunfall |
| fuel consumption | der Benzinverbrauch, der Treibstoffverbrauch |
| to raise | anheben, erhöhen |
| to leak | lecken, auslaufen, undicht sein |
| to weld | schweißen |
| to receive | erhalten |
| to signpost | ausschildern, hinweisen |

### Changing tyres

| | |
|---|---|
| wear and tear | die Abnutzung |
| to inflate | aufpumpen, aufblasen |
| to coat | beschichten, ummanteln |
| fibreglass | die Glasfaser |
| fabric | der Stoff, das Gewebe |
| to seal in | einschließen |
| loop | die Schlinge, die Schlaufe |
| rim | die Felge |
| anti-clockwise | gegen den Uhrzeigersinn |
| (pneumatic) car jack | der (pneumatische) Wagenheber |
| hazard triangle | das Warndreieck |
| cross pattern | überkreuz |
| valve | das Ventil |

### Transporting a vehicle

| | |
|---|---|
| to tow (away) | abschleppen |
| carrier | das Transportunternehmen |
| to scrape | verkratzen |
| loader | der/die Belader/-in |
| undercarriage | das Fahrwerk |
| acceleration | die Beschleunigung |
| chassis | das Fahrgestell |
| tight | fest, eng |
| to bend | biegen, verbiegen |
| tiltable | kippbar |
| to jump-start | Starthilfe geben |
| jumper cable | das Starthilfekabel |
| grounded | geerdet |

### Working with electricity

| | |
|---|---|
| precaution | die Vorsichtsmaßnahme |
| to prevent | verhindern, vermeiden |
| exposure | das Ausgesetztsein |
| fatal | tödlich |
| surroundings (pl) | die Umgebung |
| puddle | die Pfütze, die Lache |
| moisture | die Feuchtigkeit |
| to de-energize | (von der Stromversorgung) trennen |
| to neglect | außer Acht lassen, vernachlässigen |
| vapor | der Dampf |
| decomposition | die Zersetzung, der Abbau |
| hydrocyanic acid | die Blausäure |
| to assess | einschätzen, beurteilen |
| casualty | das Opfer, der/die Verletzte |
| CPR (cardiopulmonary resuscitation) | die Herz-Lungen-Wiederbelebung |

### Safety in your workshop

| | |
|---|---|
| common | häufig, verbreitet |
| to be required to | verpflichtet sein zu, erforderlich sein zu |

211

## Vocabulary

### Module 7 Maintenance and repair work

**Important words**

| | |
|---|---|
| braking system | das Bremssystem |
| catalytic converter | der Katalysator |
| chassis and body | das Fahrgestell und die Karosserie |
| coolant | das Kühlmittel, die Kühlflüssigkeit |
| corrosion | die Korrosion |
| diagnostic (trouble) code | der Diagnosecode |
| engine mount | die Motoraufhängung |
| exhaust emissions | die Abgase |
| exhaust system | die Auspuffanlage, die Abgasanlage |
| (transmission/axle) fluid | die (Getriebe-/Achsen-)Flüssigkeit |
| gear oil | das Getriebeöl |
| leakage | das Leck |
| low/high beam | das Abblend-/Fernlicht |
| reverse light | der Rückfahrscheinwerfer |
| to service | warten |
| signalling device | das Signalgerät |
| steering system | das Lenksystem |
| tread depth | die Profiltiefe |

### Servicing a vehicle

| | |
|---|---|
| combustion engine | der Verbrennermotor |
| engine | der Motor, der Antrieb |
| windscreen wiper | der Scheibenwischer |
| wear | die Abnutzung, der Verschleiß |
| appointment | der Termin, die Verabredung |
| to vary | variieren, (sich) ändern |
| inconvenient | ungelegen, unangenehm |
| manual | das Handbuch |
| to schedule | planen, vereinbaren |
| alert | der Alarm |
| spark plug | die Zündkerze |
| to perform | durchführen, ausführen |
| spare part | das Ersatzteil |

### The main inspection

| | |
|---|---|
| cost estimate | der Kostenvoranschlag |
| warranty | die Garantie |
| car dealership | das Autohaus |
| powertrain | der Antriebsstrang |
| to flash | aufleuchten |
| headlights (pl) | die Autoscheinwerfer |
| indicator | der Blinker |
| dipstick | der Ölmessstab |
| to shift (gears) | schalten |
| to grind | schleifen |
| to stall | stehen bleiben (Motor) |
| rust | Rost |
| gauge | das Messgerät, das Eichmaß, die (Prüf-)Lehre |
| power surge | die Überspannung |
| to sputter | stottern (Motor) |
| to bounce | hüpfen, springen |
| to creak | quietschen |
| MOT test | die Hauptuntersuchung |
| valid | gültig |
| badge | das Abzeichen, die Plakette |

### Brakes

| | |
|---|---|
| to apply (to) | anwenden (auf) |
| friction | die Reibung |
| to be exposed to sth/sb | etw./jdm. ausgesetzt sein |

## Vocabulary

| | |
|---|---|
| wear and tear | die Abnutzung, der Verschleiß |
| disc brake | die Scheibenbremse |
| drum brake | die Trommelbremse |
| to squeeze | drücken, pressen, quetschen |
| to transmit | übertragen |
| to spin | sich schnell drehen |
| surface | die Oberfläche |
| hydraulic pressure | der Hydraulikdruck |
| to rotate | rotieren, sich drehen |
| bracket | die Klammer |
| to clamp | festklemmen, einspannen |
| regenerative braking | die Rekuperationsbremse |
| to generate | erzeugen, generieren |
| accelerator | das Fahrpedal |
| to recover | wiedergewinnen, sicherstellen |
| loose | locker, lose |
| defective | fehlerhaft, defekt |
| brake fade | der Bremsschwund |
| to lubricate | schmieren, ölen |
| to squeak | quietschen |

### Engines

| | |
|---|---|
| oil patch | die Öllache, der Ölfleck |
| beneath | unter, unterhalb |
| to idle | leerlaufen |
| to suspect | vermuten, verdächtigen |
| thoroughly | sorgfältig, genau, gründlich |
| to convert | umwandeln, umstellen |
| fuel economy | die Kraftstoffeffizienz |
| reliability | die Zuverlässigkeit, die Verlässlichkeit |
| cycle | der Kreislauf, der Zyklus |
| to ignite | zünden, entzünden |
| optimisation | die Optimierung |
| turbocharger | der Turbolader |
| to downsize | verkleinern, verschlanken |

| | |
|---|---|
| to adjust | anpassen |
| compression ratio | das Kompressionsverhältnis, das Verdichtungsverhältnis |
| octane number | die Oktanzahl |
| injection | die Einspritzung |

### Diagnostic tools in the workshop

| | |
|---|---|
| integrated | integriert, eingebaut |
| fault | der Fehler, die Störung, die Fehlfunktion |
| to access | zugreifen auf |
| error memory | der Fehlerspeicher |
| to correspond to | übereinstimmen mit, entsprechen |
| to detect | feststellen, ermitteln |
| to activate | betätigen, aktivieren |
| digit | die Ziffer |
| passenger compartment | der Fahrgastraum |
| assistance | die Hilfe |
| comfort | die Bequemlichkeit |
| convenience | der Komfort, die Bequemlichkeit |
| suspension | die Aufhängung, die Federung |
| drivetrain | der Antrieb, die Antriebstechnik |
| generic code | der Standardcode |
| to assign | zuweisen, zuordnen |
| unique | einzigartig, einmalig |
| to decode | entschlüsseln |

### Buying a vintage car

| | |
|---|---|
| bumper | die Stoßstange |
| fender | der Kotflügel |
| fender bender | der Unfall mit Blechschaden |
| to register | registrieren, anmelden |
| pollutant | der Schadstoff, der Schmutzstoff |

Vocabulary

## Module 8  Servicing a vintage car

### Important words

| | |
|---|---|
| bodywork | die Karosserie |
| chassis | das Fahrgestell |
| diagnosis; to diagnose | die Diagnose; diagnostizieren |
| to fit | einbauen, einpassen |
| frame member | der Rahmenträger |
| fuel consumption | der Benzin-/Treibstoffverbrauch |
| fuel injector; to inject | der Benzineinspritzer; (ein-)spritzen |
| fuel system | die Kraftstoffversorgung |
| fuel tank | der (Benzin-)Tank |
| gas(oline) | das Benzin |
| glove box | das Handschuhfach |
| instruction manual | die Bedienungsanleitung |
| insulation; to insulate | die Isolierung, die Wärmedämmung; isolieren |
| to kick start | starten |
| leak | das Leck |
| operation; to operate | der Betrieb; betreiben, bedienen |
| performance; to perform | die Leistung; funktionieren, laufen |
| pump | die Pumpe |
| revolution (rev) | die Umdrehung |
| service; to service | der Kundendienst, die Inspektion; warten |
| service sheet | das Inspektionsblatt |
| spare part | das Ersatzteil |

### Talking to international customers

| | |
|---|---|
| vintage car | der Oldtimer |
| common | häufig, verbreitet |
| fault | der Fehler, die Störung, die Fehlfunktion |
| workshop | die Werkstatt, die Werkhalle |
| to splutter | stottern *(Motor)* |
| incline | die Steigung |

### Researching fuel system problems

| | |
|---|---|
| engine | der Motor, der Antrieb |
| to occur | geschehen, auftreten |
| mist | der Nebel |
| to lack | mangeln, fehlen |
| raw | roh, Roh- |
| noticeable | auffällig, bemerkbar |
| to fluctuate | schwanken, fluktuieren |
| additionally | zusätzlich |
| to suspect | vermuten, verdächtigen |

| | |
|---|---|
| additive | der Zusatz, der Zusatzstoff |
| clogged | verstopft, blockiert |
| contaminant | die Verunreinigung |
| otherwise | sonst |
| lubrication | die Schmierung |
| to break down | kaputt gehen |
| cause | der Grund, die Ursache |
| malfunction | die Fehlfunktion, die Störung |
| loose | locker, lose |
| worn | abgenutzt |
| current flow | der Stromfluss |
| sufficient | genug, genügend, ausreichend |
| likewise | ebenso, in gleicher Weise |
| misfire | die Fehlzündung |
| fluctuation | die Schwankung |
| acceleration | die Beschleunigung |
| obvious | offensichtlich |
| purpose | das Ziel, die Absicht, der Zweck |

## Vocabulary

| | |
|---|---|
| protection | der Schutz |
| smooth | glatt, reibungslos |
| ultimately | letztendlich, schließlich |
| to stall | stehen bleiben (Motor), abwürgen |
| to remain idle | im Leerlauf bleiben |
| to contain | enthalten |
| to harm | schädigen, schaden |

### Planning repairs

| | |
|---|---|
| to mount | montieren, anbringen |
| fabric | der Stoff, das Gewebe |
| to disconnect | trennen, abstellen |
| to prevent | verhindern, vermeiden |
| siphoning | das Absaugen |
| to reverse | umkehren |
| procedure | das Verfahren, die Vorgehensweise |
| essential | notwendig, wesentlich |
| to ensure | sicherstellen, gewährleisten |
| to keep clear | freihalten, fernhalten |
| transmission | die Weiterleitung, die Übertragung |
| guideline | die Richtlinie |
| disposal | die Beseitigung, die Entsorgung |
| toxic | giftig, toxisch |
| benzene | das Benzol |
| to inhale | einatmen, inhalieren |
| approved | genehmigt, zugelassen |
| ignition | das Entzünden, die Zündung |
| spill | die Lache, der Fleck |
| to dispose of sth | etw. entsorgen, etw. beseitigen |
| solvent | das Lösungsmittel |

### Ordering a spare part

| | |
|---|---|
| in stock | vorrätig, auf Lager |
| availability | die Verfügbarkeit |
| delivery | die Lieferung, die Zustellung |
| shipment | die Lieferung, die Versendung |
| to charge | berechnen, verlangen |
| transfer | die Überweisung, der Transfer |

### Your favourite vintage car

| | |
|---|---|
| craftsmanship | handwerkliches Können |
| astonishing | erstaunlich |
| feat | die Leistung, die Meisterleistung |
| demand | die Nachfrage, die Anforderung |
| to seek | suchen, bitten um |
| utility vehicle | der Geländewagen |
| post-war | Nachkriegs- |
| humble | bescheiden, einfach |
| origin | der Ursprung, die Herkunft |
| to miss out on | verpassen |
| longevity | die Langlebigkeit |
| economical | sparsam (Auto) |
| founder | der/die Gründer/-in |
| desirable | wünschenswert, erstrebenswert |
| to boast | prahlen, angeben |
| disdain | die Verachtung |
| ordinary | gewöhnlich, normal |

## Vocabulary

### Module 9  Customer service

#### Important words

| | |
|---|---|
| activation; to activate | die Aktivierung; aktivieren, betätigen |
| aftermarket part | das Nachrüstbauteil |
| to break down | liegen bleiben *(Fahrzeug)* |
| charge; to charge | die Gebühr; berechnen, verlangen |
| cost estimate | der Kostenvoranschlag |
| to fix | reparieren |
| installation; to install | die Montage, der Einbau, die Installation; montieren, einbauen, installieren |
| replacement part; to replace | das Ersatzteil; ersetzen |
| roadside assistance | die Pannenhilfe |
| service sheet | das Inspektionsblatt |
| spare part | das Ersatzteil |
| to tow (away) | abschleppen |
| upgrade; to upgrade | das Upgrade, die Nachrüstung; aufwerten, nachrüsten |
| warranty | die Garantie |

#### Roadside assistance

| | |
|---|---|
| **patient** | geduldig |
| **to be likely to do sth** | wahrscheinlich etw. tun |
| **to assess** | einschätzen, beurteilen |
| **to receive** | empfangen, bekommen, erhalten |
| **hazard warning lights** | die Warnblinkanlage |
| **reliable** | zuverlässig, vertrauenswürdig |
| **contract** | der Vertrag |
| **to digitalise** | digitalisieren |
| **to process** | verarbeiten, bearbeiten |
| **scratched** | zerkratzt |

#### Repair costs

| | |
|---|---|
| **cylinder head gasket** | die Zylinderkopfdichtug |
| **faulty** | fehlerhaft, mangelhaft |
| **OEM (original equipment manufacturer) part** | das Originalteil |
| **accessories** *(pl)* | die Accessoires, das Zubehör |
| **to manufacture** | fertigen, herstellen |

| | |
|---|---|
| **performance** | die Leistung |
| **to depend (on)** | abhängen (von) |
| **to refer to sth** | sich auf etw. beziehen |
| **inconvenient** | unangenehm, ungelegen, lästig |
| **cracked** | gerissen, geplatzt |
| **rough** | grob, ungefähr |
| **availability** | die Verfügbarkeit |
| **to carry out** | durchführen, ausführen |
| **worn** | abgenutzt |
| **tread** | das Profil |
| **to perform** | durchführen, ausführen |

#### Upgrading a car

| | |
|---|---|
| **cruise control** | der Tempomat, die Geschwindigkeitsregelung |
| **infotainment system** | Info- und Unterhaltungssystem |
| **sunroof** | das Schiebedach |
| **trailer coupling** | die Anhängerkupplung |
| **ambient lighting** | die Innenraumbeleuchtung |
| **driver assistance system** | das Fahrerassistenzsystem |
| **unnecessary** | unnötig |
| **to require** | benötigen, erfordern |

## Vocabulary

| | |
|---|---|
| to **unlock** | erschließen, freischalten |
| to **acquire** | erwerben, bekommen |
| to **register** | registrieren, anmelden |
| **third-party** | Dritt- |
| to **modify** | abändern, verändern |

### Digital vehicle inspection

| | |
|---|---|
| to **automate** | automatisieren |
| **administrative** | Verwaltungs-, administrativ |
| **contactless** | kontaktlos, berührungslos |
| **diagnostic** | Diagnose- |
| **invoice** | die Rechnung |
| **ailing** | marode |
| to **review** | begutachten, überprüfen |
| **approval** | die Zustimmung |
| **issue** | das Thema, das Problem |
| **clipboard** | das Papierklemmbrett |
| to **enable** | ermöglichen, befähigen |
| **instant** | sofortig |
| **concise** | präzise, kurz, prägnant |
| **approach** | die Herangehensweise, der Ansatz |
| **transparency** | die Transparenz |
| **reference (to)** | die Bezugnahme (auf) |
| to **enhance** | verbessern |

| | |
|---|---|
| **template** | die Vorlage, das Muster |
| **consistent** | gleich bleibend, stetig, konsistent |
| **resolution** | die Auflösung |
| to **boost** | steigern, fördern |
| **confidence** | das Vertrauen, die Zuversicht |
| to **generate** | erzeugen, generieren |
| **engagement** | die Verpflichtung, das Engagement |

### Dealing with a complaint

| | |
|---|---|
| **satisfied** | zufrieden, überzeugt |
| **valuable** | wertvoll |
| **measure** | die Maßnahme |
| to **mistrust** | misstrauen |
| **equipped** | ausgestattet |
| **stage** | der Abschnitt, die Phase |
| **claim** | der Anspruch, die Behauptung |
| **occasion** | der Anlass, die Gelegenheit |
| **reasonable** | vernünftig, angemessen |
| **bumper** | die Stoßstange |
| **brake pad** | der Bremsbelag |
| to **request** | anfragen, anfordern |
| **response** | die Antwort, die Rückmeldung |
| to **reconsider** | überdenken |

# Vocabulary

## Module 10  Electric vehicles

### Important words

| | |
|---|---|
| acceleration; to accelerate | die Beschleunigung; beschleunigen |
| advanced driver-assistance system (ADAS) | das Fahrerassistenzsystem |
| automation; automated | die Automatisierung; automatisiert |
| battery pack | der Batteriepack, der Akkupack |
| to charge | (auf-)laden |
| to connect; to disconnect | verbinden, anschließen; trennen, abstellen |
| to convert | umwandeln, umstellen |
| DC/DC converter | der Gleichspannungswandler |
| onboard charger | das Ladegerät (im Fahrzeug verbaut) |
| to plug in | einstecken |
| steering; to steer | das Lenken; steuern, lenken |
| thermal system | das Kühlsystem |
| transmission | das Getriebe |

### Modern driving systems

| | |
|---|---|
| to **handle** | umgehen mit, handhaben |
| **sensor** | der Sensor |
| **charging station** | die Ladestation |
| **natural gas filling station** | die Erdgastankstelle |
| **hydrogen refuelling station** | die Wasserstofftankstelle |
| to **power** | antreiben, mit Energie versorgen |
| **liquid** | die Flüssigkeit |
| **(internal) combustion engine** | der Verbrennungsmotor |
| **fuel cell** | Brennstoffzelle |
| **socket** | die Steckdose |
| to **account for** | ausmachen, erfassen |
| **recuperation** | die Rekuperation, die Rückgewinnung |
| **sales figures** | die Verkaufszahlen, die Umsatzzahlen |

### How to handle EVs

| | |
|---|---|
| **fluent** | fließend, flüssig |
| **electrical drive** | der Elektroantrieb |
| **energy supply** | die Energieversorgung, die Energiezufuhr |
| **powertrain** | der Antriebsstrang |

| | |
|---|---|
| **purpose** | das Ziel, die Absicht, der Zweck |
| to **manage** | steuern, verwalten, organisieren |
| to **contain** | enthalten |
| **operator** | der/die Betreiber/-in |
| **voltage** | die Spannung |
| **hazard** | die Gefahr, das Risiko |
| **awareness** | das Bewusstsein |
| to **be exposed to sth/sb** | etw./jdm. ausgesetzt sein |
| **recovery service** | der Abschleppdienst, der Bergungsdienst |
| **access** | der Zugriff, der Zugang |
| **electrical circuit** | der Stromkreis |
| **current** | der Strom |
| **lethal** | tödlich |
| **electrocution** | der Tod durch Stromschlag |
| to **short-circuit** | kurzschließen |
| to **release** | freigeben, freisetzen, loslassen |
| **fatal** | tödlich |
| to **vary** | variieren, ändern |
| to **undertake** | durchführen |
| **towing service** | der Abschleppdienst |
| **barrier** | die Absperrung, die Schranke, die Barriere |
| to **prevent** | verhindern, vermeiden |

## Vocabulary

| | |
|---|---|
| to **measure** | messen |
| to **adjust** | anpassen |
| to **deactivate** | abschalten, ausschalten, deaktivieren |
| **cable** | das Kabel |

### Advanced driver-assistance system (ADAS)

| | |
|---|---|
| **drivetrain** | der Antrieb, der Antriebsstrang |
| to **implement** | einführen, umsetzen |
| **obstacle** | das Hindernis, die Hürde |
| **autonomous** | autonom, selbstständig |
| **partial** | teilweise |
| **conditional** | bedingt |
| **manually** | manuell, von Hand |
| **cruise control** | der Tempomat, die Geschwindigkeitsregelung |
| **lane assistance** | der Spurhalteassistent |
| to **adapt to** | sich anpassen an |
| to **alert** | alarmieren, benachrichtigen |
| **obstruction** | das Hindernis |

### Sensors in EVs

| | |
|---|---|
| **beam** | der Strahl |
| **radio wave** | die Radiowelle |
| to **reflect** | reflektieren, widerspiegeln |
| to **measure** | messen |
| to **detect** | feststellen, erkennen |
| **park distance control** | die Einparkhilfe |
| **ultrasound** | der Ultraschall |
| **measuring range** | der Messbereich |

| | |
|---|---|
| **blind** | die Blende |
| **lens** | die Linse |
| to **spin** | sich schnell drehen |
| **detection** | die Erkennung, die Ortung |
| **malfunction** | die Fehlfunktion, die Störung |
| to **fail** | scheitern, fehlschlagen |
| **trailer** | der Anhänger |
| **elevation** | die Erhebung |
| to **brake** | bremsen |
| to **process** | verarbeiten, bearbeiten |
| **rear-end collision** | der Auffahrunfall |
| **surface** | die Oberfläche |
| to **issue a warning** | eine Warnung aussprechen, warnen |
| **investigation** | die Ermittlung, die Untersuchung |
| **public authorities** (pl) | die Behörden |
| **misleading** | irreführend |

### Electric vehicle or petrol car?

| | |
|---|---|
| to **consider** | bedenken, berücksichtigen |
| **drawback** | der Nachteil, der Haken (fig.) |
| to **depend (on)** | abhängen (von) |
| **harmful** | schädlich |
| to **be concerned (about)** | beunruhigt sein (über) |
| **carbon dioxide** ($CO_2$) | das Kohlendioxid |
| **driveway** | die Einfahrt, die Auffahrt |
| **convenient** | bequem, angenehm, passend |
| **eco-friendliness** | die Umweltfreundlichkeit |

# Mathematical terms and conversion table

## Mathematical terms and symbols

| | | |
|---|---|---|
| **Addition:** | 2 + 3 = 5 | (Two **plus** three equals five.) |
| **Subtraction:** | 8 − 4 = 4 | (Eight **minus** four equals four.) |
| **Multiplication:** | 9 x 4 = 36 | (Nine **multiplied** by four equals thirty-six; or nine **times** four …) |
| **Division:** | 55 : 11 = 5 | (Fifty-five **divided** by eleven equals five.) |

**Fractions** (Brüche)
1/2 – one half, a half
1/3 – one third, a third
1/4 – one quarter, a quarter
3/4 – three quarters
1/5 – one fifth, a fifth
5/8 – five eighths

$\sqrt{\phantom{x}}$ – square root: $\sqrt{9}$ the square root of nine equals three
$\sqrt[3]{\phantom{x}}$ – cube root: $\sqrt[3]{8}$ the cube root of eight is two
$3^2$ – three squared equals nine
$4^3$ – four cubed equals 64
$2^4$ – two to the power of four equals 16

% per cent
‰ per thousand

≠ does not equal, is not equal to
\> is more than / greater than
\< is less than
° degree

## Conversion table inch – cm / foot – metre

**1 inch (in) = 2.54 cm    1 foot = 30.48 cm**
Die Angaben sind gerundet. Die bei den Umrechnungen in *inches* und *feet* angegebene Dezimale dient nur der Verdeutlichung.

| in | cm | cm | in | ft | m | m | ft |
|---|---|---|---|---|---|---|---|
| 1 | 2.54 | 3 | 1.18 | 1 | 0.3048 | 1 | 3.28 |
| 2 | 5.08 | 4 | 1.57 | 2 | 0.6096 | 2 | 6.56 |
| 3 | 7.62 | 5 | 1.97 | 3 | 0.9144 | 3 | 9.84 |
| 4 | 10.16 | 10 | 3.94 | 4 | 1.2192 | 4 | 13.12 |
| 5 | 12.70 | 15 | 5.91 | 5 | 1.5240 | 5 | 16.40 |
| 6 | 15.24 | 20 | 7.87 | 6 | 1.8288 | 6 | 19.68 |
| 7 | 17.78 | 25 | 9.84 | 7 | 2.1336 | 7 | 22.96 |
| 8 | 20.32 | 30 | 11.81 | 8 | 2.4384 | 8 | 26.24 |
| 9 | 22.86 | 35 | 13.78 | 9 | 2.7432 | 9 | 29.52 |
| 10 | 25.40 | 40 | 15.75 | 10 | 3.0480 | 10 | 32.80 |
| 11 | 27.94 | 45 | 17.72 | 11 | 3.3528 | 11 | 36.08 |
| 12 | 30.48 | 50 | 19.69 | 12 | 3.6576 | 12 | 39.36 |

## Classroom phrases

### Asking about words and meanings

| | |
|---|---|
| What does (the word) … mean? | Was bedeutet (das Wort) …? |
| I don't understand the word …/ the expression …/this sentence. | Ich verstehe das Wort … nicht/ den Ausdruck … nicht/diesen Satz nicht. |
| How do you say … in English? | Wie sagt man … auf Englisch? |
| Could you repeat that/say that again? | Würden Sie das wiederholen/nochmal sagen? |

### Giving your opinion

| | |
|---|---|
| I think (that) … | Ich denke/meine, dass … |
| In my opinion … | Meiner Meinung nach … |
| I find … (really) good/interesting/boring. | Ich finde … (echt) gut/interessant/langweilig. |

### Agreeing and disagreeing

| | |
|---|---|
| I agree (with Martina). | Ich stimme (Martina) zu. |
| I disagree/don't agree (with Bernd). | Ich stimme (Bernd) nicht zu. |
| Yes, I think the same/I think that, too. | Ja, ich denke das Gleiche/das meine ich auch. |
| Rubbish! | Quatsch! |

### Talking about texts

| | |
|---|---|
| In the text the reader learns that … | Im Text erfährt der Leser/die Leserin, dass … |
| The first paragraph tells us that … | Der erste Absatz sagt uns, dass … |
| In the second paragraph we read/learn that … | Im zweiten Absatz liest/erfährt man, dass … |
| The last paragraph is about … | Im letzten Absatz geht es um … |
| Finally, we learn/read that … | Zuletzt erfährt/liest man, dass … |

### Working in class

| | |
|---|---|
| Would you write that on the board, please? | Würden Sie das bitte an die Tafel schreiben? |
| I'm not sure what we have to do. | Ich bin nicht sicher, was wir tun müssen. |
| I haven't got a partner. | Ich habe keinen Partner/keine Partnerin. |
| We need another person in our group. | Unserer Gruppe fehlt eine Person. |
| Our group's finished. | Unsere Gruppe ist fertig. |
| We need a bit more time. | Wir brauchen noch ein bisschen Zeit. |

| | | | |
|---|---|---|---|
| complete | ergänzen Sie | imagine | stellen Sie sich vor |
| find (out) | finden Sie (heraus) | invent … yourself | erfinden Sie (selbst) |
| missing | fehlend | talk about/discuss | diskutieren Sie |
| match | ordnen Sie zu | do a survey | machen Sie eine Umfrage |
| choose | wählen Sie | give a talk | halten Sie eine Rede |
| translate | übersetzen Sie | which mean the same/ have the same meaning | die die gleiche Bedeutung haben |
| put in the correct order | stellen Sie in die richtige Reihenfolge | which mean the opposite/have the opposite meaning | die die entgegengesetzte Bedeutung haben |
| make notes/note down | notieren Sie | in your own words | in eigenen Worten |
| make a summary | fassen Sie zusammen | | |
| correct | korrigieren Sie | | |
| practise | üben Sie | | |

## Quellen

**Bildquellennachweis**

**6.1** Getty Images, München (Johner Images); **6.2** Getty Images Plus, München (FG Trade); **6.3** Getty Images Plus, München (The Image Bank / Mikael Vaisanen); **6.4** iStockphoto, Calgary, Alberta (sturti); **6.5** Getty Images Plus, München (E+ / fotografixx); **7** Getty Images Plus, München (E+ / GrapeImages); **8.1** plainpicture GmbH & Co. KG, Hamburg (Melanka Helms); **8.2** ShutterStock.com RF, New York (Microgen); **8.3** Getty Images Plus, München (iStock /Smederevac); **10.1** stock.adobe.com, Dublin (xiaoliangge); **10.2** Ernst Klett Verlag GmbH, Stuttgart; **10.3** TEBITRON GMBH, Edward Eckstein, Gerlingen; **11** Getty Images Plus, München (Teera Konakan / Teera Konakan); **13** Ernst Klett Verlag GmbH, Stuttgart; **14** Oser, Liliane, Hamburg; **15** plainpicture GmbH & Co. KG, Hamburg (Stock4B / Chris Harding); **18** stock.adobe.com, Dublin (rh2010); **20.1** Getty Images Plus, München (Tom Werner / Photodisc); **20.2** Getty Images Plus, München (DigitalVision / Luis Alvarez); **20.3** Getty Images Plus, München (E+ / franckreporter); **20.4** Getty Images Plus, München (Moment / wera Rodsawang); **22.1, 4, 10, 14, 20, 23** ShutterStock.com RF, New York (Benjamin Marin Rubio); **22.2, 3, 5, 15, 17** ShutterStock.com RF, New York (medicalstocks); **22.6, 16, 18, 19, 21** ShutterStock.com RF, New York (Dirk Chudzinsky); **22.7, 8, 9** ShutterStock.com RF, New York (Versatiline Studio); **22.11, 12, 13** ShutterStock.com RF, New York (Versatiline Studio); **25.1** Getty Images Plus, München (E+ / kyonntra); **25.2–4** ShutterStock.com RF, New York (Carboxylase); **26.1–6** ShutterStock.com RF, New York (Carboxylase); **26.7** ShutterStock.com RF, New York (weberjake); **30.1–4** ShutterStock.com RF, New York (TMvectorart); **31.1** Getty Images Plus, München (E+ / jeffbergen); **31.2** Getty Images Plus, München (E+ / xavierarnau); **31.3** ShutterStock.com RF, New York (Mongkolchon Akesin); **31.4** ShutterStock.com RF, New York (Chachamp); **32** Getty Images Plus, München (filadendron/E+); **33.1–6** ShutterStock.com RF, New York (mtkang); **34.1, 2, 4** jani lunablau, Barcelona (Jani Spennhoff); **34.3** iStockphoto, Calgary, Alberta (Nathan Shelton); **36.1** ShutterStock.com RF, New York (goodluz); **36.2** ShutterStock.com RF, New York (Atelier211); **40** Oser, Liliane, Hamburg ; from: The Conflict Resolution Tool Box, ©2006 Gary T. Furlong; **42** ShutterStock.com RF, New York (TarikVision); **45** Getty Images Plus, München (Klaus Vedfelt); **46.1–3** ShutterStock.com RF, New York (Faber14); **47** Getty Images, München (Westend61); **49** Oser, Liliane, Hamburg; **51.1–4** Ernst Klett Verlag GmbH, Stuttgart; **52** ShutterStock.com RF, New York (Salov Evgeniy); **54.1** ShutterStock.com RF, New York (Darkdiamond67); **54.2** ShutterStock.com RF, New York (Zapp2Photo); **54.3** ShutterStock.com RF, New York (ezphoto); **54.4** ShutterStock.com RF, New York (Anton Starikov); **54.5** ShutterStock.com RF, New York (Pattani Studio); **54.6** ShutterStock.com RF, New York (donvictorio); **55** Oser, Liliane, Hamburg; **56** Getty Images, München (Stone / Howard Kingsnorth); **58** ShutterStock.com RF, New York (BOLDG); **60** ShutterStock.com RF, New York (ChristianChan); **62** Ernst Klett Verlag GmbH, Stuttgart ; Data: Acutiy Training, March 2023; **63.1** ShutterStock.com RF, New York (Denys Drozd); **63.2** ShutterStock.com RF, New York (Gherus Store); **63.3** ShutterStock.com RF, New York (Vlad Ra27); **63.4** ShutterStock.com RF, New York (GANJIRO KUMA); **63.5** ShutterStock.com RF, New York (phipatbig); **63.6** ShutterStock.com RF, New York (UI); **65** Getty Images Plus, München (E+ / Juanmonino); **66** ShutterStock.com RF, New York (Maksim Safaniuk); **67** ShutterStock.com RF, New York (ALPA PROD); **68** ShutterStock.com RF, New York (REDPIXEL.PL); **69.1** ShutterStock.com RF, New York (CreativeX Studio); **69.2** ShutterStock.com RF, New York (CreativeX Studio); **70** Getty Images Plus, München (metamorworks); **72** Dekelver, Christian, Weinstadt; **73** ShutterStock.com RF, New York (hvostik); **74.1** stock.adobe.com, Dublin (krasyuk); **74.2** ShutterStock.com RF, New York (Shutter Baby photo); **74.3** ShutterStock.com RF, New York (suradech123yim); **74.4** ShutterStock.com RF, New York (Khotenko Vladymyr); **74.5** ShutterStock.com RF, New York (Photo Love); **74.6** stock.adobe.com, Dublin (PRILL Mediendesign); **74.7** stock.adobe.com, Dublin (freezeframe); **74.8** ShutterStock.com RF, New York (Pawel G); **75.1** stock.adobe.com, Dublin (Nur); **75.2** Getty Images Plus/Microstock, München (prill); **75.3** Getty Images Plus, München (Goodboy Picture Company); **75.4** ShutterStock.com RF, New York (Yellow Cat); **75.5** stock.adobe.com, Dublin (Natallia); **75.6** iStockphoto, Calgary, Alberta (Stensoenes); **75.7** Getty Images Plus/Microstock, München (pepifoto); **75.8** ShutterStock.com RF, New York (Nikitin Victor); **75.9** stock.adobe.com, Dublin (Coprid); **75.10** stock.adobe.com, Dublin (New Africa); **76** ShutterStock.com RF, New York (Gorodenkoff); **77** Getty Images Plus/Microstock, München (Nikolamirejovska); **77** Getty Images Plus/Microstock, München (Nikolamirejovska); **78.1, 2** Dekelver, Christian, Weinstadt; **79.1–6** Dekelver, Christian, Weinstadt; **80.1** ShutterStock.com RF, New York (Belozersky); **80.2** ShutterStock.com RF, New York (AVA Bitter); **80.3** ShutterStock.com RF, New York (KurArt); **80.4** ShutterStock.com RF, New York (Belozersky); **80.5** ShutterStock.com RF, New York (Belozersky); **80.6** stock.adobe.com, Dublin (lyudinka); **82.1** ShutterStock.com RF, New York (CreativeX Studio); **82.2** ShutterStock.com RF, New York (CreativeX Studio); **83** ShutterStock.com RF, New York (noPPonPat); **86** ShutterStock.com RF, New York (Gorodenkoff); **87.1** Getty Images Plus/Microstock, München (designer29); **87.2** Getty Images Plus/Microstock, München (A Mokhtari); **87.3** Getty Images Plus/Microstock, München (dzphotogallery); **87.4** Getty Images Plus/Microstock, München (de-nue-pic); **88.1** Getty Images Plus, München (iStock / industryview); **88.2** Getty Images Plus, München (iStock / Zephyr18); **88.3** Getty Images Plus, München (iStock / RossHelen); **88.4** ShutterStock.com RF, New York (Mikko Lemola); **89.1** Getty Images Plus, München (E+ / franckreporter); **89.2** Getty Images Plus, München (iStock / loco75); **89.3** ShutterStock.com RF, New York (YimJi WK); **89.4** ShutterStock.com RF, New York (Rito Succeed); **92.1** Alamy stock photo, Abingdon (Marcin Rogozinski); **92.2** Alamy stock photo, Abingdon (Alan Novelli); **93.1, 2** Oser, Liliane, Hamburg; **95** Getty Images Plus, München (iStock / Dmytro Varavin); **96** ShutterStock.com RF, New York (BAHA HAM); **97.1** Ernst Klett Verlag GmbH, Stuttgart; **97.2** TEBITRON GMBH, Edward Eckstein, Gerlingen; **99** ShutterStock.com RF, New York (Nomad_Soul); **100** stock.adobe.com, Dublin (Alex Segre); **101.1** ShutterStock.com RF, New York (CreativeX Studio); **101.2** ShutterStock.com RF, New York (CreativeX Studio); **102** Getty Images Plus, München (iStock / DragonImages); **103.1** stock.adobe.com, Dublin (Jacob Lund); **103.2** ShutterStock.com RF, New York (jimmonkphotography); **104.1** Getty Images Plus, München (iStock / Ladanifer); **104.2** Getty Images Plus, München (iStock / 3DFOX); **104.3** Getty Images Plus, München (iStock / madsci); **106** Dekelver, Christian, Weinstadt; **107** Oser, Liliane, Hamburg; **108** Dekelver, Christian, Weinstadt; **109.1** ShutterStock.com RF, New York (CreativeX Studio); **109.2** ShutterStock.com RF, New York (CreativeX Studio); **110.1** stock.adobe.com, Dublin (Vova); **110.2** https://creativecommons.org/licenses/by-sa/4.0/deed.de, Mountain View (Herranderssvensson); CC-BY-SA-4.0 Lizenzbestimmungen: https://creativecommons.org/licenses/by-sa/4.0/legalcode, siehe *3; **110.3** ShutterStock.com

RF, New York (James Hime); **110.4** Getty Images Plus, München (iStock Unreleased / Maxian); **110.5** ShutterStock.com RF, New York (Nadezda Murmakova); **112.1** Getty Images Plus, München (DigitalVision / Luis Alvarez); **112.2** Getty Images Plus, München (DigitalVision / Luis Alvarez); **112.3** Getty Images Plus, München (iStock / Domepitipat); **112.4** ShutterStock.com RF, New York (ALPA PROD); **112.5** Getty Images Plus, München (E+ / RealPeopleGroup); **112.6** Getty Images Plus, München (iStock / fatihhoca); **114** ShutterStock.com RF, New York (ARTPROXIMO); **115.1** ShutterStock.com RF, New York (CreativeX Studio); **115.2** ShutterStock.com RF, New York (CreativeX Studio); **116.1** ShutterStock.com RF, New York (DenPhotos); **116.2** ShutterStock.com RF, New York (Aleksandr Kondratov); **116.3** ShutterStock.com RF, New York (Azami Adiputera); **116.4** ShutterStock.com RF, New York (RSplaneta); **116.5** ShutterStock.com RF, New York (Alexey Ryazanov); **116.6** Getty Images Plus, München (iStock / Aleksandr Potashev); **117.1** ShutterStock.com RF, New York (Ground Picture); **117.2** ShutterStock.com RF, New York (socrates471); **117.3** ShutterStock.com RF, New York (aphatai Thailand); **117.4** ShutterStock.com RF, New York (Kostas Restas); **119** ShutterStock.com RF, New York (KLingSup); **120** Getty Images Plus, München (E+ / izusek); **122.1** ShutterStock.com RF, New York (Literator); **122.2** ShutterStock.com RF, New York (ALEXSTAND); **122.3** stock.adobe.com, Dublin (Sarah); **122.4** ShutterStock.com RF, New York (Anetam); **124** Dekelver, Christian, Weinstadt; **126** Dekelver, Christian, Weinstadt; **127** graphitecture book & edition, Bernau am Chiemsee ; Aus Qualifizierung für Arbeiten an Fahrzeugen mit Hochvoltsystemen, 08.2021, Deutsche Gesetzliche Unfallversicherung e.V.; **129.1** ShutterStock.com RF, New York (Roman Zaiets); **129.2** ZF, 2024; **130** stock.adobe.com, Dublin (zapp2photo); **131** Getty Images Plus, München (iStock / metamorworks); **132.1–3** Dekelver, Christian, Weinstadt; **134** ShutterStock.com RF, New York (elenabsl); **135** ShutterStock.com RF, New York (petovarga); **155.1** ShutterStock.com RF, New York (CreativeX Studio); **155.2** ShutterStock.com RF, New York (CreativeX Studio); **156.1** stock.adobe.com, Dublin (lyudinka); **156.2** ShutterStock.com RF, New York (Belozersky); **156.3** ShutterStock.com RF, New York (Belozersky); **156.4** ShutterStock.com RF, New York (AVA Bitter); **156.5** ShutterStock.com RF, New York (Belozersky); **156.6** ShutterStock.com RF, New York (KurArt); **159.1** Getty Images Plus, München (DigitalVision / Luis Alvarez); **159.2** Getty Images Plus, München (DigitalVision / Luis Alvarez); **159.3** Getty Images Plus, München (iStock / Domepitipat); **159.4** ShutterStock.com RF, New York (ALPA PROD); **159.5** Getty Images Plus, München (iStock / fatihhoca); **191** Oser, Liliane, Hamburg; **192.1** ShutterStock.com RF, New York (algre); **192.2** ShutterStock.com RF, New York (Kolonko); **193.1** ShutterStock.com RF, New York (Virrage Images); **193.2** Getty Images Plus, München (iStock / structuresxx); **193.3** ShutterStock.com RF, New York (iqrologo); **193.4** ShutterStock.com RF, New York (Fusionstudio); **193.5** ShutterStock.com RF, New York (Dusan Petkovic); **193.6** ShutterStock.com RF, New York (Thomas Soellner); **193.7** ShutterStock.com RF, New York (Ground Picture); **193.8** Getty Images Plus, München (E+ / skynesher); **193.9** ShutterStock.com RF, New York (KONSTANTIN_SHISHKIN); **193.10** ShutterStock.com RF, New York (PakulinSergei); **193.11** ShutterStock.com RF, New York (mahc); **193.12** ShutterStock.com RF, New York (Phol Pimsim); **193.13** ShutterStock.com RF, New York (anatoliy_gleb); **193.14** ShutterStock.com RF, New York (Baloncici); **194.1** ShutterStock.com RF, New York (Dan70); **194.2** ShutterStock.com RF, New York (Madlen); **194.3** Getty Images Plus, München (iStock / doomu); **194.4** Getty Images Plus, München (iStock / Valentyna Yeltsova); **194.5** ShutterStock.com RF, New York (OlegSam); **194.6** stock.adobe.com, Dublin (freezeframe); **194.7** Getty Images Plus, München (iStock / Veni vidi...shoot); **194.8** Getty Images Plus, München (iStock / Dave Collins); **194.9** ShutterStock.com RF, New York (magicoven); **194.10** ShutterStock.com RF, New York (Shutter Baby photo); **194.11** stock.adobe.com, Dublin (PRILL Mediendesign); **194.12** ShutterStock.com RF, New York (Photo Love); **194.13** stock.adobe.com, Dublin (krasyuk); **194.14** ShutterStock.com RF, New York (Khotenko Vladymyr); **194.15** ShutterStock.com RF, New York (donatas1205); **195.1** ShutterStock.com RF, New York (PTZ Pictures); **195.2** ShutterStock.com RF, New York (suradech123yim); **195.3** ShutterStock.com RF, New York (Rynio Productions); **195.4** ShutterStock.com RF, New York (except_else); **195.5** ShutterStock.com RF, New York (Jiri Hera); **195.6** ShutterStock.com RF, New York (nito); **195.7** ShutterStock.com RF, New York (Pawel G); **195.8** Getty Images, München (Westend61); **195.9** ShutterStock.com RF, New York (Ratthaphong Ekariyasap); **195.10** ShutterStock.com RF, New York (pryzmat); **196.1, 2** Dekelver, Christian, Weinstadt; **197.1, 2** Oser, Liliane, Hamburg; **197.3** ShutterStock.com RF, New York (BAHA HAM); **198** Dekelver, Christian, Weinstadt

*3 Lizenzbestimmungen zu CC-BY-SA-4.0 siehe: http://creativecommons.org/licenses/by-sa/4.0/legalcode

**Textquellennachweis**

**76** https://www.prudentialuniforms.com/blog/safety-rules-automotive-repair-shops/; **81** https://intercitylines.com/how-auto-transport-companies-load-cars-onto-their-trailers/; **84** https://www.autotrainingcentre.com/blog/5-must-have-safety-tips-working-automotive-electrical-systems-auto-technician/; Zur besseren altersgemäßen Verständlichkeit wurde der Originaltext verändert, ohne den Inhalt und/oder Sinn zu verändern.; **90** Madeleine Burry, 22.06.2023, mwg.aaa.com; Zur besseren altersgemäßen Verständlichkeit wurde der Originaltext verändert, ohne den Inhalt und/oder Sinn zu verändern.; **94** 03.06.2022, autoguide.com; Zur besseren altersgemäßen Verständlichkeit wurde der Originaltext verändert, ohne den Inhalt und/oder Sinn zu verändern.; **98** https://www.obdautodoctor.com/tutorials/diagnostic-trouble-codes-explained/; **104** 2023, Automotive Training Centre. https://www.autotrainingcentre.com; **106** Workshop Manual: Roll-Royce Silver Cloud, Roll-Royce Silver Cloud II, Phantom V... ©1961 The Technical Publications Department, Rolls-Royce Limited.; **110** James Dwyer, 21.09.2017, www.creditplus.co.uk; Zur besseren altersgemäßen Verständlichkeit wurde der Originaltext verändert, ohne den Inhalt und/oder Sinn zu verändern.; **118** 2021, FiiviQ (5iQ) Pvt Ltd., fiiviq.com; Zur besseren altersgemäßen Verständlichkeit wurde der Originaltext verändert, ohne den Inhalt und/oder Sinn zu verändern.; **125** 13.06.2023, Peninsula Business Services Limited, https://www.peninsulagrouplimited.com/resource-hub/risk-assessment/electric-hybrid-vehicles-hazards/; Zur besseren altersgemäßen Verständlichkeit wurde der Originaltext verändert, ohne den Inhalt und/oder Sinn zu verändern.; **128** Aus Qualifizierung für Arbeiten an Fahrzeugen mit Hochvoltsystemen, 08.2021, Deutsche Gesetzliche Unfallversicherung e.V.; **141** Ricardo Izzi, Elektroauto: Die Vor- und Nachteile

## Quellen

(2022), unter: https://www.net4energy.com/de-de/mobilitaet/elektroauto-vor-nachteile; **145** Patrick Jackson, V2X explained: what is vehicle-to-everything communication and how does it work?, v. 17.05.2020, unter: https://www.drivesection.com/tech/vehicle-to-everything-explained/ (Zugriff: 03.11.2023); **147** Oponeo: LIDAR vs RADAR: What Is the Difference Between LIDAR and RADAR?, v. 06.12.2021, unter: https://www.oponeo.co.uk/blog/lidar-vs-radar (Zugriff: 03.11.2023); **148** Raimund Schesswendter, Autonomes Fahren: Das bedeuten Level 0 bis 5, v. 15.06.2021, unter: https://t3n.de/news/autonomes-fahren-assistenz-fahrautomatisierung-level-stufe-1332889/